Biblical Nonsense

Biblical Nonsense

A Review of the Bible
for Doubting Christians

Dr. Jason Long

iUniverse, Inc.
New York   Lincoln   Shanghai

Biblical Nonsense
A Review of the Bible for Doubting Christians

Copyright © 2005 by Jason Long

iUniverse books may be ordered through booksellers or by contacting:

iUniverse
2021 Pine Lake Road, Suite 100
Lincoln, NE 68512
www.iuniverse.com
1-800-Authors (1-800-288-4677)

ISBN: 0-595-34182-9 (Pbk)
ISBN: 0-595-67074-1 (Cloth)

Printed in the United States of America

To the billions who have died believing in myths

"I prayed for twenty years but received no answer until I prayed with my legs."
Frederick Douglass, on escaping slavery

CONTENTS

AN INTRODUCTION TO BIBLICAL NONSENSE

This book is not about enforcing human limitations on the Christian perspective of God. Instead, it's about rendering a verdict on the possibility of the Bible being a divinely inspired representation of such an incredible being. If the Bible is, in fact, the word of the universe's omnipotent creator, the abilities of this being to alter science and logic would seemingly supersede the legitimate questions posed upon these pages. Thus, in order to derive an unbiased conclusion on such an important matter, we must read the Bible from an impartial perspective and carefully decide if we can truly attribute the book to such a magnificent entity.

If one can successfully demonstrate the accuracy of the Bible, the opinions expressed within this book disintegrate into mere rubbish. If, on the other hand, we can deduce that the possibility of the Bible having a link to this god is exceedingly remote, the book must be able to stand on its own merit to maintain its freely given credibility. If the Bible cannot be self-sufficient in this manner, it's not entitled to the aforementioned leniencies of breaking multiple rules set by science and reason. With this balanced paradigm in mind, you should discover one recurring theme while reviewing the upcoming chapters: the link between divinity and the Bible is simply nonexistent. This idea is anything but novel since thousands before me have demonstrated the abundant biblical complications that establish the logical impossibility of a supernatural force ever dictating or influencing it.

People often ask me why I spend a great deal of time denouncing and disproving the Bible. Although I can't offer an exact reason, my passion is probably driven by the salient danger created by Christianity and its subsequent influence on nearly two billion people every day. While the evil forces of certain deceitful religions have somewhat subsided in more recent times, the hatred inadvertently generated by these belief systems remains the greatest threat to humankind's continued existence. In the past 2000 years, Christianity has been guilty of initiating several wars and crusades resulting in thousands of needless deaths, blatantly oppressing women to the point of worthlessness, abhorrently justifying the enslavement of Africans and perpetuating cruelties upon them we would rather just forget, shamelessly driving its followers to hang or burn alleged witches, nearly exterminating the entire Native American population, and inconspicuously robbing billions of people of countless man-hours that could have been much better spent on improving our planet. Someone certainly needs to address these issues, and the book most of the Western world swears by demands a thorough critical analysis.

I was born agnostic, as are all children, but both of my parents were Christian. Naturally, my mom enrolled me in church at a young age because she wanted to do what she felt was best for me. Having also been enrolled in church at a young age, however, she's never had the opportunity to see the religion from an honest and impartial perspective.

By the age of seven, I acquired the typical boyhood interest in dinosaurs. As a result, I wondered how the divine creation of man could have preceded the existence of these creatures. I learned in school and from my outside reading that dinosaurs had been around for millions of years; Adam and Eve, on the other hand, were divinely created during the earth's first week only about six thousand years ago. No matter how many scenarios I considered, I couldn't think of a way to resolve this important incongruency. I asked my mom for an answer, but she didn't have one either. Instead, she advised me to ask my Sunday School teacher. The shameless answer I received the following Sunday was, "We don't know there were dinosaurs." It was then that I realized the religion had fundamental flaws if it resorted to such claims in order to explain scientific discrepancies. As time went on, however, cognitive dissonance drove me to justify further scientific contradictions as "explainable in some way" while holding onto the word of "absolute truth." *Please don't read this book and prejudicially justify the Bible's problems in the same incredulous manner.*

A great inspiration struck me while sitting in church one Sunday that made me realize billions of people who didn't accept Jesus as their savior were imminently bound for Hell. Even so, they were over on the other side of the globe thinking the exact same thing but with the roles reversed. However, what if they were right and we were wrong? Exactly who decided that Christianity was true while Islam, Buddhism, and Hinduism were demonstrably false; and how did this individual make these determinations? I remember justifying this interesting perplexity by burying my head in the sand and declaring Christianity to be a morally superior religion. I'm patently ashamed of ever forming such a notion.

By the age of seventeen, I began composing a list of all the absurd Old Testament rules and regulations that God and Moses suppressed upon us. Soon after, I gained the courage to disregard the Old Testament as fiction due to the cruelty and scientific errors that it relentlessly presents. The Bible was no longer a perfect book, but Jesus and the New Testament were still solid proof of a god to me.

By the age of twenty, I finally undertook an unprejudiced analysis on the prerequisites of entering Heaven. They simply weren't fair. If the New Testament is true, so was my original realization that members of other religions are going to Hell because their teachers mentally conditioned them to believe their respective religious systems. These individuals were simply doomed from the beginning;

they had no chance. After I factored in the lack of evidence for any of the events surrounding Jesus, the exception being a handful of contradicting accounts written decades after the alleged events, it was just a little too convenient that God decided the fate of the world in a highly superstitious age void of testable records. Because of this painfully poor choice, no one could know for sure what really happened in Jerusalem 2000 years ago. All the while, he supposedly watches us in total silence as we continue to kill each other over who has the correct religion.

When I was twenty-two, I browsed the increasingly popular Internet out of interest in seeing if there were others who had made similar discoveries. I was amazed to find that there were millions of these freethinking individuals in America alone. Using enlightened rationale in conjunction with the enormous amount of counterevidence, hundreds dedicated their time to freeing others from lives of conditioned thought. In fact, a select few had an understanding of the Bible far beyond what I ever realistically hoped to ascertain. As for the Christian defense of these findings, I could see a *lot* of straw grasping. Their best representatives, having obtained bogus doctorates from self-accredited paper mills, stretched and twisted biblical text in order to make it fit with their predetermined agendas. Besides, how objective can one honestly remain while analyzing evidence that's contrary to the belief system in which an enormous emotional investment has already been made? After a long childhood journey, the ultimate answer had finally become obvious to me. If you undertake an honest, dispassionate, and emotionless analysis of the Bible, you can easily conclude that it's not the word of a supreme being. Contrary to what many Christians would like the world to believe, certain facts can't just be absolute truth.

Once I completed my minor in psychology, I had a better grasp on how religious systems tend to work. As a general rule, individuals exhibit their desire to be in groups by surrounding themselves with those who hold similar interests in order to reinforce the perceived appropriateness of their beliefs and opinions. I recognized that I, too, underwent a near-universal conditioning process and tried to recruit/assimilate others into my group because that's what I was told God wanted me to do. I also realized that many Christians don't even know *what* they believe because they never take the time to read the whole Bible. Because of this shockingly lazy choice exercised by the vast majority of Christians, they're mentally unequipped to answer challenges to their belief system. As a result, the common response to presented complications is usually this: "The Bible says it. I believe it. That settles it."

When it comes to religion, the mainstream believers exhibit no more in-depth thinking than the cult members everyone watched burn in Waco, Texas not too long ago. Christians are normal people in the outside world, but their brains seem to switch over to standby mode on Sunday. Cult members usually exercise the ability to live normal lives, too. Regardless of the actions such religious people take, I could never deem them as evil because I understand that they're victims of an unfortunate destiny misleading them down a path of ignorance and unwitting gullibility.

Agnostic once again, I began to realize the full impact of Christianity on our society just a few months before the completion of this book. I was particularly interested in the wealth of scientific evidence against the occurrence of a global flood. Using common sense and knowledge from my scientific background, I decided to compile my own list of reasons why Noah's flood couldn't have feasibly taken place as told by the Bible. A Christian friend of mine who always asked to hear about biblical problems was fascinated by my research. I later decided to convert my list into a publishable essay in hopes of being acknowledged as a beneficial freethinker. In the process, a few additional topics worthy of discussion came to mind. While scholars, historians, and philosophers have thoroughly covered these issues, they scribed most of their material on an extremely sophisticated level. Even with a bachelor's degree and a doctorate in the sciences, much of it went over my head. For this reason, I decided to write on a level that everyone could enjoy and comprehend. After the first few essays were completed, I knew I had more than enough ideas to write a book.

You're not holding an exhaustive scholarly study into the issues covered, but rather a brief introduction to the facts we have and analyses we can make concerning pertinent biblical issues. By no means did I intend for this manuscript to be an exclusively novel, methodically referenced, meticulously comprehensive volume of perplexities plaguing the Bible. I designed this book to be my own careful summation of these discoveries, occasionally accommodating some innovative philosophical questions that the findings should naturally provoke. Since the presented conclusions of a single individual shouldn't be the only component incorporated with your personal judgment, you owe it to yourself to investigate the points raised in this book by reviewing some of the recommended reading material and subsequently considering the arguments offered by both sides. After doing so, I hope you'll realize how disappointing it is that this book, in a scientific age of progressive thought, still needs to be written.

Seemingly countless volumes of work have been written on each subject I cover, but an extensive review of a lone topic is rarely the best place to direct someone's curiosity. Alternatively, I hope this introductory condensation of biblical perplexities will be of some foundational use to doubting Christians and beginning freethinkers. If you already consider yourself a biblical scholar, you probably won't find any groundbreaking or earth-shattering ideas in this book. However, I think it's a wonderful overview of one of the world's greatest problems: Christianity.

Society And The Bible

From Jerusalem To The West

The question of why particular countries in Africa, Europe, and the Americas are essentially Christian nations is best resolved in a two-step process of first analyzing the origins of Christianity and then determining how the belief is passed from generation to generation. This chapter will explore the origins of Christianity and the voyage it made before establishing itself as the dominant religion of the West. We'll see how mere chance determined this part of the world's Christian beliefs and how just a few minor alterations in history would have created an entirely different planet due to the subsequently altered religious distribution. The next chapter, *The Psychology Hidden Behind Christianity*, will discuss religious convictions as they pertain to individuals and their offspring.

Jerusalem To Rome

The early spread of Christianity is almost entirely attributed to the Apostle Paul. His letters to neighboring regions, especially the one to the Romans included in the New Testament, were widely influential in changing local religious views. Before the purported arrival of Jesus Christ, the original Hebrew religion, as found in the Old Testament, was an unfathomably harsh one. If you've taken the time to read the Old Testament in its entirety, you've probably noticed that God was consistently angry and vengeful for what appear to be petty reasons. He even threatened to kill people for excuses most of us would consider insane if offered by an ordinary earthly individual. Records made shortly before the Common Era (otherwise known as the BC period) indicate that the support for this deity had about run out of steam. This natural fizzle is nothing new considering that dozens of religions have flourished and vanished over the past few millennia. Paul, however, was convinced that the idea of Christ renovated the old religion. Thus, he altered the formerly distant and spiteful God into a loving and fair ruler. In fact, the makeover was so drastic that some virtually extinct sects of the new religion believe the god of the New Testament is an entirely different god than the one depicted in the Old Testament.

Paul also dropped an array of incorrigible requirements for converting to this new persuasion, including the most deterring one of all: circumcision. In order to garner a larger following, he also emphasized the aspects of Christianity possessing universal appeal. The most notable of his addendums, the gift of an afterlife, may have been essential for the conversion to be successful. Furthermore, Paul took an additional step toward creating a more accessible belief system by proclaiming that anyone could get into this afterlife regardless of any immoral behavior previously exhibited by the new believer.

Because few people are readily content with the idea of their own mortality, it's perfectly understandable that many would want to jump to a religious persuasion offering a gift of eternal life. Paul was clearly one of many who was self-convinced that he would never truly cease to exist. Quite predictably, fossil records from the era in which historians now think that beliefs of an afterlife began indicate a concurrent expansion of the human skull around the frontal lobe of the brain, the location at which we appreciate our mortality. In essence, religion was born when we saw death coming. God's afterlife could be nothing more than the product of a human defense mechanism against death. All creatures fight for their earthly survival; man has tricked himself into believing he's immortal.

In the first century CE, Rome was in an obvious state of religious and governmental flux. The traditional Roman and Greek religions were rapidly falling out of favor with the citizens of the Empire. Zeus, Jupiter, and company were scarcely observed in religious ceremonies. The Caesar was the closest thing to a god that the people of Rome had ever experienced. In addition, many of the other government officials were corrupt without a thriving religion to provide moral guidelines. At the same time of this spiritual downfall, a highly advanced road system was being laid throughout the Empire to expedite information exchange. These coalescing factors provided the perfect environment for a novel way of thought to remodel their society. Had the citizens of Rome enjoyed a solid religion and governmental stability, they certainly would have quickly rejected Christianity on the grounds of having no practical use for it. Thus, the fate of Christianity as a dominant world religion would have already been doubtful without its acceptance by the powerful and influential Roman Empire.

Christianity eventually arrived in Rome to a warm public reception because the religion was the first with intricate detail and organization to reach this region of the globe. A large collection of recorded events and stories from which potential members could gain the religion's essential lessons also accompanied the movement. Such inclusions were great new concepts for the Romans who previously had religions founded on abstract ideas. Before Christianity, the closest thing to an afterlife that previously established religions ever offered the Romans was the concept of Hades. While this mysterious idea permitted their souls to be saved, it wasn't clear exactly what transpired after their deaths. Heaven, on the other hand, was a remarkable refuge where they would sit alongside their god and savior while singing praises to them. Furthermore, this wonderful gift had only one prerequisite: accept Jesus as a personal savior. Such coherent simplicity was obviously a vast improvement over the older vague religions. While Christianity did have strict guidelines, the followers were seemingly immune from God's post mortem punishments if they had received forgiveness for their sins. Even though Christians are adamant about living what they consider a respectable and moral life, they cannot deny that God also admits rapists and murderers into Heaven under the provided guidelines.

Christianity had a couple of great psychological factors working in its favor centuries before modern psychologists recorded the foundations of the science. First, Jesus prophesied his own return within the lifetime of certain individuals who personally witnessed his miracles. There are several passages in the New Testament reinforcing this essential idea, and we'll discuss these statements at length in future chapters. If the Romans desired to avoid eternal damnation in Hell, they absolutely needed to act quickly before it was too late. Once Jesus returned, the offer was seemingly void. A sense of urgency is always useful in coercing people to behave a certain way. For example, if product discounts in a store are only valid for an extremely short period, researchers have demonstrated that people act impulsively by making purchases they would not have otherwise made in a normal setting. If a significant percentage of people behave this way with small discounts on material possessions, how many would take the chance with eternal damnation by postponing one simple task? When Jesus' return prophecies eventually failed, however, it was necessary to alter the predictions into ambiguity.

The second great attraction was the initial ban of Christianity from practice and observance within Rome. As we all know, when you can't have something, you want it even more. This rule of human nature fueled the desire for the religion, similar to the way that Prohibition fueled a desire for alcohol in 1920s America. The fact that the government didn't allow people to drink made the idea of consuming alcohol more enticing than ever before. Coincidentally, the height of the Empire's expansion in the early second century was concurrent with the prohibition of Christianity. As a result, word of Jesus Christ spread throughout the entire European continent via their improved road system. By 380 CE, Christianity had become such a widespread belief that Emperor Theodosius recognized it as the official religion of Rome. Even though the Empire was collapsing during his reign, it still held large portions of present-day France, Spain, Portugal, and England. As we will see in a moment, these countries were the most vital in shaping the West.

Christianity's Failure

While Christianity was making its numerous rounds throughout Rome, missionaries also pushed the beliefs on societies farther to the East. However, in deep contrast to the citizens of Rome, inhabitants of these regions didn't welcome the religion with open arms. The key difference between Eastern Asia and Rome was the presence of previously established, easily understandable, and consistently observed religions. By 1000 BCE, India already had Hinduism, a set of beliefs founded on their sacred Veda books. These written tales of the world's verifiably oldest surviving religion were widely distributed centuries before Paul was even born. Since Hinduism was firmly rooted in Indian culture, Christianity had very little impact in the region. Likewise, large portions of Asia, including China, had Buddhism by 500 BCE and a written moral guideline, the Tripitaka, by 200 BCE. Needless to say, efforts in bringing Christianity to China overwhelmingly failed as well. Hinduism and Buddhism still respectively stand as the third and fourth largest religions of the world.

By the dawn of the Middle Ages, followers of Christianity, Buddhism, and Hinduism had long established their respective belief systems as the dominant world religions. However, Christianity was the only one of the three that often resorted to violent tactics of conquest and conversion. Its only competitor in crime would be Islam, which was already several centuries behind its more ancient counterparts. Shortly before Columbus rediscovered the Americas, Christians cast a quickly growing Islamic following out of Europe through a series of wars and crusades in the eleventh through fifteenth centuries. Their access to the Atlantic Ocean effectively closed, Muslims would have to be satisfied with forcing their religious beliefs across the Eastern Hemisphere. Consequently, we see a great expansion of Islam throughout large parts of Africa and Asia. Israel, a predominantly Jewish country, is now completely encompassed by Muslim nations. Because Islam was virtually unopposed in the East, it rapidly flourished to become the second largest religious preference in the world. Christianity, on the other hand, stood unopposed at the gateway to the West.

Europe To The Americas

The Roman Empire may have been a distant memory by the 1600s, but it left its mark on Europe through the continued presence of its last principal religion. English Christians made their way to North America in order to escape persecution of harsh religious governments. It wouldn't be long before these immigrants succeeded in murdering or converting several native tribes out of a desire to occupy the eastern third of the continent. France was a trifle more humane to the natives, but they still forced their way into occupying the middle third of the continent. Roman Catholic Spain claimed the western third of the continent as well as most of Central and South America. Portugal, another Roman Catholic country, occupied present-day Brazil. In short, all four countries that conquered the Americas had some form of Christianity as their only publicly accepted religion.

The United States, the region formerly held by England, would eventually buy France's claim in the Louisiana Purchase, an acquisition of definite threat to Spain's presence in North America. The idea of Manifest Destiny, the popular belief that the Judeo-Christian god wanted Americans to rule the continent and firmly impart their ideologies to others, spread quickly in the 1840s. Because of this misguided belief, Christian Americans murdered large numbers of native inhabitants and started wars with Mexico, the region formerly held by Spain, to force them out of the western territories. Greatly weakened by their recent war for independence, Mexico eventually agreed to give up their claims as far south as the present-day border.

By 1865, the Union freed the slaves held by the Confederate States of America. Some of these former human possessions decided to return to Africa, bringing their coerced Christianity with them. To this day, Protestant Christianity dominates the land above the US/Mexico border, while Roman Catholicism is dominant in the regions to the south. Africa is now a balanced mixture of Islam and Christianity.

Why Does Christianity Dominate The West?

One very influential missionary had a desire to spread the idea of Christ. Paul passed the new Hebrew religion onto the Romans through his persuasive skills for writing and speaking. As the citizens of the Empire were desperate for a new religion, they were quite open to the change that Christianity offered. The vastness of Rome then allowed Christianity to spread throughout much of Europe. Before the Empire collapsed, Christian believers had well established their religion in the regions that would play a key role in shaping the West. No other religions, with the exception of the much weaker Islam, were interested in conquering and converting societies with contrasting religious viewpoints. Thus, a lack of viable threats allowed the European Caucasian population to flourish unopposed across the Atlantic Ocean. With this unmolested liberty, the proportion of the Christian world increased to nearly one-third of the present-day religious preference.

If Paul had decided against becoming a Christian, or if Rome wasn't in need of stability, Christianity may have never survived in Europe. In this case, the West could have been free from the burdens and oppressions of religious nonsense. If Islam had formed quicker or sooner, Muslims may have been capable of forcing Christians to release their hold on the Atlantic. The West would then be susceptible solely to Islamic faith. As it stands, the West is a Christian region because Christianity was simply in the right place at the right time.

THE PSYCHOLOGY HIDDEN BEHIND CHRISTIANITY

In the previous chapter, we investigated how Christianity arrived in Europe and the Americas. It's readily observable how expansions of a country's borders will help proliferate its religious views, but how do these views propagate within the country itself? To answer that question, this chapter will look at the passing of religious beliefs from parent to child and the maintenance of the child's beliefs throughout life. I'll illustrate how parents unknowingly condition their children from birth to believe religious stories no matter how absurd these tales may seem to an outside observer. I'll also explain what happens when ideas from sources of contradictory information are presented to children later in life.

From Parent To Child To Grandchild To Great-Grandchild...

It's not a shocking discovery that parents pass on their religious beliefs through their children. Muslim parents tend to have Muslim children; Christian parents tend to have Christian children; atheist parents tend to have atheist children. These traditions simply cannot be maintained by chance alone. Because religious beliefs are certainly not in our DNA, a child's environment must necessarily affect his religious affiliation in some manner. In fact, all children are born agnostic and remain so until influenced by the religious convictions of their parents. I think it would be more than fair to say that if the most avid Christian preacher of your hometown had been born in Israel to Jewish parents, he probably would have been the most avid Rabbi in a comparable Israeli city. Subsequently, he would have been just as certain that he was preaching the truth about Judaism as he is now doing for Christianity. It also follows that he would view Christians as misguided and pray to God for them to stop acknowledging Jesus as his son.

In almost every case, individuals become members of their respective religious groups because their parents were also members. Likewise, the parents are only members because *their* parents were also members. This pattern should prompt the question of how far back this visionless trend continues. To answer, recall the primary reason from the previous chapter why America and Europe are Christian regions: the citizens of the Roman Empire needed stability in their government. Roman acceptance probably had nothing to do with what they analytically believed was the most accurate religion. Instead of initiating an honest and impartial analysis of the new evidence that science and enlightened thinking have provided, people simply bury their heads in the sand and observe whatever beliefs they were conquered with or whatever religion their ancestors needed thousands of years ago. Moreover, this type of reckless behavior goes unnoticed because religious individuals exhibit it throughout almost every culture around the globe.

As for the individual, we can easily observe how a child's religious beliefs originate from the influence of the parents. To what extent does this coerced indoctrination occur? I won't be the first to propose that children are mentally conditioned, more commonly and inaccurately known as brainwashed, to believe whatever their parents desire them to believe without question. If this claim sounds absurd, it's probably due to an ignorance of what the mental conditioning process actually entails.

The activity in question is nothing more than establishing a belief system in a person's mind, intentionally or not, using a series of simple manipulative steps. The necessary stages for such conditioning are exhausting the subject, getting the subject to admit that the current support system isn't perfect in some way, removing the subject's support system, introducing the subject to a new support system, explaining the consequences of not accepting the new support system, keeping the subject isolated from other support systems, explaining the urgency of accepting the new support system, offering a reward for accepting the new support system, and maintaining the subject's new support system for the length of time desired. The first three steps are part of the cleansing phase. However, no cleansing is necessary if there's no conflicting information already present within the subject's beliefs. Thus, there is no need to tire a young child or remove an existing support system to install the new one.

These methods aren't fantasy; they're science. The United States experienced the phenomenon firsthand when some of our soldiers captured in the Korean War underwent this process and made a conscious decision not to return after their captors coerced them into believing America was a treacherous country. The Chinese government forces their prisoners to go through this process as well. Only five percent of their prisoners are repeat offenders whereas fifty percent of prisoners in the United States will repeat a criminal offense if released. Even though the prison sentences are much shorter in China, their prisoners are considerably less likely to repeat a crime. It wouldn't be because they actually rehabilitate them, would it?

When children are at a very young age, their parents unknowingly initiate the conditioning process by informing them that everyone is imperfect. Because they're not perfect, they must take a role model who seemingly defines perfection: Jesus Christ. By turning their lives over to Jesus, they receive forgiveness for their imperfections and inadequacies. Next, parents must make their children fear the consequences of remaining alone with their imperfections. As a result, they are convinced that Hell is the ultimate destination for people who don't rely on the support system. In this place called Hell, those who choose not to accept Jesus will burn in perpetual agony. Since the consequences of not accepting the support system are so horrific, and the steps necessary to eliminate the consequence are so simplistic, children will learn to adopt these beliefs if only to keep a distance from the supposed punishment. By this point, children certainly become willing to follow those who know this system best.

To continue the conditioning process, parents must successfully keep their children free from external contradicting influences by encompassing them within a Christian environment in a Christian country with weekly Christian refreshment. Other religions would obviously present conflicting information and weaken their bonds with Jesus Christ, the head of the support system. The other religions would also illustrate the contradictions and consequential uncertainties shared amongst all beliefs. This mental havoc would also create cognitive dissonance, the tendency driven by uncomfortable feelings to repel or justify contradictory information, before there is enough conditioning to stabilize the belief.

Just as Paul told the Romans that there was a sense of urgency in accepting Jesus, parents tell their children that they'll go to Hell if they know about Jesus and refuse to worship him. Since Jesus could possibly return today or tomorrow, time is of the utmost essence. They absolutely must accept Jesus as soon as possible in order for God to save them from the perpetual punishments of Hell. If they choose not to accept Jesus before they die, that trip to Hell would certainly be in order. Finally, we must not forget about the ultimate reward for accepting Jesus: an eternal stay in Heaven with infinite happiness. How many impressionable young children could possibly refuse this "genuine" offer?

At the tender age this process usually begins, children typically aren't able to rationalize these assertions or challenge their validity. Just the opposite, children habitually give benefit of the doubt to their parents and role models. As time goes by, the vast Christian American environment consistently pounds the imperative system into their heads day after day, week after week, month after month, and year after year. By their teenage years, most Christians couldn't possibly consider the presence of an error in the Bible, much less a completely erroneous foundation, because it's unquestionably the perfect word of God to them. They believe this notion because they're lifelong members of a society that has continually reinforced the "special" nature of Christianity. Needless to say, every religion is "special" in its own isolated environment of observance.

When skeptics ask Christians why they think their religious beliefs are absolute facts, a semi-logical response is rarely produced. Unfortunately, they are never able to see the world as clearly as those who have freed themselves from the intangible bonds of false religions. No Christian would deny that the blood-drinking cult down the street is full of brainwashed members, but Christianity is "the one true religion" with an "authentic savior" who suffered and died for their sins. This nonsensical response comes directly from the conditioning statements reinforced *ad nauseam*. The defensive assertion offered is a logically unsound loop that has been centrally repeating in their minds for years.

We can utilize the exact same conditioning techniques on unwitting subjects in a number of situations. For example, these methods would work wonders in convincing obese people to lose weight through diet and exercise. First, we must make the subjects realize that they don't have a healthy body if they haven't already made this casual observation. Next, we must inform them of the opportunity to join a weight loss support system capable of improving their appearances. We should then warn the overweight people of consequences to their well-being if they refuse to accept the weight loss system. Along the way to losing weight, we must keep the overweight individuals free from external influences that would support their "natural shape." We should also design the system in a way to avoid influences offering an alternative method, such as liposuction, to meet their goals. Then, we should make sure the overweight people realize that every passing day is a drastic step toward a premature death if they're still in excess of their scientifically determined ideal weight. Following that, we should tell them that they could even suffer a heart attack tomorrow if they don't immediately begin to lose weight. All the while, we continuously remind them that losing weight will result in obvious rewards of improved health and appearance. In fact, this change could subsequently open doors for job promotions, better-looking partners, more respect, etc.

The method used on these obese subjects matches systematically with the process of introducing developing children to Christianity. However, the overweight people are at an age where they can investigate the legitimacy of the claims by using a variety of analytical methods. Impartial studies will typically support these weight loss claims. Furthermore, these claims are much more ordinary and readily believable than the incredible ones made in the Bible. However, people can't necessarily be conditioned with the truth as long as they're willing to question their present beliefs upon the arrival of new evidence. In other words, we're not presenting the weight loss system as "absolute truth." There's an enormous amount of evidence debunking the extraordinary claims made by the Bible, yet those who are aware of the evidence and still believe it's the inerrant word of God are not willing to impartially analyze what's being discussed because of the conditioning's lasting effects.

Cognitive Dissonance

To explain cognitive dissonance more thoroughly, I'll start with a hypothetical experiment. Suppose we wanted to test the power of God and prayer in order to verify or debunk related Christian claims. To begin the study, we gather a group of fifty atheists and a group of fifty Christians who volunteer to have an extremely lethal dose of bacteria injected intravenously. Following the injection, we provide the fifty atheists with a regimen of broad-spectrum antibiotics to counteract the infection. We then isolate the atheists in a secret location and tell no one that they are involved in the experiment. Essentially, they don't exist to the rest of the world. Likewise, we isolate the Christians in a secret location but refuse them the antibiotic regimen.

News of the fifty Christians injected with the lethal bacteria will then be broadcast over the entire Christian world. The report will ask everyone to pray to God for their facilitated recovery from the infection so that deductive reasoning will force the world to acknowledge the one true religion because of the unquestionable and verifiable power of God and prayer. Because no one knows about the atheists in isolation, no one is specifically praying for them. All they have are antibiotics, while the Christians have the power of prayer from hundreds of millions of certain volunteers and the omnipotence of God. After two months, we will end the experiment and see which group has the most survivors.

Whether or not the public is willing to admit it, I think everyone knows which group would fare better in this study. No semi-rational Christian would *ever* sign up for this deadly experiment even with the added promise of a great monetary compensation for the survivors. They know that God isn't *really* going to answer the divinely directed requests of hundreds of millions of Christians because God only seems to answer prayers in some mystical and unobservable fashion. Deep down, these Christians may even realize that they can't consider prayer dependable. Thus, the failure to acquire volunteers who won't receive antibiotics creates friction with what the typical Christian believes is absolute truth. The uneasy feeling felt throughout the body creates a drive within the mind to explain and/or separate from the logical contradiction. We call this internal phenomenon *cognitive dissonance*.

As a way of irrationally explaining the lack of activity from God, a Christian would quickly assert that the almighty doesn't like us putting him to a test. In addition, we would also hear that God wants us to believe in him based on faith, not what we determine from our own limited human understanding. As I mentioned previously, because of this proposed choice, God performs his miracles in superstitious ages or in scenarios disallowing falsifiable tests or independent observation. In other words, the power of God is there even though there's no logical way to draw such a conclusion. This irrational explanation is a little too convenient for me. An enlightened person will realize that Christians receive answers for prayers just as often as atheists receive answers for problems. Sometimes prayers are "answered," and sometimes they're not; sometimes problems will have solutions, and sometimes they won't.

It's because of this suppressed "futileness-of-prayer" realization that I feel there is a subconscious mechanism trying to protect individuals from illogical thinking. In such a case, this hypothetical defense mechanism has simply been repressed from years of conditioning. Naturally, I don't have the means to prove this hypothesis and wouldn't expect any believer to accept it without the necessary support, but it makes perfect sense when you've been on both sides of the fence.

Matthew 21:22 and a few other biblical verses tell us that we will receive whatever we ask for in prayer. This statement is not taken out of context, and we can easily disprove a literal interpretation of Jesus' proposal through objective testing. 2 Chronicles 16:12 condemns Asa for consulting physicians with his health problem rather than seeking God's help. As you can see, the Bible is unambiguous on its demand for prayer over medicine, yet common sense and observation tell us how deadly a combination of prayer and medical rejection can be. This is why no Christian would sign up for the experiment. This is also why it's illegal for parents in America to refuse medical services for their children, regardless of the parents' personal beliefs. Medicine has proven its effectiveness; prayer has not. Because the evidence contradicts their deepest convictions, Christians provide nonsensical solutions to the perplexity and ignore valid rebuttals when they can't answer them.

Cognitive Dissonance And The Average Christian

Cognitive dissonance also has a crescendo effect based upon the amount of belief invested in the disputed claim. Let's consider a few more examples to illustrate this point.

Roger, our hypothetical Christian friend, bought a car for $30,000 yesterday thinking it was a great deal. He obviously doesn't want to hear that it's on sale for $25,000 today. In fact, he may have to "see it to believe it." The realization of losing $5,000 by not waiting one more day creates an uneasy feeling within Roger. Although he can't truthfully deny his losses once he sees the new price for himself, he may predictably make several casual comments along the lines of "I can't believe it."

The following week, a criminal burglarizes Roger's house. The police eventually arrest Roger's coworker, Larry, in connection with the crime. If Larry seemed like a decent individual, Roger will probably find it hard to believe that Larry was the one who robbed him. Despite tangible evidence pointing to this conclusion,

Roger may not be fully convinced that Larry was acting on his own accord. He *personally* needs to hear Larry's confession in order to believe the police report.

Years later, Roger's mother is the victim of a violent murder. This time, the police arrest his father for the crime. Unlike the situation with his coworker, Roger will require a much greater amount of evidence before he even begins to acknowledge that his father may be the one who committed the heinous crime, regardless of how obvious the situation is to an impartial observer. Understandably so, he desperately wants to believe the murderer is someone other than his father. Because it's perfectly natural for people to avoid information contradictory to what they rigidly believe, Roger may refuse to accept the story even if his father admits his guilt. The stronger the conviction in question, the stronger the resistance against contradicting evidence will be.

Now, imagine how Roger feels after receiving information that's contradictory to the core religion that has served as his life's foundation for the past forty years. These solid ideas tell Roger that there's no good reason to accept the existence of his version of God or the presence of his slain mother in Heaven. Most people in Roger's situation will repress such "baseless" information and simply not acknowledge it. Some will defer the argument to so-called experts in the same religious camp. Others will find a quick quasi-plausible justification and forget about what they heard. While these actions will successfully alleviate the uncomfortable feeling accompanying the realization of conflicting information, the individual experiencing these emotions has not actually rectified the problem. To Christians, the invalid dispute is now gone; to everyone free of conditioned thinking, it still requires a logical and justifiable resolution.

Roger's latest problem should lead us to another important question. To what extent has society mentally conditioned Christians to believe the perfect nature of their religion? Allow me to use an unusual example to answer.

Suppose the world witnesses the descent of a great entity from the sky. This being proclaims that its name is God and the time for the world to end has finally arrived. Needless to say, most people are going to want to see proof of its claims. Whatever miracles one requests of God, he is happy to oblige. He has the power to make mountains rise and fall at will. He can set the oceans ablaze at the snap of a finger. He can even return life to those who died thousands of years ago. God can do *anything* asked of him. Then, someone from the gathered crowd makes an inquiry as to which religion holds the absolute truth. God replies, "The religion of truth is Islam. The Qur'an is my one and only holy word. All other religious texts, including the Bible, are entirely blasphemous. All those who don't acknowledge my word will undergo a lengthy punishment for not following my teachings. Now is your chance to repent."

What choice does Roger and the Christian community make in this situation? This deity has already demonstrated that it possesses the omnipotence and omniscience of a supreme being. Do Christians readily switch over to the side of observable and testable evidence, or do they declare that this being is the Devil tempting their faith in God? Think about it for a minute because it's an interesting predicament. I believe we all know that a good portion of Christians would denounce this new being in order to please "the one true God, Heavenly Father of Jesus." As a result of their collective decision, the supernatural entity forces them to undergo unimaginable torment for a few weeks before offering them a final chance to repent. Do the Christians embrace the teachings of this creature after experiencing its capabilities firsthand, or do they still consider it the final test and refuse to denounce their faith in the Bible?

What exactly is the meaning of this example? No matter what level of sophisticated evidence contrary to their beliefs might be provided, some Christians will always find a way to set aside reasoned thought in favor of what they have always been thoroughly conditioned to believe. If Christians won't accept the answers of such a powerful creature, how would they ever have the capacity to make informed and impartial choices based on evidence presented by their peers?

When You Can't Handle The Truth

In this introductory material, we investigated how and why religious beliefs have been passed on from parent to child for centuries. Parents unwittingly continue this tradition through a repeated process of mental conditioning that sharply influences the child to think along a certain path about their religion from a very mentally immature age. We can successfully utilize the same process in a variety of other real world situations to verify its utility. Psychological defenses against the absurdities of religion may be deeply repressed by those who experience a high level of religious influence. When opposing data meet the conditioned beliefs, cognitive dissonance takes over and represses such information or irrationally justifies the discrepancies in a manner that allows the confronted people to forget them. For centuries, this psychological phenomenon has prevented people from accepting rational conclusions about Christianity.

CHRISTIANITY'S IMMINENT DOWNFALL

As John Lennon once said, "Christianity will go. It will vanish and shrink. I needn't argue with that; I'm right, and I will be proved right." Shortly after John made this bold and unpopular declaration in the 1960s, society began to reveal the truth in his words. Since 1990, the percentage of Christians comprising the US population has been dropping rapidly. For this reason, we should look at recent trends in religious affiliation and extrapolate what they might indicate on an individual basis. We'll also examine various proposals as to why Christianity is starting on a downward trend and speculate as to which factors may play a part in an individual's decision to leave the practice of blind faith.

The Numbers

The United States has *finally* become the absolute last modernized country to see a sharp drop in the proportion of Christians comprising its population. The landmark ARIS 2001 study indicates that the percentage of Americans who consider themselves Christian has dropped about one percent every year, from 86.2% in 1990 to 76.5% in 2001. Less than half that number will ever satisfy the simplistic purported requirements of entering Heaven. Meanwhile, the percentage of Americans who have no religion grew about one-half percent every year, from 8% in 1990 to 14% in 2001. Furthermore, 13% of Christians joined the faith after belonging to a different religion, while 17% of Christians will eventually leave the faith. On the other hand, 23% of those with no religion left Christianity or some other belief, while only 5% will eventually leave a state of agnosticism/atheism to join a religion.

What factors could account for the sudden drop in Christian percentages and the increased observance of secular views? If anything, it seems that the percentage of Christians would be rising in America given the dramatic influx of immigrants from predominantly Roman Catholic Mexico. The immigration of people from nations with non-Christian views isn't high enough to account for this decline. In fact, Hindus and Muslims have only increased an additional 1-2% in the US over this eleven-year span, while the non-religious have acquired an additional 6% over the same period.

There are also millions of instances where individuals switch from one religion to another. Polls have shown that the most common reason for such changes is the wish of the partner in a relationship. In other words, people are switching religions to please someone else, not God. Without a doubt, there are a large number of people sitting in church every Sunday who couldn't care less about the preacher's message, yet the church unknowingly counts them in their Christian census. On the other hand, how often would Christians renounce their faith if an atheist or agnostic partner made a similar request? Consequently, it's far more likely that a person will switch *into* a religion to please someone than the other way around. This point allows us to assume that the number of non-religious individuals joining an organized belief artificially inflates the percentage of Christians in America above its already dwindling share.

To explain this recent positive phenomenon, I propose that an increase in enlightened thinking about scientific discoveries contradicting the Bible and an increasingly global culture have given people a more accurate view of the world as it truly exists. The Internet, for example, has been instrumental in distributing harsh critiques of the work undertaken by Christian authors. Regardless of the cause, one fact is certain: children are no longer remaining with their parents' Christian religion, as they once were, just because cues in their environment told them that the belief system is true. Some undetermined factor has obviously begun working in America to free people from the bondage of this blatantly false religion. Once a person finally sees the ancient religious myths from an impartial perspective, they're highly unlikely to return to the previously sacred belief system.

Who Will Be Among The Millions This Year?

I believe that the decision to denounce the faith and leave the comfortable confines of Christianity has a strong correlation with a combination of two factors: high levels of intelligence and low levels of exposure. From my anecdotal observations, I've noticed that individuals who leave Christianity are either fairly intelligent or received relatively less conditioning from their parents. Once I made this discovery, I noticed that those who had both of the aforementioned qualities left at an exceedingly early age, while those who had only one quality left the religion in their late teens or early adulthood. Christians probably won't deny that a strong influence persuades a person to remain active in church. Likewise, it's only logical to conclude that a lack of the same influence increases the chances a person will leave the faith. The intelligence element to my hypothesis, on the other hand, is surely insulting and certainly difficult for Christians to swallow. Even so, I strongly feel that a line exists where a certain level of intelligence and a certain level of influence reach equilibrium.

As I just mentioned, an intelligent person with a low level of Christian influence has the best chance of leaving the religion at a young age, whereas an unintelligent person with a high level of influence is almost certain to remain within the church for life. The interesting scenario created with this hypothesis is that an intelligent person with a high level of influence would have two competitive forces at work. One would seemingly free the individual from bunk religious thought while the other would presumably fight to keep the individual within the faith. Since there are more people who stay within the church than those who leave, we can reasonably assume that the influence is a stronger factor than the intelligence. Similarly, an unintelligent person with a low level of influence has no competitive internal forces at work. Consequently, this individual wouldn't develop groundbreaking theories on the existence of God or have external influences pressuring them to believe one way or another.

Weeks after I thought I had written the final draft of this book, I came upon a wealth of experiments collected by Burnham Beckwith and published in the Spring 1986 issue of *Free Inquiry* that effectively demonstrated parts of my hypothesis. Nearly three-fourths of all studies since the 1920s that investigated a correlation between intelligence and religious affiliation have found that the proportion of atheists, agnostic individuals, and deists increases dramatically as you move up the scale in school grades, exam scores, and IQ tests. The remaining fourth of the studies show no correlation; zero reviews suggested that people in organized religions are more intelligent than those with secular beliefs. The apparent conclusion to draw from the data is that people who are more intelligent tend to disbelieve religious superstitions.

Additional recent polls, such as the Harris 2003, suggest that individuals who attend college, live in regions of the country where standardized test scores are higher, or belong to the male gender are less likely to believe in the Christian god. (A side note explanation for those of you getting in a huff: Men comprise more than 50% of the extremely intelligent and extremely unintelligent ends of the spectrum. In other words, while the average man and woman are of equal intelligence, men are more likely to be extremely intelligent/unintelligent and less likely to have normal intelligence. Because I suppose that only those near the highly intelligent extreme of the spectrum have an increased chance of escaping the religion, this may explain why the data are skewed toward men.)

We Will Overcome

As we've recently witnessed millions of people becoming more aware of their surroundings by breaking the restraints of the conditioning commonly associated with religion, the percentage of those affiliating themselves with Christianity is currently dropping at a tremendous rate within the United States and the rest of the world. On an individual basis, achieving freedom from this conditioned way of thinking is probably more likely if the individual has a high level of intelligence and/or a low level of Christian influence. For the previously discussed reasons, Christianity has begun quickly losing ground to enlightened and rational thought. However, the deceitfully sinister and scientifically erroneous religion holds its position as an influential and dangerously robust juggernaut in our society. As Thomas Paine once lamented, "These are the times that try men's souls." For those of you who are aware of his intended connotation, his statement seems to have taken on an entirely new meaning.

POOR CHRISTIAN REASONING

Perhaps the most aggravating ordeal in discussing religious theory is the burden of listening to logical fallacies used by someone with an opposing viewpoint. Logical fallacies are arguments outside the bounds of reality, commonly used by zealous defenders of their respective religions. While some of the arguments used by such an individual may seem sound or valid to a lay audience, especially one with beliefs deeply rooted in the debated system, this chapter should assist you in being able to recognize when such disingenuous methods of argumentation are used. In fact, the illogical attributes of Christianity itself prematurely handicap the ability for a Bible defender to use sound logic in defending his position. I will support examples of these poorly developed techniques with hypothetical religious arguments in order to reinforce the often-confusing explanations.

It's important for the freethinker to avoid these faulty methods of argumentation in order to remain above an intellectually dishonest level. As the tools of logic and reason are on the side of those who don't blindly delve into the comforts of false superstitions, there's no foreseeable excuse to ever resort to the use of logical fallacies in the "defense" of disbelief.

Baseless Assertions

This section will discuss a variety of general arguments that use unreliable methodologies to arrive at a desired conclusion. The first example is *argumentum ad ignorantiam*, which means an argument from ignorance. This is a proposal that something is true (or false) because it has yet to be proven otherwise. A Christian might say, "The crucifixion is a historical fact because no one has found any documents conspiring to invent the story." In the same manner, I could claim that Jesus had four arms. Since no one can solidly disprove my ridiculous assertion, the previous speaker's fallacious logic allows my statement to be considered a historical fact. Needless to say, a lack of evidence against a claim doesn't make the proposal a historical certainty.

Some apologists (those who defend a religious doctrine) will consider an argument more valid if the audience hears it more than the opposing viewpoint. We call this erroneous consideration an *argumentum ad nauseam*, which is an argument that depends on mere repetition. A speaker using this method of argumentation will go to great lengths in order to ensure that he voices his opinion as often as possible. Although the argument itself may be perfectly sound, it's no more or less true the thousandth time that the speaker used it than the first. A silent form of this argument may be self-utilized when someone forms an opinion on the legitimacy of Christianity based on the abundance of related literary works. While Christian nations tend to publish extraordinary amounts of Christian material, the arguments contained therein do not increase in soundness based solely on the number of times that writers regurgitate the information.

Christians will often make arguments that imply something is true because society has generally accepted it as the truth for a lengthy but arbitrary period of time. This is an example of *argumentum ad antiquitatem*, which means an argument based on age. A Christian might say, "People have believed in God for thousands of years. This belief has existed for so long that there must absolutely be some truth to it." Apologists of even older religions could also make such bankrupt claims, but such assertions would no doubt go unheard by a close-minded Christian apologist. In short, the age of the belief in question is independent from the legitimacy of the belief itself. Conversely, some Christians will argue that certain beliefs are true because they're newer than others. This would be an example of *argumentum ad novitatem*, an argument from novelty. "Jesus Christ was crucified during the time of recorded history. Many people wrote about his death, and it's much harder to forge such a record in this era. Therefore, the account is true." Scholars have adequately disproven several modern beliefs, religious or otherwise, in the past 2000 years. While there may be an increased obstacle of difficulty in forging records of a modern event, a belief isn't true just because it's newer than others in the same field.

Apologists often cite the attributes and qualities of people during arguments as evidence to support an assertion. Let's suppose there's a multi-billionaire preacher who has dedicated his life to serving God. This hypothetical character might often be apologetically used as an example of how Christianity is more likely to be true than other religions. Because this rich individual obviously made many correct choices in life, his belief in Jesus, according to the apologist, only makes sense. We call such a ridiculous proposal *argumentum ad crumenam*, an argument based on wealth. If this rich man also believed in the Easter Bunny, the mythical rabbit doesn't leap into the bounds of reality. Conversely, another Christian might consider a poor individual to be more virtuous since he isn't preoccupied with materialistic possessions. Therefore, according to the apologist, we should hold his religious viewpoints in higher esteem than those of the common person. That's an example of *argumentum ad lazarum*, an argument based on a lack of wealth. What if the poor man also believed in the Easter Bunny?

If a person is famous, Christians will often appeal to that individual as an additional example for the legitimacy of their religion. For instance, "Since the past few Presidents of the US have adhered to Christianity, it is certainly the most correct religion." We call this absurd notion *argumentum ad verecundiam*, an argument based on authority. George Washington and Abraham Lincoln were non-Christians, but this doesn't mean the belief system is any less reliable. However, you should make an important discrepancy between this logical fallacy and the referencing of an authority on a given subject. If the speaker sufficiently explains the authority's position, the proposal then becomes an acceptable supplementary argument. Cutting the debate short by exclaiming things like "you just need to read this book by John Q. Public" isn't a satisfactory procedure because two speakers citing books back and forth all day would accomplish nothing.

If an ignorant debater considers a single person to be good evidence, then billions of people probably seem like pure gold. *Argumentum ad numerum* is an argument based on the number of people who believe something to be true. Christians often suggest that Jesus Christ must be an actual historical figure because close to two billion living people now believe that he is the son of God. However, over one billion people believe that Muhammad split the moon in half. Where is the imaginary boundary for the number argument to work? What happens when the world's Muslim population inevitably exceeds the number of Christians? Will biblical apologists then accept Islam as the truth based on this reasoning? Of course not, and they shouldn't. The number of people who subscribe to a religion doesn't make the belief system any more or less factual than it already is (or isn't). Similarly, *argumentum ad populum* is the use of a statement that appeals to some popular notion in society. A Christian might argue, "To insinuate that the Bible is a hoax is to call a countless number of our past heroes misguided." Even though such a statement might successfully enrage the audience against the speaker's opponent, it's a blatantly dishonest but often unintentional utilization of the audience's emotions to turn them toward a certain viewpoint. No matter how popular or widespread a religious belief can be, these qualities don't add to the soundness of the facts.

Distorted Timelines And Irrational Congruencies

Those who overly claim that certain events are dependent and/or evident of other events commit logical mistakes as well. Thus, we'll look at a few examples of these common fallacies in this section.

Christians often falsely attribute one event to another because they concurrently took place. This is called *cum hoc ergo propter hoc*, translated as "with the fact, therefore because of the fact." An example might be a reference to a study demonstrating that crime rates have dropped steadily in an area over the previous two years because of increased church attendance. Note that this is a *possible* explanation for the drop in crime, but there's no conclusively causal relationship between the two events. The person making the claim ignores other possible reasons why the crime rate may have dropped (e.g. an increased budget for the police department). A similar fallacy is *post hoc ergo propter hoc*, translated as "after the fact, therefore because of the fact." An example along the lines of the previous proposal might cite the improved emotions in those who attend church for two years. An apologist might conclude that the improvement resulted from church membership, but this individual once again ignores a plethora of other possible explanations, such as lifestyle modifications or antidepressant medications. Both of these logical fallacies are more specific forms of *non causa pro causa*, which is an attempt to draw a link between two events without any good evidence of a relationship.

In addition to the previous unsuccessful arguments attempting to bridge two events, there are some fallacies attempting to create a link between two theoretical events. *Denial of the antecedent* is a form of argument that concludes a proposal isn't true because it was implied by another proposal now proven to be inaccurate. A Christian could say, "The theory of evolution was dependent on modern man descending from Neanderthals. Since the Neanderthal descent hypothesis has proven to be false, the theory of evolution also fails." While it's true that scientists once speculated that Neanderthals could be ancestors of modern humans, by no means does this advancement in knowledge disprove the entire field of evolution. Similarly, *affirmation of the consequent* is a fallacious argument suggesting that if one event implies another event happened, the first occurrence is true because someone has proven the second true. A good example might be similar to this: "Jesus said that there would be war and famine in the last days of this world. Since we see prevalent war and famine, Jesus truly made this statement." Events simply don't take place for the sole purpose of fulfilling prophecies. Besides, I'd like to hear about a point in history void of these unfortunate circumstances.

I've actually known some people who have suggested that meditation is a form of prayer. Consequently, they think those who meditate are actually praying to God. However, individuals making this baseless suggestion fail to expand on *why* prayer is the same as meditation. They simply want you to accept the premise that they're similar and accept the conclusion they provide. We refer to this irresponsible method of assertion as *the fallacy of the undisturbed middle*. Christian believers also tend to utilize such an inconsistency in order to harmonize a discrepancy between the Bible and known scientific data. The most common example is the timeline for the creation of the earth's contents. These individuals may concede that the earth was created billions of years ago while simultaneously maintaining the accuracy of the Genesis account. However, both statements simply cannot be true because they're in direct conflict. The speaker would need to justify this proposed harmonization in order to avoid making an erroneous and fallacious argument.

An often-used logical fallacy is *ad hoc reasoning*, or an explanation offered after the fact. It's a common apologetic practice to fall back on an alternative solution once the foundation of the original position has crumbled. For example, a Christian might state, "There's great evidence that the earth is only a few thousand years old." Once someone exposes the error in such a blatantly false statement with the overwhelming counterevidence, the Christian might then say, "God made it look that way to mislead those who rely on their own opinions rather than having faith in his word." The speaker has totally dropped the original indefensible claim and substituted it with an alternative explanation, one that only makes sense after the fact. In other words, the speaker is justifying the problem with an invented solution in order to protect his position.

Those attempting to obtain approval for an idea often unknowingly use the *slippery slope* argument. For example, a Christian might suggest, "If you take prayer out of school, children will learn to be less dependent on God throughout the rest of their lives. When the methods these children use to solve their problems fail, they'll often result to other means that may endanger them. If they don't end up getting killed, they'll wander into a life of crime in order to fill their needs instead of turning to God." I hope you can see why it's called the slippery slope argument. The speaker insinuates that if we take a certain action, a cascade of other events will inevitably follow. As is the case here, the speaker typically offers no evidence on which to connect the series of crude assertions.

Miscellaneous Accidents

The logical fallacies included in this section are most likely the result of accidents or ignorance. We'll discuss intellectually dishonest methods of argumentation in a moment. The first such accidental case is the reliance upon *anecdotal evidence* to prove a point. Such "evidence" is nothing more than assumed conclusions based on casual observations and personal experiences rather than honest and impartial scientific analyses. For instance, "Childbirth is the result of a divine miracle. There's no other way to explain it." On the surface, childbirth may appear to be beyond our comprehension. However, once a thorough study is made of the biological events leading up to childbirth, it should become an extraordinary but explainable natural bodily process.

Special pleading is another foolish and unsuccessful method of argumentation frequently used within the Christian community. This fallacy is committed when the speaker directs a plea toward his opponent or the audience in an attempt to win them over to the desired position. For example, a Christian apologist might say, "Only a small part of my opponent's counterevidence works against my claim. If you ignore that small bit, my position stands unscathed." While it may sound intentional, the speaker is most often unaware of the erroneous nature of his request. We can't simply ignore or wish evidence away when we don't like it.

A *sweeping generalization* is the act of applying a general rule on a specific situation. For example, when apologists often claim that most atheists have never read too far into the Bible, they conclude that one atheist in particular must not have read the Bible. While it's probably true that the majority of atheists have not bothered with reading the Bible, it's improper and prejudicial to apply this general guideline to a particular individual. Similarly, a *hasty generalization* is the making of a claim based on a limited number of examples. Imagine a story running on the news about three Muslims burning down a number of churches across a city. Someone committing a hasty generalization would conclude that all Muslims are radical terrorists. Likewise, apologists will also use a very similar argument known as the *fallacy of division* to make favorable remarks about their fellow worshippers. "Roger is a Christian. Therefore, he could not have killed Larry." While the vast majority of Christians aren't murderers, this statement underhandedly applies the overall quality of the group to a specific individual.

Many Christians truly believe that none of their peers would engage in something as heinous as kidnapping people to sell them into slavery. Once we're able to convince an apologist that many slave traders were members of the Christian faith, he might alter the meaning of what it is to be a Christian by claiming that no *true* Christian would ever commit these acts of treachery. We refer to such desperation as the *no true Scotsman fallacy*. Even if the apologist's definition of what he felt comprised a Christian included being unable to kidnap and sell slaves, he's only offered a baseless and arbitrary guideline. Someone else could easily assert that no *true* Christian would ever tell a lie. Such a bold proposal would undoubtedly eliminate all two billion Christians at the blink of an eye.

Christian apologists will often use references to the natural world via the *naturalistic fallacy* for their justifications or condemnations of particular behaviors. In addition to quoting Bible verses condemning homosexual acts, they will often refer to the absence of these behaviors in the natural world. As a result, they will conclude that homosexuality isn't a natural practice for humans. The problem with this argument is that the natural world doesn't offer a glimpse at *many* of the things humans do. The use of birth control devices isn't seen anywhere in nature, yet many Christians partake in this "unnatural" act. Such a counterpoint perfectly exemplifies why the argument goes down in flames. Incidentally, much to the chagrin of ultraconservatives, there *are* homosexual acts currently taking place in the natural world.

An extremely common logical fallacy often serving as the sole foundation of a Christian argument is *petitio principii*, more widely known as *begging the question*. This mistake occurs when the premise used to support a conclusion is as equally questionable as the conclusion itself. For example, "The Bible is the word of God. Because it tells us that accepting Jesus is the only way to enter Heaven, there's no other way to avoid Hell other than accepting Jesus." The speaker predicates his conclusion upon the premise of his argument being true. In other words, he bases the conclusion of non-Christians going to Hell on the assumption that the Bible is the word of God. However, the premise is definitely a questionable one. A conclusion based solely on a questionable premise must, of course, be questionable as well. It would then be the speaker's responsibility to provide proof for his premise or withdraw his conclusion.

There's an interrogative form of begging the question called a *complex/loaded question*. This is where the speaker assumes certain facts when asking a question. "Are you still sending people to hell by convincing them to turn away from God?" The question contains a predetermined conclusion that turning people away from God will send them to Hell. Again, the speaker is required to present proof of a causal relationship between a disbelief in God and banishment to Hell. A one-word response will not satisfactorily answer the question even though the speaker has phrased it in such a manner.

Another similar logical fallacy is termed *circulus in demonstrando*, otherwise known as *circular reasoning*. Here's a painfully common example: "The Bible is the word of God. Since God wrote the Bible, we know that it contains only truthful accounts. Since the truthful accounts are inspired by God, we know that the Bible is God's word." In other words, the Bible is the word of God because the Bible says so. If you can't spot the enormous gaping hole in this argument, I'm afraid that I'm not doing you much help. The Qur'an says Muhammad is Allah's prophet, but that doesn't make it a fact. There must be good evidence to support these claims.

I find circular reasoning to be a particularly aggravating method of argumentation, especially when a Christian denies those with different religions the luxury to make the same bald assertions. It's even common for apologists to make the extremely frustrating claim that relying on complimentary evidence, such as the discrete sets of scientific data yielded by radiometric dating and fossil deposits, is the same thing as invoking the use of circular reasoning. In other words, they believe the only validity that we can derive from these two tests is that one supports the other. This is simply not the case. Each test independently yields the same conclusion; therefore, each test *reinforces* the validity of the conclusion made by the other. No one is saying that the age from radiometric dating is true because it agrees with the age from fossil layers and that the age from fossil layers is true because it agrees with the age from radiometric dating; *that* would be circular reasoning.

When the going gets rough for Christian apologists trying to defend their biblical views, they'll often say, "You can't prove God doesn't exist." They're exactly right. Similarly, they can't prove the Easter Bunny doesn't exist. However, they can be *reasonably certain* of its nonexistence when they make a judgment based on all available data. The proposal for the other party to disprove the positive assertion is a logical fallacy known as *shifting the burden of proof*. It's never the responsibility of the person denying the claim to prove otherwise, nor is it possible to prove something doesn't exist unless we burden this hypothetical phenomenon with rules and logic of our universe (e.g. disproving squared circles). The person who makes the positive claim is always responsible for proving it's factual. Whether or not you believe that a god who makes a magical egg-delivering rabbit is more ridiculous than a god who is pleased by the smell of burnt flesh is simply a matter of perspective. Each demands the same amount of proof.

Smoke And Mirrors

Unfortunately, many apologists use arguments that they know are wholly lacking in credibility. Perhaps some part of them even realizes the absurdity of their position and creates the need to resort to such tactics in order to defend their beliefs. This section will discuss those logical fallacies most often intentionally used under intellectual dishonesty.

A good starting example is the use of *bifurcation*, commonly known as the *black and white fallacy*. This is a way of offering only two possible answers to a scenario when there are credible alternative solutions. An individual practicing bifurcation might say, "Either Mark knew about Jesus and wrote the Gospel account, or he didn't. Since Mark records Jesus' miracles several times, we can conclude that he knew Jesus." The problem with this particular statement is the lumping of Mark's knowledge and authorship into one inseparable unit. The speaker ignores the possibility that Mark wrote about Jesus but didn't know him, or vice-versa. There's also an interrogative form of bifurcation known as *plurium interrogationum*. This fallacy is committed when the speaker requires a simple affirmative or negative answer to a more complex question. "Did the biblical characters exist? Answer *yes* or *no*." If you wish to retort by saying that some existed while others didn't, such a question requires a more detailed explanation for a satisfactory answer than the one word allotment provided by the speaker.

An apologist defending his position may even resort to force, *argumentum ad baculum,* as a way of getting an audience to adhere to his belief. This cunning individual might say, "If you don't accept Jesus Christ as your savior, you'll burn in Hell for eternity." While the apologist obviously believes he's speaking the truth, the statement by itself isn't any truer than "If you accept Jesus Christ as your savior, you'll burn in Hell for blaspheming Allah." However, this shamefully dishonest method is an appreciably effective scare tactic to use on a gullible audience.

A Christian speaker might also attack the credibility of his opponent by using factors unrelated to the credibility of the opponent's position. An example of such an *argumentum ad hominem* would be this: "The man who stands before you is an atheist. He claims Christianity doesn't have a good moral code, but I happen to know that he's verbally abusive toward his peers." Such an unwarranted attack against the opponent has no value toward supporting the issue of Christianity's moral code. While the hostility doesn't have any logical credibility as a valid argument, it speaks volumes about the credibility of the individual resorting to its usage.

An *irrelevant conclusion* is self-explanatory. This act of deception is committed when a speaker makes a conclusion that has absolutely no relationship with the point he wishes to defend. Perhaps a Christian wants to protect the notion of Jesus being the son of God. He might consequently say, "Jesus died on the cross for our sins. This took away all our sins and gave us eternal life. Many people have now turned to Jesus. This tells us that Jesus was the son of God." Notice how the supporting ideas do nothing to prove Jesus was the son of God. The conclusion is, therefore, irrelevant.

A similar argument might have a *non sequitur*, the use of a premise having no logical connection with its proposed conclusion. For example, "Because Mark wrote a biography of Jesus, he must have been well versed in ancient Hebrew Scriptures." The premise does nothing to support the conclusion, nor can you logically infer the conclusion from the given premise.

The immensely popular *red herring* occurs when someone attempts to introduce irrelevant material into a discussion. Suppose two sides are debating whether the followers of Christianity or Islam have committed the most historical atrocities. A Christian apologist might say, "Christianity hasn't committed more atrocities than Islam. I know many loving Christian people who go out of their way to help others regardless of the religious faith to which the beneficiaries subscribe. Everyone in my church does volunteer work for the community. We've all donated our life savings to the homeless. You never hear about Muslims doing any of these things. Thus, Christianity hasn't committed more historical atrocities than Islam." In this instance, the speaker did nothing more than offer a few anecdotal evidences to support the notion that Christianity is a kinder religion than Islam. However, the speaker's examples did not deal with the issue of which religion has committed more atrocities in its history. Whether or not Christians perform caring acts is entirely irrelevant to the debate. The speaker is deceitfully attempting to divert the audience's attention away from the topic at hand by distracting them with irrelevant material.

Next, we have the cleverly titled *straw man*. This fallacy is committed when the speaker alters or misrepresents the position of his opponent in order to enable an easy but unwarranted attack. Suppose two sides are debating over the existence of the Hebrew god. After side one proclaims that he probably doesn't exist, side two might reply, "You say that God probably doesn't exist as though you had all the answers yourself. Tell us how you know the universe didn't need a creator." Notice how the speaker begins his retort by mentioning a specific god but quickly broadens his opponent's stance to include a decoy position of atheism. Side one never claimed that a god doesn't exist, nor did he say that the universe didn't require a creator. Side two has maliciously misrepresented his opposition because side one only claimed that the *Hebrew* god probably doesn't exist. There's an obvious and crucial difference between these two positions.

Finally, no overview of poor logical reasoning would be complete without mentioning *the universal reply*. If apologetic responses repeatedly have no more value than "You just need to read the Bible to understand Jesus and God's word," you're probably wasting your time trying to talk some sense into the speaker. Any statement capable of being recycled by another religion never qualifies as evidence. Change *Bible* to *Qur'an, Jesus* to *Muhammad*, and *God* to *Allah* to produce an equally irrational "special insight" assertion ready for Muslim consumption. If anything, belief only poisons the ability to make an unbiased judgment of the evidence. Similarly, we cannot consider personal experiences to be solid evidence for the legitimacy of a religious system because members of all religions claim to have the same experiences. How many times have you heard of God getting credit for curing someone's cancer? Strangely enough, so does Allah!

Now You're Ready To Understand

This chapter should provide you with a sufficient overview of disingenuous arguments commonly used by apologists to support their beliefs. Any Christian readers who have utilized these illogical methods of argumentation should understand why they are not valid. Likewise, anyone wishing to engage an apologist in biblical debate should always be very mindful to avoid utilizing these logical fallacies. This successful avoidance will no doubt facilitate the use of logically sound arguments. Thus, it would serve anyone well to memorize these fallacies and be able to explain why they are considered to be blatantly foolish methods of misguided argumentation. Now that you have a basic understanding of the common apologetic stance, let's analyze the Bible, without relying on such desperate measures, to derive plausible explanations for its content.

Science And The Bible

SCIENCE TO THE RESCUE

The presence of observable and falsifiable scientific evidence is perhaps the most compelling reason we can conclude that the Bible is not free from error. Because this evidence clearly yields certain conclusions that are contradicted by direct statements from biblical authors, we can safely say that the Bible is an imperfect book containing flaws of human origin. Due to the overwhelming amount of scientific errors the book possesses, you should have great comfort in deciding that there was no divine inspiration or intervention involved during its creation. Furthermore, the vast categories of errors contained in the Bible demonstrate that the mistakes are not confined to a single author or field of study, a realization that should question the foundation and intent of the book as a whole. We'll focus considerably on the first chapter of Genesis, astronomy, and biology because each of these topics unmistakably contributes to the *faux pas* of apologetics.

"The Beginning"

Anyone with a decent background in natural science who undertakes an impartial but critical look at the first chapter of Genesis should have no trouble denouncing its claims as rubbish. At best, the author has offered a poorly constructed allegory for the creation of the universe; at worst, and far more plausible, Genesis 1 is a total fabrication. This section will of course demonstrate why the creation account in the opening chapter fails miserably to be scientifically accurate.

Early in the creation, God allegedly separated the waters into two distinct bodies so that land could appear between them. He called the water below *seas* and the water above *sky*, which he presumably held aloft by the use of a *firmament* (Verses 6-10). While the NIV translated this verse using *expansion*, the Hebrew word utilized by the author is *raki'a*, which the KJV more accurately translated as a *solid* body.

Why is the KJV translation more in line with the author's intent? First, it's the primary use of the word. Second, it reinforces the aforementioned idea of a sky ocean because a solid protective layer would be required to suspend the water if there truly were an ocean above us as the Bible suggests. Third, it complements the known widespread primitive beliefs. Take the mindset of an ancient Hebrew for a moment by ignoring any contemporary understanding you have of the world. You can glance at the sky above and observe that it's the color of water, while, periodically, water falls from above. With no further evidence to consider and no further understanding of this phenomenon, the perfectly logical conclusion would be that there's a mass of water in the sky. If this is true, it certainly follows that a solid body, a firmament, would be necessary to contain this oceanic reservoir. Perhaps windows even open in the firmament to allow rainfall (Genesis 8:2).

Although the pursuit of knowledge has proven these outdated beliefs untrue, we are far richer in scientific understanding than our Hebrew predecessors and should not scoff at the author for his proposal. We now know that the sky is blue due to the scattering of a particular wavelength of light passing through the atmosphere at a certain angle, not because there's an ocean in the sky. While we cannot fault the author for believing this ancient hypothesis, we *can* conclude that his guess on the properties of the sky was incorrect. Already, a critical analysis has demonstrated the Bible to be scientifically inaccurate and undeniably imperfect.

God allegedly created the sun and moon on the fourth day of the creation (14-19), but this curious statement creates a plethora of troubles because God had already divided the day into lightness and darkness as his first creation (3-5). How can there be night and day without the sun, the only appreciable source of light for our planet? Again, we must take the probable mindset of the author to understand his position. Look into the sky away from the sun. It's unreasonable to conclude that the earth is bright at its distal boundaries just because the sun is shining, unless you have solid evidence to the contrary, because the light originating from this enormous ball of fire appears to stop very near its edges. Besides, everyone knows that the horizon is luminous well before and well after the sun is in the visible regions of the sky. Thus, there's no solid reason to conclude that the sun has anything to do with creating the illumination, only that it accompanies the somewhat concurrent periods of lightness. In fact, the Bible explicitly states that the sun and moon are merely symbols "to divide the day from the night" (14). In the biblical world, however, God controlled morning and evening by this mysterious force called *light* (3-5), an entirely different entity created much earlier than the sun. We now know that the sun is the determining factor between morning and evening, yet the Bible clearly proclaims morning and evening existed prior to the sun's creation.

In addition to the sun gaffe, the scientifically ignorant author commits the mistake of listing the moon as a light (16). If we were to be rigidly technical about the Bible's claim, this verse is another scientifically erroneous notion because the moon merely reflects illumination from the sun. Isaiah and Ezekiel also make this mistake in their prophecy accounts (30:26 and 32:7, respectively). Again, we often take our modern knowledge about the universe for granted, yet such a gift was completely unforeseeable to the ancient Hebrew.

Another problem arises from the sun not appearing until the fourth day when you consider that plants suddenly appeared on the third day (11-13). While it's definitely possible, even very likely, for plants to survive without the sun for a single day, many apologists have attempted to rectify the obvious timeline problems in Genesis by altering the meaning of a day. Once they consummate this amendment, they've created a timeline in which the plants exist without sunlight for however long these "days" are to them. In most cases, a biblical day must necessarily be no less than a period of millions of years in order to be congruent with scientific data. While the general Hebrew term for day, *yom*, doesn't necessarily mean a twenty-four hour day, we still understand it to be a short time period based on every contemporaneous instance of its use. Millennia simply do not qualify using this unbiased criterion. Furthermore, the author provides us with the precise definition of *yom* in every creation instance: morning and evening. Naturally, we'll revisit these creationary intervals in the upcoming *Thousands Or Billions*. For now, let's return to the problem of the plants thriving without the sun's existence.

Most vegetation requires sunlight to undergo photosynthesis, the process of using light energy to convert carbon dioxide and water into nutrients. I wouldn't bet on plant survival much more than a month without the sun. While it's true that the biblical creation has this mysterious *light* existing prior to the arrival of plants, the only thing we can conclude about its existence is the probable lack thereof. The sun, on the other hand, is fully compatible with plant life. Once again, this obtuse blunder can be justified by the limitations of the ancient Hebrew's knowledge because he obviously wasn't aware that plants were feeding off sunlight for their survival.

As one final minor point on plants for now, God says he has given us every plant for food (29). However, we're now aware of plants with qualities poisonous enough that make us avoid physical contact with them. Such disturbingly reckless advice hardly seems to be the kind likely given out by an omniscient deity.

The "Heavens"

God allegedly created the stars on the fourth day (16), but what were they, and what was their purpose? Biblical authors believed that stars were small sources of light contained within the imaginary firmament covering the earth. In other words, they exhibited no divine inspiration, whatsoever, telling them that stars were actually unfathomably enormous gaseous spheres seemingly countless miles away. In short, the authors' celestial hypothesis was incorrect on location, number, and size. Verification for the location part of this position is quite easy to demonstrate. After God made the sun, moon, and stars, he "set them *in* the firmament of the heaven to give light upon the earth" (17). So along with the sun and moon, the stars are apparently housed in this imaginary physical boundary separating the sky ocean from the open air above earth's inhabitants.

The Bible also remarkably claims the outdated belief that stars were extremely small in size. After the disclosure of their location in the firmament, and after God tells Abraham several times that his people would be as numerous as the stars (which is also impossible, yet it's claimed to have been fulfilled in Hebrews 11:12), the next clear reference to size and position of these celestial bodies is found in the book of Isaiah. Here, the prophet speaks of exalting a throne "above the stars of God" (14:13). Likewise, Job says, "behold the height of the stars, how high they are" (22:12). Stars are not high; they are distant. One would expect these two divinely inspired individuals to make this distinction in their records; instead, they boldly demonstrate that they shared the popular yet erroneous belief that God fixed the stars at the sky's apex.

The book of Psalms states that God tells the number of stars and calls them all by their names (147:4). That's quite an impressive accomplishment considering scientists estimate that there could be as many as 10,000,000,000,000,000,000,000,000 in the known universe. If God truly told anyone how many stars surrounded our planet, the ridiculous firmament belief should have ceased without delay.

Daniel speaks of a vision that he had concerning a giant goat's horn knocking the stars down to the ground where the goat "stamped upon them" (Daniel 8:8-9). Passing comment on the vision, we can also be decidedly certain that Daniel believed stars were tiny lights hanging above the earth. Otherwise, how could his monstrous goat stamp upon them? More importantly, how could someone divinely inspired write something so blatantly preposterous? In the New Testament, Matthew and Mark both record Jesus foretelling of an era when the stars shall "fall from heaven" (24:29 and 13:25, respectively). Jesus, a supposedly perfect human being who was supposedly the only son of a supposedly perfect god, wasn't immune to scientific ignorance either.

Revelation was the grandiose vision of John, yet another man who God allegedly inspired, but John also thought that stars were bright objects of insignificant size directly above the earth. In this record of his dream-like hallucination, he claims to see Jesus holding seven stars in his right hand (1:16). While John may have seen what *looked* like seven stars in Jesus' hand, this is not what the text clearly states. The passage unambiguously says Jesus *was* holding seven stars in his hand. Thus, John's statement is certainly in error. In addition, John mentions a dream in which "the stars of heaven fell unto the earth" and compares this event to a fig tree shaking off its leaves (6:13). Furthermore, he describes a great star falling into "the third part of the rivers, and upon the fountains of the waters" (8:10). If a star were to "fall" to our planet as John indicates, it would annihilate the earth upon impact because these bodies are generally hundreds of times larger than our world. Finally, John sees a dragon swing its tail around, consequently knocking a third of the stars in the sky down to the ground (12:4). There's no need to discuss how enormous such a hypothetical tail would have to be in order to accomplish this impossibility. After all, Revelation was only a vision. On the other hand, we must expect Christians to accept that this man had a unique foreknowledge of humankind's imminent future. In other words, these ridiculously fantastical events must remain futuristic certainties to biblical apologists. At this point, we can safely say that anyone attempting to harmonize the scientifically determined position, size, and number of our celestial neighbors with a literal interpretation of the Bible is veraciously wasting his time.

Zoological Pseudoscience

The ancient Hebrews apparently didn't have abundant knowledge of the animal kingdom, and the supposedly omniscient deity neglected to grant them with such insight before they started working on his timeless declaration to the world. Following Noah's flood, the Bible says that all terrestrial and marine life would have fear and dread toward humans (Genesis 9:2). That's simply not the case because there are vast numbers of animals, ranging from pets to fearless predators, that have no fear whatsoever toward humans. This erroneous complication was simply a matter of the fallible author's confined knowledge. While the animals inhabiting Mesopotamia may have very well been scared of humans, this prospect doesn't alter the clear connotation of the biblical text.

Later in Genesis, Jacob successfully alters the color patterns on lambs and goats so that he could differentiate the stronger ones from the weaker ones. He purportedly accomplished this feat by placing peeled tree branches in front of the mating livestock (Genesis 30:37-39). Following his absurd achievement, an angel of God visits him in a dream and praises him for his work in genetics (Genesis 31:11-12). As someone with a thorough background in human physiology, I hold the opinion that this is easily the single most embarrassing error contained between the Bible's covers. Peeled branches have absolutely no effect on an organism's appearance; DNA does. As an extremely quick summary of the topic, the general rule is that half of an offspring's DNA comes from each parent with the more dominant type being physically expressed. The specific genes in the DNA sequence are the determining factor for the animals' colors. Of course, such advanced understanding was *way* beyond the scope of the ancient Hebrew. Divine inspiration obviously doesn't resonate from this passage either.

The story of Moses relaying God's commands to the people also drops the ball when you consider which animals the almighty deemed unclean. He says hares are not clean enough to eat because they chew their cud (Leviticus 11:6 and

Deuteronomy 14:7). I'm not sure where he gets this impression because it's the exact opposite of reality. The obvious solution to this problem is that no all-knowing deity told Moses anything of the sort.

The book of Job depicts ostriches as birds that bury their eggs in the earth so that they can depart and leave them unattended (Job 39:13-16). It's sufficient to say they're biblically painted as careless parents. Nothing, however, could be further from the truth. Ostriches are extremely meticulous about how they take care of their offspring. Even the father helps out, which is the overwhelming exception in the animal kingdom. This is another example of a flat-out error that often goes shunned by biblical apologists due to the absence of a reasonable response.

A more popular story centered on zoological blunders is that of Jonah being swallowed by a fish and living inside its stomach for three days (Jonah 1:17). Even if we ignore how strange the story might seem, we can still conclude that the author lacked the knowledge of gastric juices and bile acids more than capable of digesting a human body.

The New Testament doesn't offer any enlightenment on the animal kingdom either. James declares that every kind of animal has been tamed (James 3:7). Although James asserts nearly the exact opposite of the earlier Genesis authors, perhaps due to a widespread effort to tame all wildlife over the preceding few centuries, he runs straight into the same problem: limitations of an individual human perspective. Like the earlier writers, James probably never ventured too far outside of Mesopotamia. If he had taken the time to make this journey, he would have eventually realized that there were other animals yet to be discovered, let alone tamed. James' premature proclamation hardly seems consistent with what I would consider a divinely inspired statement.

Anthropological Pseudoscience

Once again, we return to the Pentateuch (a.k.a. Books of Moses, Torah, or first five chapters of the Bible) to find additional scientific errors, this time committed with regard to human beings. Let's begin with a consistent problem throughout the Old Testament: population growth. The first such example takes place during the post-flood era when the population inexplicably mushrooms from eight to a million plus, counting the women, in only a few hundred years (Exodus 1:5, 38:26). By the time the events of 2 Samuel are said to have been taking place, there were well over a million men in two armies alone (2 Samuel 24:9). Not only is this exceedingly accelerated for a believable population growth spurt, the living conditions were not exactly primed for such a magnificent, logarithmic eruption of life. Furthermore, there's no reliable archaeological evidence that there was ever a number remotely close to that many people living simultaneously in the Middle

East until just very recently. The numbers were certainly exaggerated, as are many details of centuries-old stories handed down via oral tradition. A common apologetic argument used in response to this problem will cite God's supposed tendencies to allow miraculous growth rates (Genesis 15:5, Exodus 1:7), but what actual evidence do they provide to support this explanation? As it stands, simple ignorance or an oversight by the error-prone author created this obvious difficulty.

Genesis 5 and 11 contain chronologies for the first important people in the Bible, as well as the number of years each person lived. The average lifespan is about eight hundred years with Methuselah taking the cake at 969. People simply do not live that long, especially considering the treacherous conditions necessarily burdened thousands of years ago. To answer this dilemma, biblical defenders will simply quote where the spirit of God left man to end his longevity (Genesis 6:3). However, there's a realistic approach to solving this curiosity. We know from other ancient religions that their own important figures also have extremely abnormal lifespans, sometimes reaching into thousands of years. Due to the accompanying stories behind this consistent practice, historians are easily able to conclude that the founders of these religions commonly stretched the lifespans of individuals whom they wished to exalt as having increased importance. In other words, the incredible ages of these biblical characters are nothing more than the product of folklore resulting from someone's wishful thinking.

The Book of Esther accommodates the story of a man who thinks with his heart (6:6). While this appears to be a symbolic meaning, much like how we say people think either with their heads or with their hearts, it's important to realize that people originally believed thought originated from within the heart. During Egyptian mummification, morticians often removed the brain from the corpse, leaving the heart with the deceased individual due to its perceived over-importance. Even the Egyptians certainly shared the same erroneous belief as the technologically inferior Hebrews. The Bible could have easily distinguished itself from other religious texts by establishing some reputable authenticity with such an advanced declaration, but it conveniently failed to do so.

Yet again, the Bible fails to improve upon a field of science when it moves into the New Testament. Matthew, Mark, and Luke all believed that the inabilities to speak and hear were the result of possessions by evil spirits (9:32, 9:17, and 11:14, respectively). This is an interesting and quiet creative hypothesis, but one we currently know is not true. The inability to speak is usually due to a physical abnormality in the region of the brain known as Broca's area, while the inability to hear is typically due to physical trauma of the inner ear. If these regions don't operate properly, the affected individual lacks the auditory and phonetic capacities made possible by a normal physiology.

Matthew also believes that blindness is a result of the devil's inhabitance (12:22). Again, you don't need the unverifiable nature of this wild claim explained to you. Damage to the optic nerve or detachment of the retina usually causes blindness. No devils or demons have ever demonstrated their involvement in this impairment. Luke purports that a woman's crippled nature is also due to possession by a devil (13:11). While there are multitudes of unfortunate factors that can cripple a person, spiritual possession has never proven to be one of them. Luke and Matthew commit an additional medical error when they claim that devils cause seizures (9:39 and 17:15, respectively). Suffice to say, devils, demons, evil spirits, or any other fiendish creatures have never been known to cause seizures. These violent neurological events are the result of some physiological abnormality, such as a brain tumor, or an imbalance in electrical activity. When radical epilepsy manifestations are observed, however, it's certainly understandable how a person with limited knowledge of human physiology could leap to the erroneous and fantastic conclusion that a demon might have possessed the individual in question. The Hebrew god once again fails to distinguish himself from the countless other ancient gods because his writers weren't the least bit scientifically believable.

In every instance of alleged demonic possession I mentioned, Jesus cured the people suffering from these ailments via exorcism, the act of casting demons out of the body. This heavily implies that Jesus also thought evil spirits were responsible for these conditions. Because Jesus himself even says it was through God that he casts out demons (Matthew 12:28 and Luke 11:20), one could even insinuate that he's obviously relying on the ignorance of the crowd to further his stature. Otherwise, the stories of exorcisms could very well be nothing more than fabrications.

The take-home message about these purported exorcisms is that they could not have happened if we are to believe the means by which they occurred unfolded exactly as recorded in the Gospels. Even if the *perceptions* of the authors served as the basis for the exorcism claims, the text is still incorrect and, therefore, unreliable. Thus, the Bible has once again demonstrated its own hilariously fallacious nature.

Further Scientific Nonsense

Another embarrassing tale of biblical nonsense is the construction of the Tower of Babel in Genesis 11. According to the bogus legend, everyone on earth spoke the same language when the erection of the tower began. Because the people of earth had a great desire to catch a glimpse of God, they built this supposed tower intending to breach the sky. As God didn't like the possibility of people spotting him, he confused their languages to prevent the architects from understanding one another. Unable to continue construction, everyone with different languages went separate ways.

This story is unfeasible for *many* reasons. The first problem with the incredulous account is the incongruency of the common language theme. We know that many different languages existed centuries before the story's setting around 2500-2000 BCE. Not only that, but another Pentateuch author had said Noah's sons separated according to their own tongues in the previous chapter (Genesis 10). At the very least, we have a major timeline discrepancy in need of an acceptable resolution. Furthermore, the notion that nineteenth century man had the architectural knowledge to build a tower even a mile high is ridiculous. To fathom that a group of ignorant ancient Hebrews could make an equivalent accomplishment is ludicrous.

Interestingly, no divine inspiration is available as a possible excuse for the illogical story because God wasn't siding with his people on this occasion! If he didn't wish for the people to see him, he wouldn't have provided the means for them to do so. Of course, the most obvious blunder is God's supposed fear of us actually reaching him in the sky. To suggest that an omniscient god would destroy a building because he felt he was in danger of humans catching a glimpse of him is an equally ludicrous proposal. The aspects of this story once again go back to the ancient Hebrew belief that God eternally resided on top of a dome covering the earth. Since an omniscient deity would know that the people could not possibly reach him, he would not have stopped the tower's construction for the specific reason provided by the Bible. The story cries of a myth.

We also have fanciful tales about giants roaming the earth during the Pentateuch era. There's a lot of room for interpretation here because the exact nature of these mysterious giants is unknown. However, we understand that the Bible has them living both before and after the flood (Genesis 6:4 and Numbers 13:33). Some Christians have argued these giants are the dinosaurs, but this proposed explanation fails to be consistent with the "flood caused the dinosaur extinction" hypothesis offered by others in the same crowd. While the text is most likely referring to a race of people, archaeologists have found no reliable evidence that these creatures existed. Given the track record of the Bible thus far, it's reasonable to conclude that the Genesis giants are, at best, an exaggeration of an otherwise normal species of life.

Jesus also commits another scientific blunder when he declares the mustard seed to be the smallest seed of the earth (Mark 4:31). There are, in fact, many seeds smaller than the mustard, such as the South American orchid, but the Hebrews were obviously ignorant of most everything outside of their homeland. Had God presented this bit of information to the author of Mark, it seems unfeasible that the writer would portray Jesus as a man so careless with his diction. This example is clearly another biblical error on the growing accumulation that arises from the same limitation of divinely uninspired perspective.

The Tentative Verdict For Science Versus The Bible

The suggestion that the Bible is lacking a scientific foundation is nothing less than a colossal understatement. The Bible has failed fair, impartial, and universally applicable tests in multiple fields of science. If God truly is the inspiration behind this purportedly divine declaration to the world, he shows absolutely no interest in its understandability or accuracy in astronomy, cosmology, zoology, botany, anthropology, geology, ecology, geography, physiology, and several other disciplines not covered in this chapter. In fact, the Bible handicaps those who use their "God-given" talents of reason and logic to settle blatant biblical problems. Nothing can be more detrimental to the authenticity of a statement than contradictory phenomena that we readily observe and experience. With no other evidence to consider, these natural manifestations should *always* override what we might hope and think to be correct explanations for unignorable discrepancies. Such is the power of science and reason. They are the impartial pursuit of an answer to a question, not the search for supplements to a predetermined answer.

101 Reasons Why Noah's Story Doesn't Float

I can think of no superior example thoroughly demonstrating why the Bible is not the holy word of any deity than the tale of Noah and his ark. Although this book is intended to be a short introduction of biblical problems for those still hanging onto their programmed beliefs, I'm unable to fathom how I can be concise with the tale of the global flood. Rather than bogging you down with some mind numbing scientific data, I'll try to present the various problems in an organized yet fun to read manner.

A Dose Of Common Sense

Let's begin by looking at this highly questionable account from a common sense point of view. Within the story, we have a god who has to modify virtually all of his creations for the solely expressed reason of the people having become wicked and evil (Genesis 6:5), yet wicked and evil people continue to exist throughout the Bible. Right off the bat, the foundation for the story fails to make sense. Why would an omniscient god have to destroy all of his work for a specific quality that he knew would continue to exist even unto this very day? The flood was for naught, yet God carried out his horrific genocide anyway. I find this to be the most disturbing and perhaps the most ridiculous premise ever conjured by the human mind.

The author clearly tells the story from the perspective that God had just recently realized the way the world had become. This, too, fails to make sense because biblical authors repeatedly claim that God is omniscient. By definition, his omniscience requires him to have known at the time of Adam and Eve that he would later desire to start from scratch at Noah. This unnecessary and foreseeable correction is hardly the logical course of action for an omnipotent god to take. If you let your inhibitions loose, however, it should be painfully obvious that the original authors of Genesis didn't consider these salient points as they were writing. One might even ask if they bothered to proofread their work. Such casual observations work well against the hypothesis of an all-knowing god, a consideration we'll revisit repeatedly. At this point in our study, one must *already* concede that God is not omniscient, God behaves in an acutely illogical manner, or the flood simply never took place for the reasons provided by the Bible.

Appallingly, God drowned unborn children in the flood. This indisputably necessary consequence of his actions should ironically put a huge kink in the pro-life arguments from the church. God aborts countless unborn children for the questionable sins of their parents, yet the church expects society not to do the same? Infants and young children who do not possess the intellectual capacity to tell right from wrong were also casualties of the flood! How could they be among the wicked and evil? These are hardly the actions of the loving God depicted in the New Testament. The innocent children didn't deserve the fate God inexcusably dealt them, end of story. Helpless animals also suffered the horrible fate of the children. However, given the apparently twisted love that God has for smells from animal sacrifices (Genesis 8:20-21), that last point shouldn't have been very surprising to someone familiar with the Bible.

No one has ever found the enormous ark even though we know its final resting place is among the mountains of Ararat located around present-day Turkey (Genesis 8:4). All evidence presented as proof of the ark's discovery has been admitted to be a hoax, proven a hoax, or withheld from testing. Although one could reasonably anticipate that someone would have discovered a tangible piece of evidence from the craft if it hasn't decomposed, multiple expeditions have turned up absolutely nothing. While many people claim they have evidence for the ark being conveniently underground, no one has ventured to exhume it from the earth.

Genesis, the only known source of Noah's story, has several hundred additional problems in need of answers before we can consider it a reliable historical source. No known individuals recorded this particular version of the global flood myth until nearly 2000 years after the floodwaters vanished. Since oral accounts of an event can obviously undergo drastic changes even over a few generations, there's really no telling how much alteration the story incorporated before existing in its present form. In short, as we have seen and will continue to see, the book of Genesis is not a reliable source of historical information by any stretch of the imagination.

Observable Facts In Any Day And Age

A little known but important piece of information about the Genesis flood is that the extremely similar Epic of Gilgamesh in the Sumerian legend predates Noah's story by at least one thousand years in the written form and at least five hundred years for the setting. The similarities between the two tales are so remarkable that we cannot write them off in good conscience as mere coincidences. In the earlier flood legend, Utnapishtim receives instructions and exact dimensions on how to construct a large ship to avoid an imminent flood (as does Noah in Genesis 6:14-16), takes animals and his family aboard to preserve life on earth (as does Noah in

Genesis 6:19-7:1), lands the ship on a mountain after the flood has stopped (as does Noah in Genesis 8:4), releases a dove and a raven from the ship in order to aid his search for dry land (as does Noah in Genesis 8:6-11), and burns a sacrifice after the flood for the gods who find its odor pleasing (as does Noah in Genesis 8:20-21). Because several additional minor parallels exist, I would encourage everyone to read Tablet XI of the short epic in its entirety in order to appreciate fully the similarities between the two legends. Since the Gilgamesh tale is the earlier version of the two, we can only surmise that the authors of Genesis copied the Epic of Gilgamesh or inadvertently patterned the story of Noah's ark on an even more ancient flood legend that we have yet to discover.

Records of flourishing civilizations in China, Egypt, Babylon, and Mesopotamia exist straight through the flood era of 2500-2000 BCE. This contingency creates a stack of obvious problems without planned solutions because the flood supposedly vanquished the inhabitants of these regions. If this was the case, why do we now possess their journals made before, during, and after this global deluge? The flood would have certainly destroyed these societal accounts if God were truly guilty of genocide. If people from each region somehow managed to survive and continue these records, why isn't the cataclysmic flood mentioned in their accounts? In fact, no sort of catastrophe on this level exists anywhere in the written histories of any society during any era. On the other hand, records of ancient civilizations frequently mention several *local* floods. This is quite possibly the most compelling reason why many Christians have abandoned a global flood hypothesis in favor of a local one, a proposal rapidly gaining in popularity that I will debunk toward the end of this chapter. Had the authors known their descendants would one day be able to date these civilizations, the story most certainly would have been different from what we have today.

Most people with a reasonable level of geographical education are aware of the existence of Mt. Everest, which has an apex well over five miles above sea level. In apparent contrast, the ancient Hebrews, as we discussed before, probably never ventured too far from their homeland and therefore knew of no such formation. If the textual description of the flood is assumed to be accurate, we know that this enormous mountain would have to be covered by fifteen cubits (about twenty-two feet) of water during the flood (Genesis 7:19-20). Had the authors been truly aware that there were mountains extending this far above sea level, they would have certainly altered the story again in order to bring the water requirement back to a somewhat more feasible level.

To this day, no one has ever been able to assemble a seaworthy boat the size and best possible composition of the ark even though the all-knowing God personally dictates the dimensions. Experts in the field agree on the long established three-hundred-foot limit for a wooden vessel, yet the ark extends 50% beyond this repeatedly verified limitation. In addition, researchers carried out their attempts to break the three-hundred-foot barrier under tranquil weather, not conditions indicative of the apocalyptic downpour depicted in Genesis. Furthermore, the modern boats used in these attempts had the benefit of iron braces to maximize cohesion. There's no indication that Noah used *any* metal when building his ark. If we accept the Bible as an accurate account of the event, Noah was necessarily confined to "gopher wood" and pitch (Genesis 6:14). Had the authors ever attempted to construct a craft the size of the one that they championed as a global flood survivor, they would have failed miserably. Consequently, the size of the ark would have been yet another factor of the flood story in desperate need of adjustment.

Hundreds of millions of animal species existed during the time of Noah, many of which could have been observed by undertaking a long journey from Mesopotamia. Had the authors spent more time researching animal life in the neighboring regions, they probably would have come to appreciate the futility in fitting two animals of every kind onto the ark. As a result, the authors would have to expand the ark's dimensions in order to accommodate Noah's guests. At the same time, however, the boat's larger design would further handicap its credibility as a seaworthy craft.

A surviving population of eight could not have rebounded quickly enough in order for the equally comical Tower of Babel story to take place only one or two centuries later. While God commands Noah's family to be fruitful and multiply, seemingly providing the story with a mirage of plausibility, the population simply could not have grown to more than a hundred or so even under ideal environmental conditions. Could this minuscule group of people have possibly posed a threat to God by building a tower so immense that Heaven would become attainable to them? Ignoring the obvious reply that God doesn't live on top of the sky, Noah's future descendents certainly didn't have the resources to accomplish this assuredly impossible task.

The Water Fiasco

As the title of this section indicates, we'll now look at a few problems created by the water supply, most notably the lack thereof. The amount necessary to produce a flood of global proportions far exceeds the current amount available on, in, and above the earth. While this doesn't prove the water wasn't present, the burden of proof is on those who defend the story to provide it with a plausible explanation. As the "fountains of the deep" (Genesis 7:11) contain only 1% of the necessary water, 99% would have to fall from the supposed sky ocean. Thus, the goal of covering every mountain with only forty days' worth of precipitation would require a rainfall of six inches per *minute*, which is far too tremendous for the primitive ark to remain intact. In great contrast, we would typically expect a rainfall of only six inches per *hour* from a category five hurricane. One can only decide that this requirement is hardly feasible to carry out, especially when the heat generated by the impact of the raindrops on the flood surface would have been more than sufficient to boil the water and prevent it from rising.

The water originating from underneath the earth's surface would erupt with noxious gases, such as sulfuric acid, that would make their way into the atmosphere and cause the earth to become uninhabitable. The lava expected to accompany the subterranean water would also bring the already scalding liquid to its boiling point. Furthermore, if the oceans somehow miraculously avoided vaporization, nothing would have prevented the water from receding beneath the earth once the outpour ceased unless the pressure exerted by the water above collapsed the previous passageways. Such a scenario would then force the water to remain or evaporate. Since the water is no longer present and the clouds in the supposed sky ocean don't have the capacity to hold this amount of liquid, we can only assume that it mysteriously vanished. However, the problems of the water's source and destination are moot points since the entire ocean should have almost instantaneously been converted to steam. In fact, the steam rising from the ocean beds would have been concentrated enough to boil off the planet's atmosphere.

Keep in mind that this tale would make sense to the early Hebrew who apparently believed there was an oceanic reservoir in the sky (Genesis 1:6-7). If a mysterious canopy of water existed above the earth at one time, as some Christians have offered as an explanation for the origin of the water, the mass of liquid would raise the atmospheric pressure enough to cause a dramatic increase of oxygen and nitrogen to toxic levels. Such a canopy would also extend beyond the ozone layer, a problem concluding with the denaturation of water molecules by high levels of ultraviolet light. If you subtract the requisite of covering the world's highest mountains, of which we have no reason to believe the story's inventors were aware, most of these problems would conveniently disappear. As it stands, however, the necessary water requirement is too extraordinary for covering the earth's surface by fifteen cubits.

The Geological Fiasco

One should also realistically expect at least a scant amount of geological or natural evidence for a global flood if the supernatural catastrophe took place, but the signs overwhelmingly point to the contrary. The flood should have created a massive extinction along the floors of the oceans. Likewise, millions of land organisms that would have certainly been victimized by the flood would also have

deposited a large layer of terrestrial fossils. Of course, neither one of these eviden-
tial necessities is apparent.

Miles of coral reef, hundreds of feet thick, still survive intact at the Eniwetok
atoll in the Pacific Ocean. The violent flood would have certainly destroyed these
formations, yet the rate of deposit tells us that the reefs have survived for over
100,000 undisturbed years. Similarly, the floodwaters, not to mention the other
factors leading to a boiling sea, would have obviously melted the polar ice caps.
However, ice layers in Greenland and Antarctica date back at least 40,000 years.

Impact craters from pre-historical asteroid strikes still exist even though the
tumultuous floodwaters would have completely eroded them. If these craters
were formed concurrently with the flood, as it has been irresponsibly suggested,
the magnificent heat from the massive impacts would have immediately boiled
large quantities of the ocean, as if it wasn't hot enough already. Like the asteroid
craters, global mountain ranges would exhibit uniform erosion as a result of a
global flood. Unsurprisingly, we witness just the opposite in neighboring pairs of
greatly contrasting examples, such as the Rockies and Appalachians.

Even if we erroneously assume there to be enough water under the earth's surface in order to satisfy the required flood levels, the size of the openings necessary
to permit passage for a sufficient amount of water would be large enough to
destroy the cohesive properties of the earth's crust. However, the outer layer is
firmly intact, and there's no evidence indicating that it ever collapsed. All this
hypothetical escaping water would have greatly eroded the sides of the deep ocean
fissures as well, but no such observable evidence exists for this phenomenon either.

We can obtain additional geological evidence suggesting that there will never
be records discovered for this particular global flood by examining fossil deposits
via radiometric dating. This scientific process isn't as complex as it may initially
sound. We know that isotopes, specific forms of chemical elements, will naturally
convert to other isotopes over time. The rate at which they undergo this change
depends on the concentration of the original isotope. Regardless of the original
amount present, half of isotope A will become isotope B over x length of time,
where x depends on the specific properties of the isotope that one wants to measure. After the same x length of time, the present amount will reduce by half again,
leaving one-fourth of the original amount of isotope A. The length of time
required by the isotope to reduce its concentration by half is referred to as the
half-life. We know that this process will continue indefinitely, but we can only
take an accurate measurement while a sufficient amount of the original isotope
remains. For example, we know that Rubidium-87 decomposes into Strontium-
87 over time. To demonstrate the natural phenomenon of radiometric decomposition, we can begin by collecting and measuring a pure sample of Rubidium-87.
After a specified period, we can again measure the sample and observe how much

has converted to Strontium-87. Now there's enough information to extrapolate the precise rate at which Rubidium-87 converts to Strontium-87. Many isotopes, such as the one mentioned in our example, have half-lives of several billion years.

Results from this radiometric dating method unambiguously indicate that many of the less complex fossils are billions of years old. This realization drives a painful thorn in the Creationist hypothesis that attempts to explain how the flood deposited the fossils only a few thousand years ago. Furthermore, time has also neatly separated the earth's fossils into distinct layers according to their radio-metrically determined age. In fact, there has never been a verifiable instance in which two fossils discovered in the same layer were dated appreciably different. Even if we entertain the possibility of the fossils being deposited by the biblical flood, the field of fluid mechanics tells us that the smaller fossils of less complex, more primitive life forms would not sink as fast as the larger fossils, yet the remains of these tiny creatures are the sole occupants of the basement layer because they obviously settled millions of years prior to the deposition of fossils belonging to more complex, more recent life forms.

We can also observe algae deposits within the fossil layers, a phenomenon that could not have formed during the flood because they require sunlight to thrive. It's quite reasonable to assume that the clouds would have thoroughly obstructed the sunlight during such a tremendous rain indicative of the flood. Setting aside this and all other known fossil inconsistencies with the Bible, archaeologists have found human footprints within the upper layers. Moving water simply could not have deposited these markings. As I alluded to earlier, this seemingly endless list of geological problems was completely unforeseeable to the primitive authors, thus the Bible offers no justifications or explanations for our discoveries.

The Animal Adventure

Shifting topics, let's tackle the various animal problems and the question even the most rigid believer has asked at one time or another: "How did Noah get all those animals to fit on the ark?" An appropriate sequential analysis should begin with the problems Noah would have faced years before the ark ever left the ground. This recently appointed shipbuilder would have had extreme difficulty in gathering some of the more dangerous and sizable animals, such as tigers and elephants; and without falling back on divine intervention once again, the apologist can't justify a reason why these animals would readily decide to return with Noah to the construction zone. Thus, there's no good way to determine exactly how long it would have taken to trap and transport all the necessary animals in order to comply with God's orders. Noah would have also been required to know, collect, and preserve the food for special diets required by certain animals. While many finicky species, such as the koala, can survive for short periods away from their primary sources of nutrition, the choice to forego these considerations compounds the great risk of killing such animals already traumatized by the drastic relocation.

As we all know, many animal species are indigenous only to certain regions of the globe. There would have been no rational means by which Noah could have traveled to Australia to catch two koalas, North America to trap two grizzly bears, Antarctica to kidnap two penguins, etc. Even if we allow a miraculous way for Noah to journey to these remote regions, we're still looking at that enormous amount of time to venture across the earth for the sole purpose of preserving an insignificant percentage of animals that God could have easily recreated after the flood. As Noah and his family are already pressed for time with the ark's assembly, successful completion of such a futile journey seems exceedingly unattainable.

As a consequence of their forced relocation, the overwhelming majority of the animals wouldn't have survived in the near-desert region of Mesopotamia due to the extreme climate. For example, many cave dwelling animals require 100% humidity to survive. Such animals couldn't have lived through months of turmoil on the boat, much less a week's stay in the desert. Additionally, many animals require residency on an island due to their nature of being easy prey. Mainland creatures would have quickly driven them to extinction due to competition among the different species during the time prior to the flood. These considerable animal anomalies were, once again, unknown to the ancient authors.

In the last area you'd anticipate having problems, the thoughtless God only provided Noah with a seven day warning to load the ark (Genesis 7:4). This designated period wouldn't have been sufficient to secure even a few thousand animals onboard even when working around the clock. However, this task would have been relatively easy to accomplish if Noah was only boarding the handful of animals known to the flood story's original audience.

We also understand that God advised Noah to take a male and a female of each kind onto the ship (Genesis 7:2). An unconditional problem with this divine order is the presence of asexual and hermaphroditic species. Because variant asexual species reproduce without a sexual partner, there's no male or female distinction of which to speak. As for the hermaphrodites, they simultaneously exhibit qualities of being both male *and* female. These two anomalous creature classifications have no distinct male and female members, thus Noah couldn't have gathered a male and female member of the kind as instructed by God unless we alter the clear meaning of the text.

Unbelievably, the hypothetical sojourn aboard the ark would have likely created problems even more numerous than those encountered before the journey. The answer to the question on everyone's mind is that the animals, babies or not, clearly could not have fit on the ark if we follow the building guidelines provided by God. Remember that according to some Christian apologists, the flood was responsible for depositing the fossil layers. The consequence of this hypothesis is the requirement for every species, including those believed to have become extinct millions of years ago, to be present at the time of the flood in order to deposit their share of fossils in the geological column. Moreover, Noah would have been required to load the ark with dinosaurs. These enormous creatures wouldn't fit onboard even if they had the crude vessel entirely to themselves. Apologists are really grasping at straws by this point if they're still asserting that the global flood deposited the fossil layers.

Ignoring the dinosaur difficulty for a moment, the ark still would not have been large enough to house the remaining animals. Once again, the size of Noah's boat would have been sufficient if you only count the variety of animals known to the authors. While the attempt at this feat doesn't even come close to approaching success when considering two of each *species*, apologists will often regress to the "*kinds* of animals" hypothesis set forth in the Bible (meaning one kind of cat, one kind of beetle, etc.) However, this foolish proposition doesn't allow enough time for the deviation of species into their present forms. Once this issue is settled, perhaps they can begin work on a method by which the dinosaurs can come aboard.

Considering that there was only an eighteen-inch opening near the roof, the boat's ventilation system would have been inadequate for the animals' oxygen requirements. To make matters worse, some of the rooms were separated entirely from this makeshift ventilation system (Genesis 6:16). Any organism attempting to thrive in this isolated environment would have fortunately died much sooner than those slowly suffering with a more proximate location to the roof. In short, almost every living thing would have eventually expired from asphyxiation. Furthermore, the buildup of toxic methane gas from animal feces would have only compounded the respiration predicaments. While I imagine the smell would have been simply intolerable, one spark would have created a far more critical problem because methane is highly flammable.

Many special types of carnivores become very afflicted when forced to live off vegetation because they typically only meet their nourishment requirements from live foods. Likewise, many herbivores will only eat fresh foods. While the biblical authors would probably like us to believe that these special need creatures survived off stored foliage, such torturous concessions would be ill advised in this unfathomably hostile environment. Even with the supposition of these animals being able to tolerate a drastic change in their diets, Noah could not have feasibly provided fresh vegetation throughout the duration of their confinement. The lack of refrigeration and open storage of the accessible rations would have solicited a number of pests to facilitate the natural rotting process. The high level of humidity would also have created an ideal environment for mold to thrive and spoil the food. Every living creature, except for the strongest carnivores eventually able to dine on carcasses, would have soon starved because there would be nothing edible remaining on Noah's ark.

Several more dilemmas imminently faced over the duration of the stay are readily apparent. Some species, such as ants and bees, need a colony to survive. Thus, two members alone would not have been sufficient for guaranteeing the continuation of their survival because each individual has a limited capacity to perform only certain tasks for the community. Host specific parasites could not have survived with only one pair of hosts. Either the parasites would have expired from a lack of nutrition, or they would have doomed their hosts' species, as well as their own, by killing their only acceptable source of nourishment. Since moderate activity is quite necessary for most organisms to remain healthy, the relatively lucky prisoners would have further suffered due to a lack of exercise from the necessary space confinement. The lifespan of many species is shorter than a few months, but the ark would not have provided a suitable reproductive environment for most of these short-lived animals. There could not have been sufficient separation in the ark to keep the violent animals from attacking the weaker ones. There were no replacement animals for many species in the certain instance that one of them met an early death. The eight-person crew would not have been large enough to feed and take care of the countless number of animals taken aboard. I could really go on and on about the animal problems on the ark, but I hope this brief discussion will be sufficient.

Once nature has ultimately dispersed the floodwaters and Noah has released the animals, the problems *still* continue. The unfathomably heavy rains would have essentially annihilated any means for nutritive support to sprout from the ground. In order for the animals to continue their unprecedented survival, they would need some form of nourishment. Unfortunately, it would take quite some time before the ground would be capable of ever yielding anything of value. Of course, God could have recreated all the plant species, but that would be incongruent with the purpose of taking life onboard in the first place.

The two flood-surviving members of each species don't provide enough genetic variation to guarantee their futuristic representation in the ecosphere. More specifically, diseases and genetic defects had a great chance of pushing them into extinction due to the lack of essential variety at the molecular level. As I mentioned in the scenario before the flood, some species require very specific environments to live. The violent downpour would have destroyed certain foods and shelter required by these animals. Finally, we have no evidence that all the animals originated from the resting point of the ark near Turkey, yet a reasonable deduction leads us to believe that the animals found their way back to their original locations. However, their assumed success in beating such overwhelming odds raises the question of why they would want to return to their original habitats. It seems that if all these species were able to survive in such radical conditions, they would be equipped to thrive anywhere they desired.

People...

All the grueling but necessary maintenance undertaken by Noah and company would have certainly led to lethal levels of exhaustion if the tasks were successfully completed. In reality, Noah's family couldn't have accomplished waste sanitation alone because the crude layout of the ark requires them to carry the manure from the lower decks above the water line for disposal. Let's also not forget that Noah's family still has feeding duties along with whatever else the enormous crew at the San Diego Zoo accomplishes every day. All the while, Noah's family would have to tackle and complete these superhuman tasks while serving as living hosts for viruses, bacteria, fungi, and other microorganisms capable of producing pathologically based ailments in humans. A population of eight obviously had no chance to survive this fatal concoction of illnesses. If everyone had gone onboard disease-free, the microorganisms would have nowhere to thrive. Likewise, the animals carrying their own specific parasitic problems could not have realistically survived such turmoil. It should be a foregone conclusion that the author wasn't well versed in the microorganism theory of disease.

Ignoring all these factors working against humans surviving the forty days of utter chaos, Noah's family *also* lacked a sufficient gene pool to guarantee continuation of our species once the ark landed. Even if we assume that they were successful in surviving against these unprecedented odds, could we have all descended from only eight original members? Genetic markers, such as DNA, are excellent timekeepers to determine the interval back to a common ancestor. Since delving into the subject in sufficient detail would require a book in itself, just understand that it's possible to observe the deviation of DNA strands by retroactively measuring them to a common strand. This period back to a common ancestor has been determined to be tens of thousands of years, an age remarkably consistent with the ones established for human civilization remains through previously mentioned dating methods. We do not see the five thousand years that our DNA would reveal if all humans descended from the sole survivors of God's flood.

...Fish...

The seemingly immune marine life could have fared no better than their terrestrial counterparts because, first of all, the rapid mixture of salt and fresh water from the conglomeration of various pure water sources would have killed all known marine creatures in a matter of hours. End of story. Of course, that is not really the end of the story. Like terrestrial creatures, some marine species have very specific requirements for their habitats. One such example would be the delicate breeding ground for salmon. The violent floodwaters would have certainly eradicated these fragile aspects of their environment. Similarly, the force of the rainfall would instigate an integration of large mud deposits with the now semi-salty water. This scenario would undoubtedly create an increasingly lethal environment for marine life requiring crystal clear water.

The required five-mile rise in the global water level would have drastically altered the pressure exerted within the ocean and forced many species to leave their only hospitable levels in order to avoid a pressure-inducing death by implosion. You may also recall that the oceans should already be boiling from subterranean lava, outer space asteroids, torrential raindrop impacts, and whatever else might be necessary to maintain apologetic proposals. Remarkably, we could consider salt and mud to be the least of the threats against aquatic survival.

…Plants

The world's vegetation should also join the growing list of organisms without immunity from the effects of the morally shameful flood. Many plant species could not have survived throughout their continuous submersion in water, especially if the flood introduced them to the new saline mixture. Even so, is it possible that the vegetation could have vanquished, yet left viable seeds to continue their species as many have suggested? The answer is *no* for several reasons.

The flood would have buried the vast majority of vegetative offspring under hundreds of feet of sediment, far too deep for successful sprouting. Similarly, many seeds cannot survive the lengthy, yet necessary duration of the flood without undergoing germination. Others cannot germinate unless they've been exposed to fire or ingested by an animal, two specific conditions extremely unlikely to occur within the drenched post-flood era of tremendously reduced animal populations.

To compound the vegetative problems further, not all plants produce seeds as a method of reproduction. The common, nontextual, apologetic hypothesis proposes that Noah brought seeds onto the ark to assure plant survival, but this amateurish guess obviously fails to address the aforementioned problems. As I mentioned earlier, these obvious errors originally went unnoticed because ancient Hebrews almost certainly didn't appreciate the living quality of plants as we do today. A wonderful case in point is the ridiculous inclusion of the dove returning and olive leaf that absolutely could not have had time to germinate after the flood (Genesis 8:11).

Outside The Box

Let's now turn to the ark and its odds for survival throughout the violent apocalypse. Even before the first raindrop descends from the clouds or rises from beneath the surface, Noah would have had no way to prevent the wood from rotting in the hot desert sun. Even so, this factor is probably the least of Noah's wood-related problems because he would need to select a grain and species strong enough to prevent separation between the ark's joints during its hazardous journey. For reasons that should be painfully obvious by now, I doubt this mysterious "gopher wood" was selected using such advanced analytical thinking.

The endurance of the ark faces several more formidable obstacles than its primitively wooden composition. Wave undulation caused by the presumably violent winds accompanying the storm would have undoubtedly capsized the makeshift craft. Incredible hydroforces would have propelled loosened rocks from the sides of subterranean fissures into the air, only to return to the surface with a great chance of doing appreciable damage to the boat. Finally, there weren't enough people available to operate essential pumps for repelling the water that the primitively designed ark would have assuredly taken on. If Noah and his animal guests didn't kick the bucket from methane poisoning, incineration, starvation, disease, asphyxiation, dehydration, mutilation, or exhaustion, they would have certainly drowned.

A Local Flood?

It's painfully obvious that the story is burdened with a number of significant problems. For this reason, many apologists will attempt a hopeless defense for it by suggesting that the tale was speaking of a local flood. This notion, however, clearly contradicts the text, which states that all the mountains of the earth are covered (Genesis 7:19-20). Although the word in the text used for earth, *erets*, has an ambiguously additional meaning of *land*, we can still easily determine the author's intended connotation for this specific passage. How else would God's flood annihilate every living thing on earth, as this was his stated intention, unless the elevated water extended well beyond the Middle East? An additional difficulty, randomly selected from the pile of problems with the local flood suggestion, is the inability of the ark to travel hundreds of miles to Ararat without water high enough to reach the oceans. Liquids seek their own level and don't stand in one area without complete confinement. Since the barriers required for this magical constrainment are not present, we can only conclude that a local flood scenario is not only logically impossible but also entirely incompatible with the biblical text.

Recent archaeological evidence, on the other hand, has shed some light on the possible origins of the ancient global flood legends. Researchers have suggested that the Mediterranean Sea had likely become swollen with glaciers during the most recent ice age. If this proposal is representative of past conditions, it's quite likely that the water pressure increased to the point where a fine line of earth previously serving as a barrier between the Mediterranean Sea and the land currently under the Black Sea collapsed. Such a scenario would then allow a violent surge of water to rush inland and create the Black Sea. Needless to say, this feasible natural process would result in widespread devastation in areas now buried under hundreds of feet of water. As a further consequence, survivors who witnessed the aftermath of the tragic event would certainly spread their contrasting stories to neighboring regions.

Additionally, secular scholars agree that the biblical version of the flood account most likely culminated during the Babylonian Exile. During this troubling period for the Israelites, their priests likely embellished the historical event with supernatural attributes, possibly as a way of manufacturing propaganda to intimidate their captors. In essence, the Israelites may have wanted to increase their own power by frightening others with a deity angry enough to decimate even his own people. If the mystery behind Noah's ark has this much simpler explanation, why shouldn't we apply the same reasoning to the remaining ridiculous, unverifiable, and supernaturally based accounts of the incredulous Old Testament?

Is There Any Chance For Noah?

There's really no need to search here for a conclusion so obvious. The story's utter ridiculousness is probably why many polls indicate that an increasing number of *Christians* no longer claim a literal belief in the Old Testament. Sure, one can easily explain the whole fiasco by use of miracles: God made all the water appear and disappear; God prevented all the water from becoming too hot; God put the animals into hibernation; God kept the ark afloat; God repopulated the earth with life; and God erased all evidence of the flood. By invoking the miracle clause, however, Christians are using unverifiable events that *any* person can insert into *any* scenario in order to maintain the legitimacy of *any* religion.

To rectify all these problems in such a deceitful manner is to go against the whole purpose of constructing the ark in the first place. Applying such implausible explanations would also mean that God, once again, intentionally misleads people who rely on their logical and observational talents that he himself gave them for deducing answers to readily apparent problems. Searching for the truth behind Noah's ark isn't a matter of coming up with any solution for a problem that makes the story fit, but rather discovering the most likely solution to the problem so that we have the most likely answer.

The intent of the story is sparkling clear. An imminent flood was coming, and Noah was to perform specific duties to keep life thriving on our planet. The eight members of his family could not have accomplished this task for the reasons discussed at length in this chapter. Like every other global deluge story that came before and after Noah, the biblical flood is a lie. The source of the entertaining tale was most likely a tremendous flood that would later be embellished to fantastical proportions. When taken literally, the tale of Noah's ark is an insult to human intelligence and common sense. If the story didn't appear in the Bible, as is the case for dozens of other flood legends, no one would be giving it a second thought.

THE FLAT EARTH SOCIETY

I borrowed the title of this chapter from a religious sect so incredibly devout to their beliefs in a flat earth that they will proliferate the bounds of logic to any extent in order to explain obvious complications with their easily disprovable hypothesis. However, we should refrain from laughing too much at people holding onto such an outdated notion because those clinging to such preposterous beliefs have merely been conditioned to think this way since birth, just as the ancient Jews casually thought that the identical belief was true for thousands of years. Nevertheless, how does the belief of a flat planet still manage to survive in the twenty-first century? The Holy Bible. In fact, the Bible provides much more erroneous detail about the earth than its purportedly planar configuration. The good book also explains how foundational pillars, which shake when God becomes angry with us, supposedly hold our planet motionless. Seeing as how I don't feel much need to convince you that the earth is a spherical body, sans pillars, in motion around the sun, we'll only look at the sources of the opposing school of thought.

From Flat To Round

Before I delve into detail of how our flat earth supposedly survives in this mystical environment, a brief historical progression on the proposed shapes for our planet is necessary to appreciate fully the erroneous hypotheses offered by the Old Testament authors. Around 600 BCE, Pythagoras became the first person we know to have proposed the idea of a spherical planet. His hypothesis subsequently grew in popularity around 500 BCE with the support of Aristotle. While Plato first gave a rough guess of the earth's size around 400 BCE, Archimedes offered a more educated hypothesis of its circumference around 250 BCE. Moreover, during Archimedes' lifetime, Eratosthenes was completing the first in depth scientific research into the circumference mystery.

Because of the work done by Greek scientists and philosophers, the idea of a spherical earth became nearly concrete before the New Testament authors began their writings. Considering the fairly acceptable record keeping found in Kings and Chronicles, as well as the presence of Jesus' genealogies in the New Testament, we can determine whether the historical Jewish writings were completed before or after the spread of the Greeks' spherical earth philosophies. Once we match the histories of the two regions, we find that almost all of the Old Testament had been penned well before the spherical earth theory became concrete. On the other hand, only a very small amount of Old Testament writings had the potential to creep in during the demise of flat earth beliefs. In short, educated people were well aware that the earth was spherical before New Testament authors arrived on the scene. Now that we have this understanding, we can analyze the different positions on the earth's confirmation taken by the two testaments.

The Shape Of The Earth

In *Science To The Rescue*, we learned of several supporting examples for how the ancient Hebrews commonly believed that a solid firmament, separating the sky ocean from the land ocean, covered the earth. Within the proposed firmament are the sun, moon, and stars. The throne of God could potentially be found on top of the earth's dome. When a group of people tried to ascend into Heaven by building a tower, God confused them to cease its construction because he was afraid of people seeing him. While there's no directly informative statement about the shape of the earth itself in these Pentateuch examples, one must assume, based on logical deductions, that the so-called divinely inspired authors held the same opinion as the general population. If divine inspiration allowed them to realize that our world was spherical, one would expect the accords to be void of such figurative, fantastic, and erroneous descriptors. Again, the Bible had a chance to distinguish itself from other ancient religious texts, but it failed to do so. Instead, God seemingly allows certain people to write whatever they please about his magnificent universal creation.

In the years following the Pentateuch completion, additional illustrative scriptures would emerge from the prophets and paint additional pictures of a flat planet. Isaiah describes how God will "maketh the earth empty, turneth it upside down, and scattereth abroad the inhabitants thereof" (Isaiah 24:1). No matter how the spherical earth is situated, however, part of it will always be "upside-down" relative to another. As you should also realize that there's no true "upside-down" to the earth, it's impossible to orient our planet in such a fashion and erroneous for Isaiah to use this absurd brand of diction. The concept of gravity and its effect among massive spherical bodies would have certainly been a foreign notion to a fallible man, such as Isaiah, when this piece was written over 2000 years ago. However, if the earth were as flat as a casual observation would indicate, and we toss all modern understanding of gravity to the side, it would be very conceivable for us to think that God could invert the earth so that its inhabitants would fall into some unknown void. As the situation stands in the natural world,

Isaiah plainly made the flat earth mistake because he had no scientific knowledge beyond that of his peers.

Daniel also commits the same error recorded by Isaiah. He speaks of his dream about a tree so tall that "the height thereof reached unto heaven and the sight thereof to the end of all the earth" (Daniel 4:11). As you may have already deduced, it's impossible to see a tree from all points on the earth, regardless of how far it ascends, because the earth is spherical. While witnessing this tree might be possible from all points on a plane or from all points on the earth known to the Hebrews, such widespread observation is simply impossible on a massive spherical body. Daniel obviously exhibited no special insight or inspiration either.

The book of Job curiously refers to the earth as "long" and having a "strong" sky with the appearance of "glass" (11:9 and 37:18). "Long" obviously isn't an accurate term for conveying the idea of a spherical planet. In addition to implying attributes of a flat world, this biblical author reinforces the widespread ancient belief of a glass dome ceiling covering the earth.

In the New Testament, Matthew and Luke record a fantastic tale in which the Devil whisks Jesus to an exceedingly tall mountain in order to show him all the kingdoms of the world (4:8 and 4:5, respectively). Again, you cannot see the entire world from a single point. However, we must recall that the belief in a flat earth began to fizzle by the time writers put these words on hardcopy. Thus, this statement probably only insinuates that Matthew and Luke believed that all the *kingdoms* of the world were in locations observable from a single point. In other words, this passage is unemphaticly suggesting that the unviewable regions of the globe were void of kingdoms. If this interpretation is the case, the statement contains an entirely different category of error because it neglects civilizations of the Far East and Western Hemisphere that were presumably unknown to Middle Easterners.

On the other side of the coin, there's a singular instance found in Isaiah that Christians often flaunt to promote an imagined harmony between the Bible and the true configuration of the earth. All the while, previously mentioned scriptures authored by Isaiah and his colleagues go completely ignored. Isaiah 40:22 says, "It is he that sitteth upon the circle of the earth." The word in question here is "circle." A circle is a flat two-dimensional object, while a sphere, the approximate shape of the earth, is a three-dimensional object. The original Hebrew term used in this verse is *chug*, meaning *circle*. The same word is used twice in the book of Job to describe Heaven and the sea, two areas that we have no reason to believe anyone ever considered spherical. Furthermore, Isaiah does not use the actual Hebrew word for sphere, *kadur*, in 40:22 even though this utilization would have been much more appropriate if Isaiah intended to convey a spherical planet. In addition to this logical analysis of the verse, historians have long determined that a disc-shaped earth was a popular belief not only in the Middle East, but also in Greece before the time of Aristotle. We even have ancient maps of Babylon and Egypt containing illustrations of a circular sea surrounding circular land. When you combine this tangible evidence with other biblical comments regarding the shape of the earth, the likelihood of Isaiah 40:22 referring to a sphere is extremely remote.

What Keeps The Earth Aloft?

If you believe the earth is flat, that's a reasonable question to investigate. The ridiculous proposal offered by imperfect Old Testament authors is a set of pillars. What do we know about these phantom pillars? They "are the Lord's and he hath set the world upon them" (1 Samuel 2:8); the earth is shaken out of its place when they tremble (Job 9:6); they shake at God's disapproval (Job 26:11); God holds them in place when the earth shakes (Psalms 75:3).

Keep in mind that no one has ever found such pillars, nor would we ever sanely explore this proposal because the earth isn't in any real danger of collapsing. Nevertheless, what is all this business about the pillars shaking? Fortunately, the Bible explains the fictitious reason behind this physical phenomenon in more detail. "The Earth shook and trembled…because [God] was wroth" (2 Samuel 22:8 and Psalm 19:7); "At [God's] wrath the earth shall tremble" (Jeremiah 10:10); God will "shake the heavens and the earth shall remove out of her place…in the days of his fierce anger" (Isaiah 13:13); "The Lord shall roar out of Zion…and the heavens and the earth shall shake" (Joel 3:16); "Speak to Zerubbabel, governor of Judah, saying 'I will shake the heavens and the earth'" (Haggai 2:21). Since the pillars are supposedly the support foundations for the earth, it's reasonable to conclude that our world would shake right along with them.

As you can see, the Bible has at least six different sources recording and prophesying earthquakes only during times when God is angry. While these so-called divinely inspired authors are supposed to be speaking on behalf of an omniscient god, they instead offer ancient superstitious explanations for a natural phenomenon known as an earthquake. Today, we know these events are the result of volcanic eruptions or tectonic plate movements in the earth's crust. Again, the chances of obtaining this knowledge were well beyond the grasp of someone living 2500 years ago. For this reason, the alleged physical manifestations of God's anger were frightening enough to coerce the scientifically ignorant population into believing these hilariously clueless explanations.

Movement, Or Lack Thereof

Thus far, we have a flat earth with pillars to keep it aloft. Since these pillars are the foundation for the earth, and objects with such foundations tend to remain relatively motionless, does the Bible also imply that the earth doesn't move? Looking into these potential implications isn't necessary because the Bible directly spells it out for its audience. "The world also shall be stable that it be not moved" (1 Chronicles 16:30), "Where wast thou when I laid the foundations of the earth?" (Job 38:4), "And the foundations of the earth searched out beneath" (Jeremiah 31:37), "And ye strong foundations of the earth" (Micah 6:2). In addition, Psalms twice mentions that the earth has foundations (18:15 and 82:5) and twice mentions that God established the earth so that it cannot be moved (93:1 and 96:10). Furthermore, Psalms also binds the ideas of a foundation and motionlessness: "Who laid the foundations of the earth, that it should not be removed for ever" (104:5).

There should be little debate over what the Old Testament authors thought of the earth's kinetics and other characteristics. Today, we know that the earth moves in at least five different ways: it rotates on its axis, causing day and night; it revolves around the sun, causing us to maintain our distance; it wobbles due to the gravitational pull toward the moon; it hovers around the galaxy with the rest of our solar system; and the galaxy as a whole is continuously moving through empty space. Did God inspire his biographers with this knowledge, or did he allow the inclusion of blatantly false superstitions in his holy book?

The Sun Plays The Earth

Since the earth is purportedly motionless upon its pillars in the biblical universe, and the sun deceitfully appears to be the body in motion, does the Bible imply that the sun has movement as it relates to the daily cycle on earth? Once again, we're not required to examine these potential implications because the Bible plainly delivers its held position to us. "[The sun's] going forth is from the end of the heaven, and his circuit unto the ends of it" (Psalms 19:6). In more comprehensible English, the sun journeys across the sky in a circular path. Thanks to the work of early astronomers, we now know that the sun is stationary relative to the planets around it. Twenty-five hundred years ago, it would only be logical for divinely uninspired individuals to assume that the sun was the body in revolutionary motion.

Other books of the Old Testament also purport witnesses to similarly strange astronomical events. Isaiah once asked God to move the sun's shadows ten degrees, and the almighty allegedly complied with this request (2 Kings 20:11, Isaiah 38:8). We can find a comparable event in the book of Joshua when the main character asks God to keep the daytime symbol in the sky longer so that he can defeat his enemies before nightfall (10:12). God allegedly complies with Joshua's request as well by creating a length of day that had never taken place in the past (10:13-14, Habakkuk 3:11).

The consequences of these two phenomena occurring would be catastrophic. The earth's gravitationally induced inertia around the sun is the sole force preventing the two massive bodies from merging. Without this momentum, the earth would move gradually yet dangerously closer to the sun. After a short while, it's quite possible that the earth would become too hot to remain inhabitable *if* it was able to survive the countless local effects of its halt. At the very least, the polar ice caps would melt and flood the coastlines. Once again, these modern understandings go far beyond the limitations of Ancient Hebrew knowledge. Even so, I suppose that if a power existed to stop the planet from moving, the same power could withhold such consequences from taking place.

A much more detrimental perplexity with these sun-stopping events lies with the presence of astronomers spread throughout different regions of the world. After Joshua's celestial miracle supposedly took place, the two recording authors specifically say that no one in history had every experienced a day like this. In other words, this extended day was a unique event. As you might have guessed, there's little credibility to this claim because astronomers in Egypt, China, Babylon, and South America would have certainly recorded an additional 12-24 hours of daytime/nighttime if such an occurrence were this atypical. We are now in possession of the records made by these astronomers. Predictably enough, there's no indication of such extraordinary and unique astronomical events ever taking place. The only rational and obvious conclusion to make concerning these wild claims is that they're totally fabricated. Thus, the Bible has once again offered falsified history as fact.

Joel offers one final misinterpretation of the earth's role in the solar system. He says, "The sun shall be turned into darkness, and the moon into blood" during the day of the Lord (2:31). While Joel would probably like his readers to remain scared of these supposedly supernatural events, we now have more advanced knowledge concerning the mechanics of eclipses. The earth goes dark on the rare occasion that the moon passes directly between us and the sun; our nighttime light turns red from the earth's sunsets projecting on the lunar surface when we sweep directly between the sun and the moon. Again, if you subtract this modern understanding, it wouldn't be too difficult to frighten a person into believing that a supernatural force was manipulating these heavenly bodies in order to foreshadow some imminent spectacle of anger. Seeing as how this ordinary Hebrew had no reasonable explanation for these extraordinary scientific phenomena, he seemingly invented one of his own.

Sailing Off The Edge

Based on their works that reveal beliefs of a flat, stationary, and pillar-supported earth surrounded by the path of a revolving sun, I don't think it's too far of a stretch to say that the authors failed to exhibit divine inspiration. In actuality, the earth isn't much different from the limitless number of spherical planets revolving around their respective stars in order to hold their positions in their own solar systems. We should expect these fallible biblical authors to have a limited knowledge concerning the true nature of the universe if they were void of inspiration allegedly available from an omniscient deity. This is, in fact, what we observe when undertaking an impartial reading of the Old Testament.

Since the authors leave us with these erroneous notions in the Bible, the majority of unbiased persons who hold the knowledge contained within this chapter would not dare defend the blind belief that an omniscient and omnipotent being directly inspired its authorship. These curious statements are just part of the growing number of solid reasons to consider biblical passages twice before recognizing them as absolute truth. We should never accept any statement based solely on the fact that we can find it in an ancient book claimed to have been co-authored by one of ancient society's many gods.

Thousands Or Billions

The ages of the earth's components and neighboring bodies are additional pieces in the elementary puzzle of evaluating the Bible's accuracy. While every relevant branch of science plainly supports the existence of life on this planet for billions of years, the Bible undeniably claims that life began only about 6000 years ago. Thus, I included this chapter to reveal the information we have that enables us to place a true age on our planet, its contents, and our celestial neighbors. You should soon understand that there's no logical way to harmonize the two conflicting accounts respectively provided by science and the Bible. When rendering a verdict on the ages of these objects, I hope you will adhere to observable data rather than succumbing to blind faith. The material contained within this chapter is an expansion of similar ideas offered in *Science To The Rescue*.

Dating The Earth

Although the Bible doesn't directly state that the earth itself is only 6000 years old, a moderate amount of common sense will verify this is the position it must take. Expanding on this point, the book ambiguously states that God created the earth "in the beginning" (Genesis 1:1). However, the earth could not have logically formed prior to the sun (even though Genesis says just the opposite), which *is* verifiably alluded to be 6000 years old in the Bible. We're also able to observe planets in other solar systems consistently forming after their celestial anchors. In fact, it's scientifically impossible for life to thrive on a planet without a proximate location to a star. Thus, Creationists feel compelled to discover evidence for a young planet in order for their dogma to remain inerrant. Even though an overwhelming amount of data suggests that the earth is older than 6000 years, these self-ordained "scientists" are not looking for any evidence disputing their *a priori* beliefs. This method of research is, to say the least, blatantly dishonest. Those of us viewing *all* the data from an unbiased perspective can throw out everything we know about astronomy and assume that the earth is a unique case where the planet formed before its star, yet still have more than ample evidence to debunk the young earth claim.

Ironically, Christian geologists made the primary breakthroughs in discovering the earth's genuine antiquity during the late-eighteenth century. Baron Georges

Cuvier was the first to publish observations of a multilayered fossil column, noting that many of the species found in these columns were extinct, settled to very specific layers, and became more complex as he spotted them closer to the earth's surface. Having no intention to contradict the church's presumably infallible teachings, Cuvier concluded that there must have been a series of creations and catastrophes omitted from the Bible that were necessarily responsible for creating the physical evidence for these phenomena. Naturally, Cuvier's discovery is also an important factor for the previously discussed fossil age determinations. James Hutton, another early Christian geologist, found mixed vertical and horizontal rock layers in adjacent areas, leading him to conclude that an exceedingly drawn out natural phenomenon had to push on the earth in order to form the vertical layers. Again, the evidence suggested that the earth was far older than the 6000-year Genesis insinuation.

Only after the aforementioned technique of radiometric dating arrived on the scene could geologists offer such an accurate guess on the earth's age. Equipped with this knowledge, scientists can now measure quantities of radioactive elements within the earth's rocks. Researchers have performed this impartial scientific analysis on several thousand rock samples located deep within the fossil columns, and the results are consistently in the billions of years for samples estimated to be this ancient via more primitive dating methods. Although researchers believe that early volcanic activity is responsible for destroying the earth's oldest rocks, we can still be certain that specimens exceeding four billion years in age are very much in existence. Similar to the rocks on the earth, most meteorites eventually finding their way onto our planet date at four billion years as well.

Those with the futile agenda of proving that the earth has aged only a few thousand years will often point out the uncertainty of how much of the forming isotope was present at the rock's conception. This much is seemingly true. However, when you consider that every measured radioactive rock just *happens* to contain the exact isotope arising as a result of the long-term decay of its parent compound, it's only logical to conclude that the secondary byproduct wasn't there at the rock's formation. While some external factors may interfere in a few isolated cases, there are foolproof methods of measuring isolated samples to correct any variance created by such influencing conditions. The only alternative left for young earth believers is to make the desperately absurd claim that God created the rocks thousands of years ago to make them look billions of years old in order to mislead anyone who went searching for truth outside of the Bible. As ridiculous as this hypothesis may seem, I must admit that the scenario wouldn't be too far removed from God's motives based on what we'll study in the upcoming chapters.

Using a procedure analogous to the radiometric dating of rocks, we can determine which radioactive elements are still present on and above the earth. If our planet is truly billions of years old, we should expect elements with short half-lives to be absent from the list of those still present in nature, while elements with long half-lives should be the ones to comprise that very list. In other words, elements that transform at a relatively rapid rate should have disappeared, but elements with lengthier survivals should still be naturally observable. We cannot consider any element with a replenishing source for inclusion in the list because its continuous production will always yield a fresh supply of the element. Unsurprisingly, we find that all eighteen criterion-meeting radioactive elements with a half-life in excess of eighty million years are still found in nature, while all others have disappeared. Thus, we can reasonably conclude that any radioactive material with a half-life less than eighty million years has been present for such a long period that we can't find it naturally unless some chemical reaction is currently producing it. After twenty half-lives, these elements were in such low quantities that they were virtually undetectable when researchers first performed this experiment many years ago. If the earth's elements had a starting point 1.6 billion years in the past, we would witness the exact scenario I just described. This discovery opened the door for scientists to place increasingly accurate estimations on the age of the earth, currently believed to be 4.3 billion years. Incidentally, the odds that all these elements would line up in this manner by chance are greater than half a *billion* to one.

Although these are the foremost techniques we have for dating the earth, there are several more indicators telling us that the earth is older than just a few thousand years. While these methods don't have the ability to directly support a multi-billion year old planet, they *do* inform us that the earth must have necessarily been present longer than the apologetically proposed length of six thousand to ten thousand years.

The Green River lakes located in the western United States have been observed to deposit one layer of bottom sediment every year. There are currently several million layers of sediment plainly indicating that the lakes are several million years old. Likewise, white algae form layers in the depths of Japan's Lake Suigetsu when they die in the spring of each year. Over the remainder of the year, dark clay covers these pale algae. As a result of this continuous process, alternating streaks of light and dark sediment form at the bottom of the lake. To the chagrin of biblical apologists, there are presently tens of thousands of layers screaming that the start of this process began prior to the controversial events depicted in Genesis.

The tides of the earth's oceans are causing the planet's rotation to slow by one second per day per 50,000 years. Consequently, the relatively accelerated spinning of the earth millions of years ago would have shortened the length of a day and increased the number of rotations our planet was able to make per revolution around the sun. In a complementary discovery, scientists had already observed coral fossil rings exhibiting the notion that they thrived during a time when the year contained nearly four hundred days.

The continuous spreading of the continents has also provided evidence for our planet's age. Once continental drifts separated the Pangea homeland of the dinosaurs into South America and Africa, these prehistoric creatures began to evolve differently due to their contrasting environments. This anticipated change is evident in fossil records from the time after we believe the continental drift caused the land bridge between the two continents to disappear. Yet again, a hypothesis based on one observation is supported by another.

Ice layers in Antarctica and Greenland assemble on the preexisting layers every year. Considering that certain layers contain ash from known volcanic eruptions, we can determine how fast the ice forms by measuring the increased thickness accumulated over the time elapsed between these events. Utilizing this simple understanding, we ascertain that some ice formations in these locations began materializing over 40,000 years ago. Similarly, the study of geology has provided examples of landmasses where a series of millennium-long ice ages have taken place. In fact, the periods in between these ice ages are even lengthier than the freezes themselves. Furthermore, there is evidence of the earth's antiquity in the mile-thick permafrost layers of the arctic. We know that it takes decades to produce a sheet even one foot thick. Therefore, the frozen mass would have required hundreds of thousands of years to form at its present rate.

In addition to radiometric tests, we can date rocks by measuring the length of their subjected exposure to cosmic rays. The observable aging occurs when a neutrino, a type of subatomic particle, strikes a rock and reacts with certain minerals to form a measurable amount of radioactive isotope. Using this analysis, rocks in undisturbed desert locations are determined to be hundreds of thousands of years old, while rocks thought to be relatively new, based on independent tests, indicate an age of only a few thousand years.

As I mentioned in *101 Reasons Why Noah's Story Doesn't Float*, we can use DNA as a timepiece. In addition to revealing that humans had a common ancestor tens of thousands of years ago, our DNA indicates that we had a much more distant common ancestor with bacteria billions of years in the past. While there are several more sources I could reference that would successfully defend the undeniable antiquity of the earth, such as the evidence for numerous magnetic pole reversals in the Atlantic Ocean, I trust that you get the important message from all this data. Simply put, the overwhelming amount of evidence points toward an ancient earth. Apologetically proposed evidence to the contrary, which we'll look at some samples of later, can be easily refuted.

Dating The Heavenly Bodies

The authors of Genesis would also have their readers believe that God created the stars on the universe's fourth day (1:16), about 6000 years ago. However, modern observations tell us that the most distant stars are considerably more than ten billion years in age. Astronomers obtained this valuable piece of knowledge by looking through the powerful Hubble telescope and performing complex number crunching over the discoveries. Because we have applicable procedures for measuring distances this great, such as redshift and parallax (too complicated to get into here), we know the approximate location of distant stars. Since we also know the universal speed of light emanating from these stars, we can now determine that it took the light x amount of years to reach the observing telescope, where x represents the distance of the star divided by the distance light can transverse in one year. Therefore, stars must be *at least* as old as the time it takes their light to reach the earth from the previously measured distance. Otherwise, we wouldn't see these stars because their light wouldn't have reached our eyes yet. In other words, if we are able to see a group of stars ten billion light years away, the distance light can travel in ten billion years, we know that the group of stars is at least ten billion years old because it took the light ten billion years to reach us.

How can light from a star be billions of years old if God created the star only 6000 years ago? The hilarious apologetic answer to this glaring complication is often that "God created the stars 6000 years ago but created their light in transit for us to be able to see them." To paraphrase this proposal, God is making us see things that never really happened. This suggestion is a classic example of what has been termed a "how-it-could-have-been-scenario," which substitutes a painfully ridiculous and nonsensical explanation for the obvious answer in the interest of apologetics. It seems that no complication is too difficult for some Christians to invent absurd justifications and phantom harmonizations even though they will consider these acts to be logical violations when used by other religious sects to justify alternative beliefs.

Thanks to the astronauts who visited the moon and returned with rock samples, we're able to use radiometric dating on lunar rocks as well. Sure enough, the rocks found on the moon's surface consistently date around three to four billion years. However, scientists calculated the approximate age of the moon well before specimens were ever available for testing. The number of craters gave astronomers the primary clue.

It's possible to observe the passing of nearby asteroids and to determine how many travel through our region of space over a set period. Considering the size of the moon, we can then determine the likelihood of a single asteroid striking its surface. If we know how likely a strike is to occur, it's possible to mathematically derive the average length of time elapsing between impacts. We can then quantify the viewable crater evidence by counting the number of strikes on the surface and determining how long it would take the moon to accumulate enough impacts to present its battered condition. Again, we get a figure in the billions of years.

Yet another clue we have on the moon's age is the layer of dust present on its surface. Because there's no real atmosphere on our moon, the dust lays virtually undisturbed. Since we know the depth of the debris and the rate at which it collects, we're able to derive a third date for the moon using only this information. Yet again, we arrive at a number far in excess of one that would support a young biblical universe.

Dating the sun proves to be a bit less conventional because it's far too thermogenic to get anywhere near it. However, we still have many clues to go on. First, as I mentioned earlier, we know that the sun is necessary to sustain our viability. Since life on our world has thrived for billions of years, it's only logical to conclude that the sun has enjoyed billions of years of coexistence with our planet. Second, we know the sun is a star. When we observe the formation of other solar systems, we discover, without exception, that the stars form prior to their surrounding planets. Third, we know stars have life cycles. These enormous bodies of gas start out as semi-organized masses of helium and hydrogen before coalescing to form yellow stars similar to our sun. After ten billion years as a yellow star, the concentration of helium in the center makes the star expand into a red giant. A relatively short while later, the star will imminently explode and collapse. Since we're able to observe countless celestial bodies in all their various stages of progression, we can determine how long they tend to remain in these contrasting phases. Extrapolating this information to our own star, we know that about five billion years were required for the sun to achieve its present state.

Dating Life

Before radiometric dating, there was the "infamous" Charles Darwin. Scholars consider his 1859 manuscript, *On the Origin of Species*, to be the most popular, if not the greatest, leap forward toward debunking the Bible's scientific accuracy. Darwin recognized how species are specifically adapted for their respective environments and speculated on how they acquired this adaptation. He also notes the struggles among members of species that lead to survival of only the fittest members. In other words, only those members of the species that are most willing and capable of adapting to changes in their environment will be among the survivors. Most importantly for our discussion, he correctly noted that these natural progressive events would take an enormous amount of time to occur. In the nineteenth century, his theories were obviously heretical to the church because anything other than a God-directed creation was incorrect according to Christian teachings. In these somewhat more enlightened times, Darwin's work remains the cornerstone of modern biology and even influences some contemporary Christian thought.

Scientists have located simple fossilized organisms, such as bacteria, within rocks well over three billion years old. According to the theory of evolution, plants and animals both evolved from similar, primitive life forms. Since plants and animals are obviously much more complex than the earthly array of prehistoric microorganisms, we would expect their fossils to appear much closer to the earth's surface. As you might recall from Cuvier's work, this is exactly what we observe. Through a battery of analytical techniques, we're solidly able to conclude that plants and animals began appearing on earth around five hundred million years ago. Furthermore, increasingly complex animals presenting advanced nervous systems appear well after the more primitive, less evolved ones.

Human beings are much easier to date because we're relatively new to the earth and because our distant ancestors left behind extremely helpful clues. Researchers were almost immediately able to conclude that tools discovered in the late-eighteenth century were much older than a few thousand years. Remains of ancient human-like creatures found in the mid-nineteenth century prompted several expeditions to search for more of these mysterious life forms. These human-like creatures would later become known as the Neanderthal, of whom we are not likely to be direct descendants. Recent fossil discoveries in Africa yielded ape-like human remains dating to around a few million years, while paleontologists uncovered two-million-year-old fossils of beings that evidently used two legs to walk upon the African grounds. Furthermore, modern humans, *Homo sapien*, began to appear around 100,000 years ago. By the time of modern man's dominating emergence, fossil remains indicating our migration to other regions of the world become readily apparent. Only 10,000 years ago, humans became advanced farmers and hunters. The aforementioned tool discoveries can now be carbon dated to verify their belonging to this era.

Anthropologists have also positively affixed dates for dozens of additional human discoveries to a time prior to the supernatural birth of Adam. Several examples are the domestication of sheep, goats, turkeys, reindeer, water buffalo, cattle, horses, pigs, and dogs; the uncovering of pottery in Japan, woven cloth in Turkey, astronomical markings in South America, cuneiforms in Sumeria, calendars in Egypt, clay tokens in Mesopotamia, paintings in Algeria, and mummies in Peru; and cultivation of wheat, barley, potatoes, pumpkins, squash, lentils, beans, cotton, dates, peas, peppers, rice, peaches, corn, flax, yams, bananas, coconuts, and avocados throughout the world.

Very recently, archaeologists discovered artifacts of a civilization on the ocean floor from inhabitants abandoning this location due to the pre-Genesis ice age.

Scientists long anticipated these findings, even though no similar traces had been previously discovered, because such expectations were simply the product of the known coexistence of humans with the latest ice age. Once again, one cannot honestly ignore the obvious biological complications with the Genesis creation story while maintaining its scientific inerrancy.

The Universe According To Genesis

Speaking of Genesis, all the information we need to place a rough biblical date for the age of the earth's contents is contained within this book and the first chapter of Matthew. Genesis 5 gives the genealogy and ages of Adam through Noah; Genesis 11 provides the genealogy and ages of Noah through Abraham; Matthew 1 offers the genealogy of Abraham through Jesus. More details on the ages of the Abraham through Jesus lineage are available in the books of Kings and Chronicles. Due to sketchy detail, we cannot place a precise value on the time elapsed between Adam and Jesus, but the period in question is roughly 4000 years. It's certainly no more than 6000 years. This is a universally accepted number by anyone who does not twist the facts in order to meet an agenda. Add on the 2000 years since the start of the Common Era to obtain the total 6000-8000 years between the purported events of Genesis and whatever's going on in your world at the present.

The genealogies provide us with a time back to Adam, but what information do they provide for the rest of God's creations? Genesis 1:1 tells us, "In the beginning God created the heaven and the earth." The Bible gives no specific date for the earth itself, but as I mentioned earlier, the earth has certain requirements to survive. However, God created the *contents* of the earth and universe during six consecutive sets of evenings and mornings, starting with light on day one and ending with Adam on day six. We can easily conclude that the earth's contents and the remainder of the universe were, according to the Bible, made only days before Adam. Therefore, biblical authors also claim the sun, moon, stars, plants, and animals to be only about 6000 years of age. Seeing as how anyone with a decent education in the past century knows that this is embarrassingly inconsistent with the wealth of scientific evidence, the search began to find a way around this complication in order to save the Bible's credibility. However, you will soon realize that Genesis is far beyond hope.

As I mentioned in *Science To The Rescue*, the Hebrew equivalent for a day is *yom*. Technically, *yom* is used to communicate a short period of time, not necessarily a day. Thus, Creationists have proposed that *yom*, in these early instances, means millions or billions of years. However, the text unambiguously says, "And the morning (*boqer*) and evening (*ereb*) were the [*n*th] day." *Yom* clearly and unmistakably refers to a twenty-four hour day in these passages. While *yom* may have slightly altered meanings in some other verses, there is no possibility for such variation due to the added specificity of mornings and evenings. Thus, Creationists must alter the length of these mornings and evenings into millions or billions of years in order to accommodate scientific observations into their ancient religious dogma.

A passage in Exodus even reiterates the literal six day creation: "Six days shalt thou labour, and do all thy work: But the seventh day is the sabbath of the Lord thy God: in it thou shalt not do any work...For in six days the Lord made heaven and earth, the sea, and all that in them is, and rested the seventh day" (20:9-11). Christian zealots inserting their "figurative days" interpolation into the text refute its obvious meaning. Genesis clearly maintains that God created his universe in six days only a few thousand years ago. This is absolutely and undeniably wrong.

An alternative explanation commonly offered for the apparent mistakes in Genesis is that even though the days are clearly ranked as being the first, second, third, etc., the numbering of days wasn't intended to be consecutive. Letting that factor slide, this baseless hypothesis still fails to consider the majority of problems created by Genesis' statements. Yet another far-fetched explanation is that the authors meant for the days to be figurative, not literal. In other words, Christian apologists deem passages *figurative* when they undeniably conflict with external information and deem them *literal* when they are not disprovable or are necessary for furthering the apologetic cause. I doubt any Christian would like it if a Jew asserted that the resurrection of Jesus was only figurative simply because it furthers the Jewish cause, but Christians are committing the same illogical method of assertion when implementing this defense. Besides, I'd really like to know how blatantly biased apologists of any religion objectively determine what is included in these *figurative* versus *literal* classifications.

In all seriousness, these explanations are additional examples of poor "how-it-could-have-been-scenarios" that ignore the obvious meaning of the religious text. The Bible is simply stuck with a clearly interpretable 6000-year-old date for everything but the earth itself. If we are to twist and turn everything the Bible clearly states, we could *literally* turn it into anything from a romance novel to a war manual. It's from this inescapable conclusion that Creation "Science" was born. Since there was no rational way to get out of the date set in stone by Genesis, the selective search for young earth evidence commenced.

Well, has anyone discovered convincing evidence for the alternative apologetic position? Let's just say that the percentage of today's scientists who believe that the earth is only a few thousand years old equals less than one percent, a distribution yielded almost certainly because the dwarfed minority holds their position out of dogmatic desperation. These self-proclaimed scientists are determined to make all evidence fit with a young earth while ignoring the completely over-whelming juggernaut of counterevidence working against their predetermined conclusions. Such research methods are very unscientific and blatantly dishonest because a true scientist does *not* start out to prove something one way or another. Such researchers should always remain impartial and undecided before consider-ing *all* of the available evidence to make a rational and logical decision that is *independent* of their hopes and beliefs.

The Young Universe Assertion

As I alluded to a moment ago, the field of Creation Science is anything *but* true science. Those who firmly trust that the earth is only 6000 years old are either ignorant of the facts or have a religious agenda to meet. To reiterate the earlier premise of this chapter, a significant piece of the Bible is flawed if the universe is not 6000 years old. It's *extremely* rare to find a scientist who has abandoned the old earth theory in favor of the new earth hypothesis. Those who firmly believe that the earth and the balance of the universe are billions of years old arrive at this con-clusion not to intentionally destroy the young earth hypothesis, but because this rational decision makes overwhelming sense in light of all the available evidence.

For brevity's sake, this section will discuss what I feel are the ten most popular arguments that Creationists use to support a young universe. A brief summary of the reasons why we can refute each erroneous apologetic conclusion will immedi-ately follow each said proposal. More detailed arguments and counterarguments for these statements, in addition to other young earth suggestions, can be found in a variety of sources for those particularly interested in the earth age "debate." In fact, modern authors have dedicated entire books or articles to each upcoming position. Contrarily, the purpose of this section is simply to provide a somewhat concise introduction to the pseudoscience of Creationism.

The sun is shrinking at a rate at which it would have been too large for life on earth millions of years ago. In 1979, researchers John Eddy and Aram Boornazian published the rate of shrinkage measurements utilized in this argument. Since we knew relatively little about the sun when they recorded their observation many years ago, it was premature for readers to assume that the sun had always been shrinking at the rate calculated. Our lungs also contract at a certain rate when we exhale, but that doesn't mean they'll collapse within a few seconds. The sun is a star, and we know that stars go through several phases in their lifetimes. It's also been demonstrated by a plethora of more recent measurements, including eclipse shadow observations, that our sun exhibits repeated stages of shrinking and expanding. In fact, we now understand that these fluctuations are necessary for the sun to provide its heat.

The depth and rate of collection of moondust tell us that the moon is only a few thousand years old. The methodology used to determine how much dust would collect over time was severely flawed when Hans Pettersson first carried out the referenced study in 1960. A series of better-controlled measurements, beginning with one by J. S. Dohnanyi in 1972, arrived at collection rates about 0.1% of the original expectation. In other words, the dust collected at a *much* slower rate than researchers originally believed. Consequently, we would anticipate much less dust on the surface of the moon. Because of these more representative undertakings, the thin layer of lunar dust provides the moon with an age far beyond 6000 years.

The moon has Uranium-236 and Thorium-230 that should have decayed billions of years ago. You'll need to recall what I mentioned earlier about radiometric dating. Th-230 is a byproduct of U-238. Of course, if U-238 still exists, Th-230 will as well. Indeed, U-238 *does* still exist; and as long as it exists, Th-230 will be created as its byproduct. However, lunar uranium ores continually produce U-236 under the right conditions. If we can presently observe the creation of certain isotopes, such as the case for lunar U-236, measurements using such isotopes are invalid for determining an object's antiquity for the previously mentioned reasons. Thus, U-236 and Th-230 are inapplicable choices for measuring the moon's age.

The earth's magnetic field is decreasing at a rate that wouldn't have allowed life tens of thousands of years ago. Thomas Barnes, the Creationist who published this conclusion in 1973, used an incorrect model of the earth's interior, measured only one component of the magnetic field that doesn't decay in correlation with the rest, and ignored the earth's polarity shifts. Taking notice of any of these factors would have greatly improved his findings. Thus, the foundation of such an argument is as flawed as Barnes' research. Like the sun's diameter, the earth's magnetic field is continuously undergoing a series of fluctuations. The overwhelming majority of other studies, beginning with those cited by T.G. Cowling in 1981, debunk these apologetically referenced calculations.

The depth and rate of formation of topsoil proves that the earth is only a few thousand years old. This is somewhat similar to the moon dust theory, but unlike the moon, the earth has a dynamic surface. Topsoil isn't going to collect in one place for billions of years, and it's erroneous to assume that it will if you take the time to make note of its constant erosion. However, topsoil *has* collected undisturbed for *millions* of years in isolated regions of The United States. Even though the thickness of topsoil has no direct relation with the true age of the earth, it ironically assists in debunking the young earth hypothesis.

The fossil layers had to be deposited quickly because of the lack of meteorites contained within them. Most meteorites disintegrate while in the earth's atmosphere. Of those that survive the scorching journey, the impact often causes them to shatter into fragments. A state of tranquility then subjects those fragments to millions of years of natural erosive forces and chemical decomposition. Considering how scarcely a meteorite strikes the earth, it would be foolish to assume that there should be an abundance of meteorite fossils readily found deep beneath the surface of the earth. We can't even spot more than a handful of craters when they're unobstructed on the surface. Why, then, would anyone anticipate an abundant discovery of meteorites in hidden places that we can barely examine?

The oldest living tree on the planet is 4300 years old, the era concurrent with Noah's ark. This desperate proposal doesn't prove anything because the tree in question will eventually die and have its title given to one of its newer counterparts. This, of course, doesn't mean that the earth will decrease in age when it happens. Nevertheless, the irony of the apologetic suggestion is yet again on the side of reason because different trees share ring formations provoked by their common environment. Consider two trees in a yard: one was born in 1750 and died in 1950; the other began growing in 1850 and is still living. They will have a common ring pattern from 1850-1950 due to the environmental phenomena that they simultaneously experienced over that period. With this knowledge, researchers were able to find fossilized trees that shared a ring system in their last days with the currently oldest living trees in their youngest days. In other words, the fossilized trees had rings dating back thousands of years before the commonalities began with the currently oldest living trees. Thus, we are able to determine that the now-fossilized trees lived a millennium before the 6000-year-old date placed on the mythical Genesis creation. Additionally, these fossilized trees should have exhibited some degree of damage caused by the global flood. And speaking of the flood...

The human population growth rate can be traced back to the size of Noah's family. While it's true that the human population has been growing exponentially in recent history, it's erroneous to suggest that it has always grown at this magnificent rate because advances in health and technology are the primary contributing factors for this recent boom. Exponential multiplication of species requires nearly ideal conditions, such as those humans enjoy now. We even know that disease kept population growth steady or in decline around the fifteenth century. Furthermore, using such foolish Creationist logic, bacteria would fill the earth in a matter of days due to their extremely high rate of reproduction. Since bacteria don't have an inexhaustible supply of resources, they are in competition with one another to survive. Thus, they don't have the means to grow at an exponential rate and cover the entire earth, which would theoretically happen in a matter of days. We can apply the same limitations to humans living thousands of years in the past because their environment was anything but ideal for rapid growth. Two children per two adults kept the population steady for a lengthy historical period. An additional problem with this proposal is that no manufactured wonders surviving from Noah's era could have been constructed if there were only a handful of people left alive after the alleged global flood.

Historical records only go back thousands of years. This is partially true, but it's probably because people didn't have both the capacity and the desire for historical records. In essence, people would only keep written accounts once two conditions were satisfied: important events came along, and people learned to write. While the public may commonly believe that these two conditions were met only a few thousand years ago, we're fortunate enough to have cave sketches depicting life tens of thousands of years before Genesis says the mystical creation took place. Perhaps if people had learned to write a lot sooner, apologists might be able to make a better case for the Bible in this regard.

Carbon dating is flawed, inaccurate, and unreliable after 50,000 years. We can check the accuracy of carbon dating by calibrating it with the tree ring data mentioned earlier. Only on rare occasion does the discrepancy ever extend beyond 5% within the first several millennia. Because of the ability to synchronize this technique with the long established dating method of counting tree rings, we can confirm the reasonable accurateness of carbon dating. However, it *is* true that carbon dating isn't reliable after 50,000 years. For this very reason, no sensible person uses carbon on objects believed to be that old. Due to the small mass of carbon left in an object after ten half-lives, about 0.1% of the original amount, a tiny error in the quantity measured can throw the determined age of the object way off. For example, consider a rock with 100.000 grams of Carbon-14. After one half-life, about 5000 years, it will only have 50.000 grams remaining. If we measure only 49.999 grams due to human error or slight variation in the decay, we're off by 0.001 grams, yielding a difference of one month in age. This variation should not be of any appreciable consequence. After 50,000 years, the rock will have approximately 0.100 grams of Carbon-14 remaining. If the same circumstances cause us to be off by the exact same amount of 0.001 grams, we will measure the sample as having 0.099 grams, which will put us off the mark by about 100 years! This is why we need to use slowly decaying elements to measure older objects. Carbon is simply the standard for measuring modern objects since it decays faster, thus yielding a smaller margin of error on these samples.

Billions

The earth, sun, moon, and stars are billions of years old. Plants and animals have been around for hundreds of millions of years. Man first appeared tens of thousands of years ago. Every piece of falsifiable evidence from every relevant branch of science tells us that these statements are undeniably accurate. The fallible authors of the Bible unambiguously purport that God created all these objects about 6000 years ago because they didn't have access to the technology utilized by contemporary scientists. The only individuals still hanging onto this outdated superstitious belief are the ones who desperately cling to dying apologetic agendas. Others have unsuccessfully sought to rectify the Genesis account with preferential scientific discoveries.

The erroneous biblical claim of the earth's creation is yet another reason why many Christians have now turned their backs on a literal interpretation of the creation tale. If we allow other religions the same amount of leniency, could we ever possibly determine which one is making the legitimate claims? Due to the overwhelming amount of observable, testable, and falsifiable evidence, we can comfortably denounce the proclaimed authenticity of the Bible solely on its erroneous, pseudoscientific claims.

Morality And The Bible

THE DARKER SIDE OF GOD

If you ask Christians to describe their quasi-chosen god of worship, you'll often hear such descriptors as "wonderful" and "loving." This choice of selective designation seems commonplace within the Christian community. In fact, most churches ignore the Old Testament all together so that the members feel comfortable propagating this view. Fueled by such blatant omission, this lengthy chapter will fill the void by offering a look at the volume of horrendous acts performed or directed by the darker side of God. However, you shouldn't interpret this chapter as an attempt at an exhaustive record of every violent act attributable to God because such a review would require another book all together.

Upon completion of reading this chapter, you should realize that God was a mass murderer among other things, often directing others to rape and kill for him. He also distributes sinister laws and explains what punishments will ensue if someone deviates from his wishes. What's worse, the ultimate penalty for disobedience is Hell: eternal torture of unfathomable proportions. Even if we ignore the previously discussed scientific problems debunking the notion of an affiliation between divinity and the Bible, you should still feel resistance against worshipping this particular Hebrew deity after learning of the details emphasized over the next few selections.

God's Genocidal Wrath

Without any conceivable doubt, I firmly believe that the Hebrew god is the most evil character of all time. Starting with the book of Genesis, we learn that he's an insanely angry deity. Of the many atrocities committed in the Old Testament, God is usually the sole participator. The Genesis authors record the first such instance in chapters 6-8 as the account of Noah's flood.

The reason that God decides to drown the entire world, killing nearly every living person and animal on earth, is his belief that people are evil and unworthy of existence (Genesis 6:5). So *what* if they were evil? As Lenny Bruce once exclaimed, "The fault lies with the manufacturer!" God allegedly created humans, yet he faults us for being guided by our desires, instincts, and natural tendencies. Since he's supposedly omniscient, God realized how we were destined to turn from the beginning. He must also have realized that his lament would fuel the urge to destroy his precious creations, only to leave himself back where he started. Even so, he creates Adam, yet hundreds of years later, he drowns nearly all the men, women, and children on the face of the earth because he deliberately chose not to make us to his liking the first time.

Even if we suppose the *adults* deserved to die slow and torturous deaths, what association could we conceivably make between their decisions and the adolescent victims of the flood? Couldn't God have just placed the innocent children and animals aside for a while so that they wouldn't drown? If not, how about a humane death at the very least? Drowning is a horrible way for people to die. As a result of hopelessly treading water for hours, their muscles burned due to large amounts of lactic acid production. Once they finally gave up, went under, and held their breaths, acidic carbon dioxide eroded their lungs until the unbearable pain forced them to inhale where there was no air for them to breathe. The water brought into their lungs robbed their bodies of oxygen, causing them to go numb. As water violently rushed in and out of their chests, the currents eventually laid their heavily breathing, slowly dying bodies at the bottom of the ocean. The inhaled water caused their lungs to tear and bleed profusely. As their blood supply dwindled, their hearts slowly came to a halt. Even so, their brains continued to process information for another couple of minutes. They were patently aware that death was imminent, yet they could do nothing to speed it or prevent it. I imagine that their final reflections would have been on what they did to deserve such treatment.

As you see, drowning is *not* a quick and painless death. Regardless, this is what God did to every man, woman, child, baby, and animal on earth because *he* made a mistake! To make matters disgustingly worse, the flood accomplished *nothing*! The omniscient God realizes *after* the flood that a man's imagination is evil from youth (Genesis 8:21). He seemingly allows us to be evil to this day, just like those he purportedly drowned in the flood. Even if this was the sole befuddled and immoral act carried out by God, I'm positive that I couldn't bring myself to worship him. However, this is only the beginning of his mass-murdering spree.

Another genocidal operation courtesy of God takes place in the cities of Sodom and Gomorrah. Above these cities, he creates a rain of burning sulfur to kill every inhabitant, save Lot and his family, because they're deemed evil by the almighty judge, jury, and executioner (Genesis 19:24-25). Now, refer back to the points illustrated in the previous paragraph. God should have assumed the responsibility of taking measures to prevent these actions from somehow becoming necessary. He even remembered that men were evil by nature after the flood. Did he suddenly forget his opinion when he destroyed two entire cities of men, women, and children? Again, we should sincerely hope that this all-knowing deity would learn to take some of the blame in these situations. Like drowning, burning is *not* a quick and painless death. Fortunately, these people didn't truly feel any pain because the tale is an obvious work of fiction. If you travel to the locations around which historians believe these cities are based, you'll effortlessly discover balls of sulfur forming naturally on the ground. In other words, as is the case for Noah's flood, we have the likely inspiration for the imaginative tale.

Another Planned Genocide

In Exodus, we find God coercing Moses into becoming his spokesperson for freeing the Israelite slaves from the Egyptian Pharaoh. Moses initially points out that he's a terrible speaker, but God's reply to this passive resistance is a set of rhetorical questions in which he takes credit for making people deaf, dumb, and blind (Exodus 4:10-11). Some of these handicapped people are a burden to others, and many die without ever demonstrating independence. Nevertheless, God takes great pride in this achievement. Most of us typically find people who relish in the misery of others to be deeply disturbed. Instead of correcting these atrociously boastful deeds, God seemingly leaves it up to us to develop ideas for combating transcendentally induced handicaps. Ironically, with advances in medical science, we're making genuine progress against God's wishes. His yearning to make certain people handicapped is useless, evil nonsense. Evidently, it's a successful argument because Moses decides to accept the offer.

In the meeting among Moses, Aaron, and the Pharaoh, God doesn't want his Israelites to go free without a fight. Instead, God instructs Moses and Aaron on exactly what steps to take so that the Pharaoh will initially become too stubborn to allow the people to leave. Obviously, God only wants an excuse to "bring forth [his] armies" against Egypt in order to punish the entire country for the decisions of one man to hold his chosen people as slaves (Exodus 7:1-14).

The plagues that God carried out against Egypt as a result of the Pharaoh's decision were turning the river to blood; sending an abundance of frogs, lice, locusts, and flies; killing every cow belonging to the people; inflicting boils upon all the citizens; creating a hailstorm to destroy their crops; instituting three days of darkness; and killing the firstborn male child in every household across the country. The darkness, boils, frogs, lice, locusts, and flies were quite punishing, but they wouldn't necessarily ruin anyone's life. The cattle slaughter, river of blood, and downpour of hail ruined the Egyptians' sole water and food sources. Worst of all, God once again feels the necessity to eradicate thousands more innocent babies, children, and animals because one man was too stubborn to free his slaves.

On the escape route, Moses miraculously parts the Red Sea and crosses safely. When the Egyptian army pursues, the waters regroup to drown the soldiers and horses (Exodus 7-14). The omnipotent Hebrew god could have easily freed the people and spared thousands of lives, but, of course, he doesn't do things this way.

One can only assume that he took sinister pleasure in murdering Egyptian soldiers for following orders from their superior officers. Thankfully, modern scholarship tells us that these events never took place either. I'll explain the logic behind this comforting declaration in *Moses And Other Historical Fabrications*.

God revisits the plague concept when he dishes one out on his chosen people for following Aaron's orders to worship a golden calf (Exodus 32:35). Recall, however, that Aaron was one of the two men to whom they owed their freedom. Why would God punish his people for actions that they didn't realize were "wrong," especially when they had implicitly learned to trust the person giving the orders? This debacle seems to have shifted Aaron over to God's bad side because God later kills his two sons for building a "strange fire" (most likely meaning that they let a forbidden item burn) (Leviticus 10:1-2). No matter how many times I read passages like this, I'm always amazed how God kills people because they do something silly like build a displeasing campfire, but as we will soon see, he allows them to rape female prisoners of war.

On the subject of fire, God later sets some of the desert wanderers ablaze for complaining about their difficulties (Numbers 11:1). Keep in mind that they were now wandering around the desert for decades doing absolutely nothing after having been slaves in Egypt for centuries. When they complain about having no meat for nourishment, God provides them with a circle of quail three feet high and a day's journey wide but immediately plagues and kills a handful of them for grumbling (Numbers 11:31-34). Later, the people become increasingly irritated over being homeless. In fact, circumstances are so miserable that they actually want to return to Egypt as slaves. Subsequently, Korah leads a group of 250 other upset individuals to stand up to Moses. Needless to say, they all pay for their mutiny. God opens the ground under Korah's household and sucks everything he has, family and all, into the depths of the earth (Numbers 16:31-33). The remaining council of 250 are burned alive (Numbers 16:35). Does the punishment fit the so-called crime? Does God have any compassion for their situation? Obviously not, on both accounts.

When the Israelites were upset that Moses caused those 250 people to die, God sends a plague to slay an additional 14,700 (Numbers 16:41-49). To close out the Pentateuch, God exterminates a number of his people who fall down and worship the gods of Baalpeor. A subsequent plague kills another 24,000 (Numbers 25:1-9). At least these people may have had some idea that what they were doing would result in a punishment...

For The Sins Of Another

God's episodes of murdering innocent individuals for the faults of their leaders, fathers, or other ancestors are not uncommon in the Old Testament. Jephthah asks for God's assistance in killing the children of Ammon and promises him the first person out of his house upon his return as a burnt sacrifice if he will agree to aid with the massacre. God concurs and lethally delivers the children of Ammon into Jephthah's hands. When Jephthah returns, his daughter, an only child, makes her way outside to welcome him home. Two months later, Jephthah regretfully fulfills his promise by burning his daughter as a sacrifice to God (Judges 11:29-39). Why would God allow a man to offer an innocent person as a reward unless God also intended for certain people to be mere possessions?

While David is King, he decides to conduct a census: a horrendous sin in God's eyes. As punishment for his poor decision, he is to select among seven years of famine, three months of fleeing from his enemies, and three days of pestilence. Unable to choose from the offered catastrophes, God picks the three days of pestilence that result in the deaths of 70,000 men. Women and children weren't mentioned, not that the Bible considered them to have any real value in the first place. Again, God murders enough people to fill a sizable city for the "sin" of one man. David subsequently cries out to God and asks him why he wants to murder innocent people who had nothing to do with the decision to execute a census. Of course God doesn't provide an impossible answer for this sensible question, but his reasons scarcely seem morally or ethically justifiable (2 Samuel 24:10-17).

David also desires a woman named Bathsheba even though she's married to one of David's soldiers. Driven by his lust, David orders her husband to the front lines of a battle so that the enemy will take care of his problem. God then becomes extremely angry with David for this relatively petty crime. Once the new couple has a child, God afflicts it with illness for a week before watching it die (2 Samuel 11, 12:14-18). Yet again, God exterminates an innocent baby for the actions of the father.

At one point, God sends a famine upon David's followers. When he makes an inquiry to God for a justification, he's told, "It is for Saul, and his bloody house, because he slew the Gibeonites" (2 Samuel 21:1). Saul died _years_ ago, yet God just now decides to punish people who had nothing to do with the decisions of their former leader.

David's new son, Solomon, turns away from the Hebrew god and decides to worship other deities. Solomon's decision infuriates God, but he isn't punished because God recently came to like David. Instead, he punishes Solomon's son by taking away part of his land when he comes to power (1 Kings 11:9-13). Once again, we see the impossibility of being free from God's anger even when living in total obedience to him. In essence, Solomon's son was divinely punished before he was ever born.

Next in the line of father-son reprimands is the account of King Josiah. "And like unto him was there no King before him, that turned to the Lord with all his heart, and with all his soul, and with all his might, according to all the law of Moses; neither after him arose there any like him. Notwithstanding the Lord turned not from the fierceness of his great wrath...because of all the provocations that Manasseh had provoked him withal" (2 Kings 23:24-26). The passage speaks for itself. Yet again, God punishes a seemingly perfect person for someone else's transgressions.

God's Novel Method of Murder

Instead of directly murdering people or using his followers to execute similar commands, the apparently insatiable God begins sending animals to kill those who displease him. On one occasion, he has a lion kill a man because he refuses to hit someone (1 Kings 20:35). God sends his lions out again to kill a group of people who were new to Samaria. The reason for this atrocity is their lack of worship, even though they were never informed of the proper worship methods (2 Kings 17:24-26). However, this supposedly insignificant detail didn't halt God from killing them. He had to have known that he would eventually murder this party, but instead of properly instructing them, God just kills them. There's not even a miniscule resemblance of justice in the Hebrew god.

In an exploit of inconceivable irrationality, God sends forth two bears to kill forty-two *children* for making fun of Elisha's bald head (2 Kings 2:23-24). Why would the omnibenevolent God feel the necessity to have two bears viciously maul little children for acting like...children? This is supposed to be the same "wonderful" and "loving" God who promises us eternal life, but an entity capable of these inane activities could certainly change his mind and banish all of his worshippers to Hell. Christians never have to justify such passages because, of course, they never read them!

A Few More For Good Measure

God commits another reprehensible act when Abraham and Sarah are journeying through Egypt. According to the story, Abraham knows that if the Egyptians see him with his beautiful wife, they'll have to kill him so that she won't have a defense when they rape her. To avoid such an incident, Abraham devises a plan in which Sarah is to proclaim that they're only siblings. Thus, they can have their way with her while sparing Abraham's life. The Pharaoh eventually has a sexual encounter with Sarah, provoking God to send plagues upon him as punishment for sleeping with another man's wife (Genesis 12:11-17). How, exactly, did God expect the Pharaoh to know she was a married woman? Was he supposed to be omniscient as well? God would have never punished the Pharaoh if Sarah wasn't the possession of another man. Based on the treatment of women we will see in *Why Women And The Bible Don't Mix*, God certainly wasn't teaching the Pharaoh to value the opposite sex; God unjustly punished him because of his ignorance.

Later in Genesis, we learn of a man named Judah who has three sons: Er, Onan, and Shelah. Seeing as how Er is "wicked in the sight of the Lord," God kills him. For what reason God found him too evil, we could only speculate. Of course, there's no reasonable guarantee that Er would have incurred a death sentence from an impartial jury. Following the slaying, God dictates Onan to impregnate and marry Er's wife in order to continue Er's family line. Since Onan seemingly believes in freewill and doesn't feel that he should be required to do something he doesn't want to do, he spills his seed on the ground instead of finishing intercourse inside of her. "And the thing he did displeased the Lord: wherefore he slew him also" (Genesis 38:7-10). Again, the omniscient God should have known that Onan would fail to comply. Because God should have also realized that he would have to kill the disobedient Onan, why did he order him around in the first place? Does he now feel the need to have an excuse before murdering an innocent person? Was Onan destined to exist only as God's slave? Are we all God's oppressed pawns, created only to be shifted around for his amusement? Onan's fate hardly seems just by enlightened standards.

The Ark of the Covenant was a sacred item that God demanded everyone to refrain from touching. The ancient Hebrews commonly believed that God even played the part of a genie by residing in the ark on occasion. Thus, when the Philistines steal this precious piece, God obviously becomes enraged. As they're carrying it through different cities, God inflicts severe cases of hemorrhoids on all the inhabitants. Why God doesn't just zap these thieves and return the ark to the Israelites without harming additional innocent bystanders is beyond me. Unbelievably, 50,070 people eventually die at the hands of God because they simply look into the ark (1 Samuel 4-6). That's the equivalent of a moderately sized modern city dropping dead just for looking at something God didn't want them looking at. It's difficult to imagine a creature that can unleash punishments more evil than that, but God is continuously setting new standards for himself.

Once we see the ark in transit again, the cart and oxen transporting it move over a rough spot in the path and nearly shake the prized object to the ground. Out of what we could only consider pure reflex, Uzzah, who was accompanying the ark, places his hand on it to keep it steady. Uzzah's instinctive, split-second decision to prevent God's home from falling angers God enough to eradicate him from the earth (2 Samuel 6:6-7).

Since God commits scores of violent acts randomly throughout the remainder of the Old Testament, let's look at a few examples. After delivering the Amorites into the hands of Joshua, he sends down a hailstorm in order to kill a large portion of the people who flee from battle (Joshua 10:8-11). God assists in the war between Barak and Sisera by surrounding Sisera's army and forcing them to dismount from their chariots. Because of his intervention, Sisera's entire army faces imminent death at the hands of Barak (Judges 4:14-15). God causes the Midianites to kill one another (Judges 7:22-23). He confuses the Philistines and causes them to kill one another (1 Samuel 14:20-23). He inflicts a number of people with blindness because Elisha asks him to do so (2 Kings 6:18). He causes a seven-year famine without specifying a reason (2 Kings 8:1). God kills Jeroboam because he's the leader of the enemies (2 Chronicles 13:20). He kills Nabal without specifying a reason, but it's probably because David desires his wife and other belongings (1 Samuel 25:38). God sends an angel to kill 185,000 men in an Assyrian camp because they're enemies of his people (2 Kings 19:31-35). He plagues Azariah, a man labeled as a good King, with leprosy for the remainder of his life because he allows people to burn incense in a location displeasing to God (2 Kings 15:1-5). This is another great example of an overbearing punishment for breaking an asinine law. Some of our fellow humans were obviously destined to meet death early in life without any chance of redemption in God's eyes.

Counting just the flood, Sodom and Gomorrah, the Red Sea incident, the ark gazers, the plagues, the census, and the battles in which God directly participated, I estimate that this terrible creature claims to have murdered one to two *million* people. Regrettably, we still haven't discussed any of the instances in which God orders his people to kill others or when he "delivers armies" into the hands of the Israelites to be annihilated in battle. By this point in our discussion, God has already joined the elite company of Hitler, Lenin, Stalin, and Zedong as the largest mass murderers in history.

Following God's Alleged Commands

When God wished certain people dead thousands of years ago, he was never confined to his own omnipotent powers. You might even agree that God was at his worst when he recruited others to assist with the scores of slaughters in the Old Testament. As initially difficult as it might be to accept, God often provided his followers with orders leading to outcomes even more horrific than before. This section will discuss the specific commands given by God and the consistently tragic results that follow. Try to keep everything in perspective. These aren't numbers; they're human beings.

Recall the setting of God dishing out a plague over the golden calf worship. Immediately prior to the plague inflicted upon his people, God had ordered Moses and his loyal followers to "slay every man his brother, and every man his companion, and every man his neighbour." Three thousand men died at the hands of their peers in addition to those killed by the second punishment (Exodus 32:26-28).

Later on, a group of followers from Moses' camp observes a man gathering sticks on the Sabbath. Since such a despicable act was illegal in those days, they escort him back to Moses and inquire how they should handle the incident. Moses answers them by declaring that God is proclaiming, "the man shall be surely put to death: all the congregation shall stone him with stones." Following what they gullibly assume are God's commands, Moses' cult members take him outside the camp and stone him to death for picking up sticks on a day that he wasn't permitted to do any work (Numbers 15:32-36). As you will soon realize, God encourages the Israelites to beat their slaves and rape women captured in warfare; picking up sticks on the Sabbath, however, will anger him enough to warrant a death sentence. Astounding!

God advises Moses on a number of matters related to his appointed leadership. He is to cast any menstruating or leprous person out of the camp because God doesn't want to be around those "dirty" people when he descends for a visit (Numbers 5:1-3). In other words, God wants no association with those who are more likely to need assistance, medical or otherwise. God also orders Moses to drive out the inhabitants of Canaan before destroying their possessions (Numbers 33:50-52). However, he should offer the people of distant cities a chance to become his slaves before killing them. If they refuse, the Israelites have the duty to kill the men and take the remaining people as plunder for themselves. In the cities that God delivers as inheritances, Moses should "save alive nothing that breatheth" because the helpless victims were taught to worship other gods (Deuteronomy 20:13-18).

In two subsequent pillages, God delivers Sihon, King of Heshbon, into the hands of Moses at the battle of Jahaz. The Israelites murder him; conquer all of his cities; and murder every man, woman, and child residing within those cities per God's instructions (Deuteronomy 2:32-35). Likewise, God delivers Og, King of Bashan, into the hands of Moses at the battle of Edrei. The Israelites faithfully obey their orders by murdering all the inhabitants so that they could acquire the land (Deuteronomy 3:1-4). This noble god orders Moses to kill anything that moves, and as the incredible list of wars in the Old Testament takes place, God's followers would continue to do exactly as their unimaginably harsh leader commands them.

When Joshua informs the Israelites of God's decision to deliver the city of Jericho over to them, they topple its walls and kill every living thing in the city, except for a single harlot on espionage missions, before burning it to the ground (Joshua 6:16-24). Afterwards, God orders Joshua to infiltrate the city of Ai because he's delivered it in likewise fashion. The Israelites also set Ai on fire and kill the 12,000 inhabitants running for their lives. The King of Ai is taken prisoner and later hanged (Joshua 8:19-29). Following the victories at Jericho and Ai, God commands Joshua to go on an unbelievable killing spree. The Israelites subsequently murder all the men, women, and children in Makkedah, Libnah, Lachish (along with the King of Gezer and his armies assisting Lachish), Eglon, Hebron, and Debir. Not a single life was spared during these invasions (Joshua 10:28-40).

When word spreads of Joshua's rapid conquests, a considerable number of cities combine their armies to attempt a victory over Joshua and Israel. The number of resistance forces is "as the sand that is upon the sea shore in multitude," but God promises to deliver them all to Joshua. Indeed, God remains true to his word and "They smote them, until they left them none remaining." Joshua then burns their chariots and brutally cuts the hamstrings on their remaining horses (Joshua 11:1-9). After the battle, the Israelite army marches into all the unprotected and defenseless cities that had offered their armies in resistance and kills every living man. In Hazor, the army kills every man, woman, and child before setting the city ablaze. One can only speculate on how many hundreds of thousands of lives God orders Joshua to take in these assuredly disputable accounts.

Following Joshua's death, God proceeds with his war strategies when the Israelites face Benjamin's army. As a result of God's unorthodox command, 22,000 of his own people die in the first battle. The next day, he orders them to face Benjamin once again. This time, they suffer an additional 18,000 casualties. Phinehas, feeling a bit hesitant to lead another hopeless skirmish, asks God if he should take command in another attack against Benjamin. God affirms Phinehas' inquiry and promises him a solid victory. In the ensuing battle, the Benjamites suffer 25,100 casualties (Judges 20). In this short series of campaigns, God orders his own troops into two battles that his omniscience tells him they won't win. On the first two days of this monstrous war, during which he wasn't about to lift a finger to help, he saw to it that 40,000 of his own people would become casualties of needless warfare. Incidentally, the death of a single person initiated these hostilities.

Centuries later, when God "remembers" what the Amalekites did hundreds of years prior to Saul's leadership, he orders Saul to journey to Amalek where he is to decimate every living thing in the city. Saul only partially obeys by killing every person but saving a few of the best animals for himself. My guess is that he was unaware of how enraged God becomes over such trivial matters. God subsequently revoked Saul's crown because of his unwillingness to follow exact orders

(1 Samuel 15). To me, however, the issue of Saul's crown isn't the one of major importance. Personally, I feel that the omnibenevolent God should not have held the people of Amalek responsible for the enterprises of their distant ancestors, but God and I are obviously in constant disagreement.

In a series of miscellaneous ethnic cleansings, God delivers Jerusalem to Judah and the Israelites. They kill 10,000 Canaanites and Perizzites in Bezek (Judges 1:2-8). Later, God accompanies Judah when he destroys the cities and kills the inhabitants of Zephath, Gaza, Askelon, Ekron, and Luz (Judges 1:17-26). When Ehud announces that God has delivered the Moabites into the hands of his chosen people, they march to Moab and slay 10,000 men (Judges 3:26-29). God delivers Sihon and the Amorites to be murdered by Jephthah and the Israelites (Judges 11:21-23). God delivers twenty men to be slaughtered by Jonathan (1 Samuel 12:14). As God orders David to exterminate a few Philistines delivered into his hands, David does so and takes their cattle as well (1 Samuel 23:2-5). As God orders David to kill *more* Philistines recently delivered into his hands, David accepts God's gift once again and kills more Philistines in two additional battles (2 Samuel 5:19-25). God delivers the Syrians to the people of Israel in order for them to murder 100,000 foreigners. Twenty-seven thousand Syrians escaped but were killed when a wall fell on them (1 Kings 20:28-30)! Likewise, God delivers the Moabites into the hands of Israel once again. The army of Israelites destroys the city of Moab along with an unknown number of its inhabitants. These instigations force the King to kill his own son as an offering in order for the hostilities to cease (2 Kings 18:27)

When God witnesses certain members of Israel turning from him, he decides to assist the tribe of Judah. God then kills the King of Israel and enables Judah to kill 500,000 Israelite men because the Judeans "relied upon the Lord God of their fathers." Abijah, their leader, takes the cities of Bethel, Jeshanah, and Ephrain (2 Chronicles 13:15-20). The supreme being forces Abijah's son, Asa, to face Zerah and his staggering army of one million Ethiopians. Asa asks for God's help, which is willingly provided. In the battle, God strikes down great numbers of the Ethiopians, perhaps killing some himself, and forces the rest to make a full retreat. Asa then chases them back into their homeland and plummets all their cities (2 Chronicles 14:8-15).

God later becomes angry with his followers when they ridicule his messengers. As punishment, he sends the army of Chaldees to kill all the occupants of Jerusalem. Control of the region now falls to Persia (2 Chronicles 36:15-23). Why does God force his worshippers to suffer through all this needless trouble when he's just going to hand the land over to someone else?

As you may have already guessed, God didn't confine the impact of his seemingly perpetual rage solely on humans. Animal sacrifices seemed particularly important to this fiendish character. Strangely enough, this is one deity out of many that seems pleased with aromas emitted by burnt flesh (Genesis 8:20-21). In fact, Leviticus chapters 1-9 are thorough instructions on how to perform animal sacrifices. The graphic details contained therein are potentially nauseating and not for the weak of stomach.

For every category of sin, God has a specific ritual that he wishes us to perform. His authors tell the readers how to break animal necks, what parts of the animal to burn, what organs to extract, where to sprinkle the blood, how much God thoroughly enjoys the spectacle, etc. If you're genuinely interested in how gruesome the Bible can be, I would encourage you to read the first nine chapters of Leviticus. There are several additional passages throughout the Bible providing complete and ridiculous instructions for these crucially important animal sacrifices, but this lengthy manual definitely serves as the most memorable example. Numbers 18:19 further declares that animal sacrifices should be performed forever. Have Christians finally appreciated the insanity of God, or do they just not read their Bibles anymore?

An estimate on the number of victims who paid the ultimate price in wars that are claimed to be instigated by God is hard to determine, but I would imagine it's somewhere in the neighborhood of two or three million. All together, God may have been personally responsible for as many as *five million* needless murders. I'm sure there are several battles and/or plagues that I omitted, but I trust you get the general message of this section. The Hebrew god is a mass murderer, plain and simple. Moreover, these estimates *still* don't include all the deaths resulting from petty religious bickering that continues to this day. On the brighter side of things, however, there's no reason to mourn for the previously mentioned victims of God's brutality because the vivid human imagination was certainly the source from which the authors derived all these accounts. Thus, these slaughters were extremely unlikely to have taken place as recorded in the Bible. Again, we will see overwhelmingly persuasive evidence to defend this position in *Moses And Other Historical Fabrications*.

God's Rules And Regulations

In addition to all the previously mentioned atrocities, God hands down a nightmarishly inhumane code for his creations to live by. In fact, there would literally be millions of murders committed every day if God still had his way. I'll certainly admit that a few of the more sane guidelines are acceptable, but many are definitely not within the bounds of justice and humanity. Those are the ones in need of a serious impartial review. A few examples allegedly handed down by God follow.

Anyone who goes uncircumcised is to be exiled from his people (Genesis 17:14).

If a man has sex with a menstruating women, both are to be exiled (Leviticus 20:18).

A man who marries a mother and daughter must burn in a fire (Leviticus 20:14).

If two men have sexual relations, both must be put to death (Leviticus 20:13).

If a mother and son have sexual relations, both must be put to death (Leviticus 20:11).

If a man and daughter-in-law have sex, both must be put to death (Leviticus 20:12).

If a man has sex with an animal, both must be put to death (Leviticus 20:15).

If a woman has sex with an animal, both must be put to death (Leviticus 20:16).

Anyone who attacks his mother or father must be put to death (Exodus 21:15).

Anyone who curses his mother or father must be put to death (Leviticus 20:9).

Anyone who commits murder must be put to death (Leviticus 24:17).

Anyone who commits adultery must be put to death (Deuteronomy 22:22).

Anyone who commits perjury must be put to death (Deuteronomy 19:18-19).

Anyone who commits kidnapping must be put to death (Exodus 21:16).

Anyone who disobeys a judge or priest must be put to death (Deuteronomy 17:12).

Anyone who works on the Sabbath must be put to death (Exodus 35:2).

Anyone who does not worship God must be put to death (2 Chronicles 15:13).

Any strangers approaching a sanctuary must be put to death (Numbers 17:7).

Any prophet who tries to turn you against God must be put to death (Deuteronomy 13:5).

Any prophet who makes a wrong prediction must be put to death (Deuteronomy 18:20-22).

Family members who tempt you with other gods must be put to death (Deuteronomy 13:1-5).

If an ox gores someone, the ox and its owner must be stoned to death (Exodus 21:29).

Anyone who claims to talk with spirits must be stoned to death (Leviticus 20:27).

A stubborn and rebellious son must be stoned to death (Deuteronomy 21:18-21).

Any woman who has had premarital sex must be stoned to death (Deuteronomy 22:21).

Anyone who worships another god must be stoned to death (Deuteronomy 17:2-7).

Anyone who curses or blasphemes must be stoned to death (Leviticus 24:14-16).

Break the neck of your donkey's firstborn or kill a lamb instead (Exodus 34:20).

If a city worships other gods, kill everyone in it and burn it (Deuteronomy 13:12-16).

Let's begin by considering the adultery law. While cheating on a spouse is certainly one of the most selfish acts a person can commit, being unfaithful is nothing deserving of death. Some couples even encourage each other to commit adultery. If that's what they want, their sex lives should remain their own business. Suggesting that this would upset a supernatural entity, one wise enough to create the universe in a week, only demonstrates the unenlightened beliefs held by that party. Since researchers have estimated that 50% of Americans commit adultery, does this mean that God *really* want us to stone 50% of America's population to death? Likewise, about 25% of men are uncircumcised. For what possible reason would God ever care what a man's penis looks like? Since there's no conclusively proven health benefit from the procedure, one can only assume that God finds it aesthetically pleasing.

As for killing men who lay with other men, I really couldn't spend enough time explaining the absurdity in such a rule. The majority of society looks down on this practice because the Bible forbids it, yet these same disapprovers break a number of similar rules detailed in the upcoming chapter, *Absurdity At Its Finest*. The love experienced between two same-sex individuals is genuine; the desire for the practice most likely originates at the genetic level; and, as was the case for heterosexual couples, a gay couple's sex life should remain their own business.

All sons are rebellious at some point, but common decency tells us that this isn't a sufficient reason to stone a child to death because such circumstances are perfectly normal during the maturation process. If the situation warrants a stern response, children should be disciplined and/or corrected on a case-by-case basis, not barbarically executed.

We shouldn't needlessly kill animals because some wacko has sex with them. The helpless creatures obviously lack the capacity to make an informed choice in the matter. Many employees work on the Sabbath every week, a realistic necessity for a variety of professionals who preserve life and maintain order. Killing your family because they worship a different god isn't a justifiable reason for homicide; that's why it's *illegal!*

The last time I checked, 67% of the world doesn't believe that the Bible is the word of God, and about 45% of the world doesn't even have the Old Testament in their preferred religion. Consequently, how many billions of people does God want us to kill now? If we are to murder someone who believes in a different god or a different interpretation of God, the Jews are to kill Muslims and Christians, the Muslims are to kill Christians and Jews, and the Christians are to kill Jews and Muslims. In essence, we can't necessarily fault Islamic extremists for their radical actions because they're obviously following what they've been thoroughly conditioned to believe are paramount, unquestionable orders. Of course, priority would dictate that all these killings should take place after those three religious sects take care of Buddhists, Hindus, and members of the minor world religions. Now that God has had his way, no one's left alive to worship him. This deity was clearly an insanely reckless invention with a poorly conceived design.

These rules do not include any of the horrendously unconscionable restrictions placed on women in *Why Women And The Bible Don't Mix* or God's slavery guidelines discussed in *God's Stance On Slavery*. There's such an extraordinary amount of unimaginable injustices against these two specific groups that I felt it was necessary to provide separate chapters in order to give their respective oppressions justice.

As you can tell from the list provided, God wants you dead for just about anything you do. While the "courts" carried out some of the sentences due to undoubtful acts of immorality, the punishments are extremely harsh and rarely reflect the severity of the infraction committed. Killing someone for murder and killing someone because his ox gores a bystander are two entirely different instances to consider. Of all the worthwhile messages that God could have included in the Bible to help us through life, he settles on a number of nonsense rules and regulations that he knew hardly anyone would still follow a short while later. Are these the likely decisions of an omniscient creator, or are they the likely product of a group of superstitious individuals playing on the gullibility of superstitious audiences?

God's Psyche

While it may seem that the preceding sections were a sufficient analysis of the oft-ignored alter ego of God, we still have quite a bit more ground to cover in order to comprehensively investigate this cauldron of evil. The focus will now shift from God's allegedly observable physical manifestations to the declarations and interpretations of "divinely inspired" poets and prophets contemporaneous with the Old Testament's creation. We'll try to tackle such issues as the human personality of God, his childish necessity to make threats, and the dark future according to this being.

We can answer many questions concerning the nature of humans by studying the things we say and do, and there's no reason that we can't apply this same principle to God if we give him the benefit of behaving in a remotely logical fashion. Moreover, this is especially true if he is, indeed, merely the product of human creation. Let's reflect on the Old Testament once again to review some of God's alleged statements and opinions in order to see what they might reveal about his personality. Of course, you should realize how facetious it is to say that we can learn about God rather than the authors molding him into their individual interpretations.

"He is a jealous God; he will not forgive your transgressions nor your sins" (Joshua 24:19). Consider this observation: God becomes jealous when we do not pay him enough attention or when we like other gods better than him. If you are guilty of either of these transgressions, he won't forgive you for making him angry. If we transpose God into a more human setting, we realize that his behavior is the quintessence of a spoiled child throwing a tantrum when you won't look to see what he's doing. This fair assessment is undeniably consistent with the remainder of God's curiously immature actions throughout the Old Testament. Even so, the Bible does an about-face in the New Testament and says that the now silent creator *does* forgive you for anger-inducing infractions. This notion exemplifies qualities of a more respectable and desirable deity, thus the New Testament creator is the one on which Christians tend to place their focus. Well, which interpretation of God should we accept as the truth? You'll no doubt see similar discrepancies reemerge in the upcoming *This Way And That: Biblical Contradictions*.

God places "the iniquity of the fathers upon the children…unto the third and fourth generation" (Exodus 34:7). As you read the Old Testament, you should take careful notice of the aforementioned recurring theme of God forcing children to pay for the sins of their ancestors. I've probably worn the topic out by now, but this cannot *possibly* be considered a fair way of treating people. God undeniably admits that he creates an unfair system in which the righteous are not guaranteed freedom from his wrath due to the contingency of him punishing us for our ancestors' actions. Thus, we can only conclude that God receives a sense of sadistic enjoyment from punishing people for things they didn't do because there's no true justification for anyone, deity or not, to treat others this way. Proverbs 16:4 even confirms this hypothesis by telling us that God made evil people so that he could punish them at some point in the future. It's an incomprehensibly evil undertaking for God to make people behave a certain way just so he can entertain himself by torturing them for eternity. Furthermore, the excessive boasting and power flaunting by God *literally* adds insult to injury. In addition, the author of the second letter to the Thessalonians says God will cause wicked people to disbelieve the truth about Jesus so that he can send them to Hell (2:8-12).

We also understand that God wants Christians to suffer through life (1 Peter 4:12-19). Why doesn't he make it less painful to follow him in order for more of us to understand the "true" way of being saved? If that's not bad enough, God even hurts the people he loves (Hebrews 12:6). Now we have even *more* evidence that God doesn't want to save some people from his punishment of eternal, perpetual damnation. However, let us not forget that this is the same deity who created his son to die an agonizing death on the cross in order to pay for everyone else's sins. If God were human, psychiatrists would certainly have him locked in an asylum.

God goes so far as to place equivalent monetary values on human life for an offering that he requires everyone to provide (Leviticus 27:1-8). This is another prime example of the total disregard God reserves for his creations. We may not be omnipotent and omniscient, but most of us would never attempt to place a specific price on the value of a human life. Incidentally, we're worth very little to him. This notion is especially true when you consider how readily he commands thousands of us to our deaths in the Old Testament. If you're interested, men are worth approximately $100 US while women are only worth about $60 US in modern currency equivalents. If you want to know why women are less valuable than men, you'll find out in the next equally disturbing chapter.

Job is an odd book in an odd place. While it's believed to have been written in an era concurrent with the Pentateuch authorship, the fable appears much later in the Bible with the books of poetry. Regardless, Christians insist that we accept it as a literal work rather than a figurative one, thus we will review it as such. As a literal work, it's a wonderful glimpse into the mind of the most primitive form of the Hebrew god. In the ridiculous tale, God allows Satan to torment the innocent Job by utilizing various methods of torture. All of this is just to prove to Satan that he couldn't make Job curse the name of God. How nonsensical is that? God's *ego* drives him to watch a good man be tortured because he feels the need to prove a point to an inferior entity of evil.

The authors of Psalms often glorify God for a number of despicable acts. The authors exalt God for giving knowledge on how to kill enemies in battle (18:34-42) and for literally bashing people who don't worship him (2:9). The authors admire God for his plans to burn some of his creations to death (21:9-10) and for the murder of every firstborn male child in Egypt (135:8, 136:10). The authors praise God for his intentions to tear disbelievers into pieces (50:22) and for making a spectacle out of people who worship other gods (52:5-7). Why would anyone sing praises of such abominations except to score points out of obvious fear? This thought reminds me of the Iraqi government officials who started praising Saddam Hussein in July of 1979 as he read a list of traitors who were to be executed. Because members of the audience obviously didn't want to be among those facing an imminent death sentence, they publicly demonstrate their loyalty to Saddam by shouting praises in order to preserve their own lives. The method works wonderfully now, and it seemingly worked many centuries ago.

Guidelines on how to secure a place in Heaven are finally set in the New Testament, but they remain inherently unfair and contradicting. Christians across the board believe that you'll burn in Hell forever if you don't accept Jesus as your personal savior (Mark 9:42-48). If we assume this belief to be factual, is it truly fair to a radical Muslim who has had the exact opposite notion drilled into his head since birth? Of course not. All God has to do for the Muslim is show him the error of his ways. Instead, the combination of God's present silence and his Old Testament approval of violence lamentably provides the radical Muslim with the notion that it pleases God when people fly airplanes into buildings. The murdering Muslim simply hasn't been instructed otherwise.

Just Empty Threats?

God invariably makes threats that if you do *this*, he will counter with *that*. Let's look at a few Old Testament examples and determine if his retaliations are justifiable. The first of which would be to not harass any widows or orphans because

God will kill you with a sword (Exodus 22:24). As in the previous section, we see a continuity of God administering unfit punishments for minor crimes. If you try to rebuild Jericho, your oldest and youngest son will die (Joshua 6:26). While such an extreme measure of revenge could hardly be warranted, God affords everyone ample opportunity to avoid his insane wrath in this instance. If you don't worship God, he'll sever your arm, revoke your eyesight, and curse you with a premature death (1 Samuel 2:31-33). Similarly, he'll wipe you off the earth if you observe other gods (Deuteronomy 6:14-15). If you take it as far as hating God, he'll totally destroy you (Deuteronomy 7:10). I think these punishments are starting to creep over that arbitrary boundary known as "fairness."

However, we see a small incongruity in making these threats. If God's orders were to kill anyone who disobeys these divine commands, why would he personally need to administer these punishments? Better yet, why isn't God making good on these threats? Incidentally, shouldn't God be angry with his followers for not killing people with different viewpoints? Regardless of the answers to these questions, we're about to see God leap past any hope of inconspicuously remaining in the background.

> If ye will not hearken unto me, and will not do all these commandments; And if ye shall despise my statutes, or if your soul abhor my judgments, so that ye will not do all my commandments, but that ye break my covenant: I will even appoint over you terror, consumption, and the burning ague, that shall consume the eyes, and cause sorrow of heart: and ye shall sow your seed in vain, for your enemies shall eat it. And I will set my face against you, and ye shall be slain before your enemies: they that hate you shall reign over you; and ye shall flee when none pursueth you. And if ye will not yet for all this hearken unto me, then I will punish you seven times more for your sins. And I will break the pride of your power; and I will make your heaven as iron, and your earth as brass: And your strength shall be spent in vain: for your land shall not yield her increase, neither shall the trees of the land yield their fruits. And if ye will contrary unto me, and will not hearken unto me; I will bring seven times more plagues upon you according to your sins. I will also send wild beasts among you, which shall rob you of your children, and destroy your cattle, and make you few in number; and your high ways shall be desolate. And if ye will not be reformed by me by these things, but will walk contrary unto me; Then will I also walk contrary unto you, and will punish you yet seven times for your sins. And I will bring a sword upon you, that shall avenge the quarrel of my covenant: and when ye are gathered together within your cities, I will send the pestilence among you; and ye shall be delivered into the hand of the enemy. And when I have broken the staff of your bread, ten women shall bake your bread in one oven, and they shall deliver you your bread again by weight: and ye shall eat, and not be satisfied. And if ye will not for all this hearken

unto me, but walk contrary unto me; Then I will walk contrary unto you also in fury; and I, even I, will chastise you seven times for your sins. And ye shall eat the flesh of your sons, and the flesh of your daughters shall ye eat. And I will destroy your high places, and cut down your images, and cast your carcases upon the carcases of your idols, and my soul shall abhor you. And I will make your cities waste and bring your sanctuaries unto desolation, and I will not smell the savour of your sweet odours. And I will bring the land into desolation: and your enemies which dwell therein shall be astonished at it. And I will scatter you among the heathen, and will draw out a sword after you: and your land shall be desolate, and your cities waste. Then shall the land enjoy her sabbaths, as long as it lieth desolate, and ye be in your enemies' land; even then shall the land rest, and enjoy her sabbaths. As long as it lieth desolate it shall rest; because it did not rest in your sabbaths, when ye dwelt upon it. And upon them that are left alive of you I will send a faintness into their hearts in the lands of their enemies; and the sound of a shaken leaf shall chase them; and they shall flee, as fleeing from a sword; and they shall fall when none pursueth. And they shall fall one upon another, as it were before a sword, when none pursueth: and ye shall have no power to stand before your enemies. And ye shall perish among the heathen, and the land of your enemies shall eat you up. And they that are left of you shall pine away in their iniquity in your enemies' lands and also in the iniquities of their fathers shall they pine away with them. (Leviticus 26:14-39, reworded in Deuteronomy 28:15-68).

That's quite a punishment for not believing in God. You'll go blind; you'll become sorrowful; you won't be able to grow food; your enemies will become your leaders; you'll run for no reason; you'll have no pride, power, or strength; your land will go bad; your children and cattle will be killed by wild animals; your cities will empty; you'll be struck by a sword; you'll receive a pestilence; your hunger won't be satisfied; you'll *eat your children*; your places of worship will be destroyed; your enemies will take your land; you'll become terrified; you'll live with injustice; and then you'll perish.

Thankfully, we can safely conclude that there's no connection between reality and these transcendental threats because it's obvious that God isn't currently enforcing these punishments. Since unfortunate episodes perpetually manifest across the religious spectrum, it's also safe to conclude that they aren't transpiring due to the absence of God in the victims' lives. Since the Hebrews contemporaneous with these threats lived in an unscientific and superstitious era, they gullibly but wholeheartedly believed that these events had a divine cause and effect relationship. As an obvious consequence of that unenlightened belief, the population rarely challenged these frightening warnings. What can we surmise about these intimidating statements? Two words: scare tactics.

In the quoted passage, God yet again exposes his childish behavior by listing a long series of punishments for failing to follow his commandments and not paying him enough attention. He sends his only son to assist us in carrying out what he feels is a positive lifestyle, yet he threatens to torture us for eternity if we don't listen to him and follow his advice. Why is God overly concerned with how we act and how we choose to worship? Since this cruel deity supposedly made us exactly how he anticipated, he should definitely know what actions we're imminently going to take. One would presumably think that an all-powerful and all-knowing god would have little regard for the opinions of his insignificant creations, turning instead to hobbies that one would think are more productive. It's now obvious that our existence is nothing but a game to him, and it should leave the reader to wonder why he would subject us to this exhibition when he already knows the outcome.

The God Of The Future

It would be quite negligent for me to approach a somewhat comprehensive piece on this perspective of God but not include references for the hundreds of evil operations that the prophets claim he will implement sometime in the future. There's such a wealth of despicable activities carried out or silently observed by God that I must once again force myself to share only a small portion of the most horrendous, inventive, or entertaining ones. Common examples of Godly justifications usually fall into one of the following categories: he has angry desires for revenge, people will turn their backs on him, or his followers will sin by finding new gods to worship. While most of the foretold events are yet to come, apologists must accept the prophecies as part of an unchangeable future because the passages are part of the inerrant, unalterable word of God. Since these promised catastrophes are imminent in their arrival, we can treat these events as though they've already materialized for the purpose of analyzing the moral justifications, or lack thereof, that God offers for his actions.

God will kill men, have their children smashed, and have their wives raped (Isaiah 13:15-16).
God will punish children for the iniquities of their fathers and distant ancestors (Isaiah 14:21).
God will lay waste to entire cities and make the lands desolate (Jeremiah 4:7).
God will set people, animals, and even plants on fire because of his anger (Jeremiah 7:20).
God will send so much evil that people would rather be dead than suffer (Jeremiah 8:3).
God will give away the property of men, including their wives, to other men (Jeremiah 8:10).
God will kill young men, and their children will die from a famine (Jeremiah 11:22).
God will cause everyone to become drunk so father and son will kill one another (Jeremiah 13:14).
God will not hear the cries of the people or acknowledge their sacrifices (Jeremiah 14:12).
God will make people hungry enough to eat their own children and friends (Jeremiah 19:9).

God will burn entire cities with the inhabitants still inside (Jeremiah 50:32).
God will break people's bones and knock their teeth out with stones (Lamentations 3:1-16).
God will force fathers and sons to eat each other and scatter their remembrance (Ezekiel 5:10).
God will be comforted by killing everyone with pestilence, plagues, and swords (Ezekiel 5:12-13).
God will lay dead bodies around idols and spread their bones around the alters (Ezekiel 6:5).
God will kill righteous men and forget their good deeds if they ever turn to sin (Ezekiel 18:24).
God will turn daughters into whores and wives into adulterers (Hosea 4:13).
God will kill children when they come out of their mothers' wombs (Hosea 10:14).
God will tear people apart and devour them like a lion (Hosea 13:8).
God will kill children and unborn fetuses because their parents worship other gods (Hosea 13:16).
God will sell the children of Israel into slavery in a far away land (Joel 3:8).
God will kill inhabitants of entire cities if they have a corrupt government (Micah 3:9-12).
God will consume every living thing from the face of the earth (Zephaniah 1:2-3).
God will send people to steal Jerusalem, rape the women, and enslave the rest (Zechariah 14:2).
God will send plagues on people and animals to rot away tongues and eyes (Zechariah 14:12-15).

The prophets warn us of the Old Testament God's frightful, futuristic return to the earth, at which point he'll initiate every category of curse imaginable on the people who ignore his commandments, refuse to worship him, or commit acts that he arbitrarily deems evil. It's remarkable how he can randomly dish out such unfathomable punishments for reasons a typical person would consider lacking in foundation, yet he becomes terribly enraged when one of us follows suit.

God brings people into this world without a choice in the matter and expects us to do certain things, otherwise he'll punish us severely without rest for an *eternity*. God's omniscience must necessarily allow him to know which names will not be included in his book of life. Therefore, we can only conclude that he purposely brings people into the world with *zero* chance of avoiding Hell. Any deviation from this predetermined course would make God wrong, but since God cannot possibly be wrong, it's impossible for us to deviate from the absolutely unalterable plan that he has already envisioned. Thus, Christians can only logically claim that we are exclusively involuntary pawns at the mercy of God's whimsical decisions as to where we will spend our ultimate eternal destinations. This heartless exercise of brutality can only be the single most hateful crime any being could ever commit.

Now that I've had time to reflect upon these considerations, if I believed for one moment that it was possible for this god to exist, I would be the first person in church on Sunday morning and the last person out the door Sunday evening. I would swallow my disgust and worship the deity that I detested in order to accept the slightly more agreeable punishment of eternal praise over eternal agony. In our universe bound by reality, however, such a personality can only be a ridiculous creation from a deceitful set of individuals who were sadly unaware of the vicious monster they created.

The God Worshipped By Two Billion

God barbarically killed millions of people in the Old Testament because they weren't "fortunate" enough to belong to the Israelite tribe. Had these alleged victims belonged to the lineage of Jacob, they obviously wouldn't have suffered the full wrath of God. However, what chances did they realistically have of converting to worship the Hebrew deity when their own parents conditioned them to think according to their local customs? Even today, God's evil demands require us to murder billions of non-Christians because their parents unknowingly continue to practice this same form of powerful conditioning. The consequences of obeying God's directions should give us the presence of mind to refrain from following such orders without first analyzing the morality of the demands in question. Widely distributed directions from a fair god should be moral or have a satisfactory explanation. Otherwise, we may be repeating the same evil accomplishments of our ancestors.

What logic is there in the fact that the being who promises us eternal life because of his love for all humankind is the same entity who orders us to kill a variety of people for morally bankrupt reasons? The biblical god is not "wonderful" and "loving" as Christians claim because these unenlightened followers base such crude assessments on the more positive New Testament. The God of the Old Testament, on the other hand, is pure evil and full of perpetual anger; he even admits as much. No one who creates and needlessly kills millions of people can honestly be called "wonderful" and "loving," deity or not. Certainly, most people wouldn't think it was fair if they saw their fellow man being tortured just because his parents raised him with a different version of the creator. God even takes enjoyment in the fact that many people will never make it into Heaven. Regardless of your position on the issue, I believe we can all agree that God has quite a unique character about him, to say the least.

We've also come to realize that we can observe the following qualities of God: he exhibits immature rage when no one pays attention to him; he makes people suffer for what others have done; he has no regard for human life; and he tortures decent people for such reasons as winning bets with Satan. If we were to extract this behavior into human terms, we would most likely draw a comparison with that of a spoiled child. Because of an obvious state of fear and panic over similar reports heard by authors of the ancient Hebrew scriptures, they wrote and sang praises to this terrible creature thinking that such measures might assist in helping them escape his unconscionable wrath.

To top it all off, God conveniently ceased his murdering and slave driving when modern philosophers, enlightened thinking, and accurate historical records began to appear. However, Jesus did not invalidate the aforementioned rules and regulations with his teachings, as some apologists often claim, because the old laws were never intended to be cast aside. "Think not that I am come to destroy the law, or the prophets: I am not come to destroy, but to fulfil" (Matthew 5:7). "For verily I say unto you, Till heaven and earth pass, one jot or one tittle shall in no wise pass from the law, till all be fulfilled" (Matthew 5:18). "And it is easier for heaven and earth to pass, than one tittle of the law to fail" (Luke 16:17). Amazingly, the perfect Jesus also tells us that we should abide by the old laws established by Moses. Something is *definitely* wrong here.

WHY WOMEN AND THE BIBLE DON'T MIX

After thousands of years of recorded history, we're just now arriving at a point where women are starting to receive fair and equal treatment in many societies. It's an irrefutable historical fact that some of the major sources of this unsolicited oppression were drawn from references of women's treatment in the Old and New Testaments. This chapter will show that the Bible takes a clear and undeniable stance in its advocation for the unequal treatment of women. Furthermore, I will prove that the authors of the Bible intended for women to play the role of a man's servant from birth until death. I will consistently and successfully defend this position using the words of God, allegedly speaking through Moses. Through this demonstration, I hope you will see that the incredibly dishonest teachings of Moses arose from an earthly source inferior to an omniscient deity. Subsequent works of Paul and his peers show only how gullible they were in so readily accepting the Old Testament scriptures as fact.

After reading this chapter, I hope you will have a greater awareness of how the Bible instructs men to treat women. More importantly, I hope you will appreciate the lack of divine inspiration behind such commands encouraging this mistreatment. The only alternative is to conclude, yet again, that a deity with desires this immoral is clearly not worthy of observance.

The Rules Of Marriage

Let's start our analysis at the "beginning." Everyone has heard the story of God becoming angry with Adam and Eve for eating the forbidden fruit in the Garden of Eden. Although God punishes both for disobeying his directions, the author clearly places the majority of the blame on Eve for tempting her husband. God says to Eve, "thy desire is to be to thy husband, and he shall rule over thee" (Genesis 3:16). Since the other suppressing punishments on the couple, such as Eve's childbirth pains, are still in effect, we have no justifiable reason to think that the servitude punishment applies solely to Eve and not the gender as a whole. If the Bible is the true word of God, this passage demonstrates his desire for women to live life in subservience to men. In actuality, however, someone most likely invented this portion of the patently unreliable story as a justification for the ongoing inferior treatment of women.

Chapter 21 of Exodus provides us with some very detailed instructions from God on women and marriage. For example, in the instance that a father *sells* his daughter to another man who is not pleased with her, she must be redeemed. Regardless of the amount of satisfaction that the girl provides for the man, God's rules still allow him to acquire another wife. If he so chooses, the first wife is not allowed to leave unless her master refuses her food, clothing, or other marriage duties (Exodus 21:7-11). These words would later serve as justification for men, such as King David, who had hundreds of wives and concubines. We've also learned in this passage that women are to be sold as slaves and treated as sex objects. If you dislike this conclusion and still believe the Bible to be the divinely inspired word of God, you must either unwillingly follow God's derogatory and dehumanizing orders or take an opposing position against the almighty.

The demoralizing instructions for daughter selling aren't the only rules of marriage that God sanctions. If a man decides he no longer wants to be married to his wife, he can attempt to have her killed by claiming that she lost her virginity prior to their marriage. Following this accusation, the woman must then provide sufficient physical evidence, such as a bloodstain, to demonstrate that his accusations are fraudulent. In the event that she fails to prove her innocence of this "crime," she is to be stoned to death because of this utmost act of disgrace. Guilty until proven innocent is the law within God's court. Any woman who accidentally tears her hymen due to an injury or other non-sexual act is simply out of luck because she could never prove her virginity. Thus, she would be at the mercy of her husband throughout her entire life. If evidence is produced to exonerate the woman in question, the accuser is fined a couple pounds of silver and forced to stay married until death (Deuteronomy 22:13-21). In this case, what does the man really have to lose?

Some rules following the death of a man are relevant to his wife's well-being. According to the rules of Moses, the deceased father's inheritance goes entirely to his sons. If he has no son, it goes to the daughters. After that, the inheritance should go to the closest male relatives (Numbers 27:8-11). Not only do the boys of the household have priority over the girls, the wife is also noticeably absent from the will. Instead, God's law forces her to marry her husband's brother, provided she doesn't already have a son with her former husband. However, the brother-in-law has the right to refuse the marriage; the woman does not (Deuteronomy 25:5-9).

Menstruation is a natural occurrence in the lives of most women. However, the God of the Pentateuch despises this biologically necessary bodily process and gives instructions on how to deal with these treacherous circumstances. During menstruation, God deems the woman unclean. No one shall have any contact with her for seven days or until the bleeding stops. God deems anyone or anything she touches unclean. If she touches another person, God deems *that* person unclean until he bathes. In fact, the same goes for anyone who touches something that *she* previously touched (Leviticus 15:19-30). All this uncleanliness is resolved by needlessly killing two doves. Admittedly, there are similar laws for male ejaculation, but men can actually suppress these events to some extent.

Childbirth is another natural event that God deems foul. If a woman gives birth to a boy, she will be unclean for seven days while she undergoes the same ritual for her menstrual period. She must then be purified for thirty-three days and barred from entering worship during this time. If she produces a girl, the sentence of solitary confinement is doubled to fourteen and sixty-six days, respectively (Leviticus 12:1-5). In addition to God unfairly designating women as filthy individuals following childbirth, this passage heavily insinuates that girls are dirtier than boys because it punishes a woman more harshly for giving birth to a female child.

Woman's Darkest Hour

Rape, the paramount fear of many women, rears its ugly head in the Bible as well. Fortunately, God ensures that the authors list it as a crime under a few circumstances. Unfortunately, God permits the sexual violation of women on more than one occasion. More unfortunately, the fine for committing one of the most heinous acts known to man without God's permission is only a pound of silver to her father and a forced marriage to the victim if she's not already engaged or married (Deuteronomy 22:28-29). Yes, God's idea of justice for the female victim is to be horrendously punished *again* by forcing her to marry the man who savagely attacked her. This disgusting rule is nowhere near what most people would consider an ethical resolution, and it's certainly not a decision rendered by any court I'd like to be facing.

If a man rapes an engaged virgin who doesn't cry loud enough to draw attention, the community should consider the attack consensual if it took place within the city. Thus, the whore must be stoned to death per God's instructions. It obviously doesn't matter if the woman is too scared to scream because the law makes no such exception. The man will be stoned to death as well, not because he committed a brutal atrocity against the woman, but only because he "violated another man's wife" (Deuteronomy 22:24). Note the shamefully sharp contrast in disciplinary action between raping a woman with a husband and raping a woman without a husband: death versus a pound of silver. Since it's all the same to the woman, it now becomes clear that God feels the *husband* is the one who is the victim of the attack.

As I previously mentioned, the Bible regrettably provides some situations in which rape is entirely permissible, even encouraged, by the Hebrew god. Recall the rule of marriage specifying how a man can force his daughter to marry and sleep with another man. This in itself is completely reprehensible and rises to the level of rape if the woman is unwilling, but the outlook for women only worsens as we continue our reading.

In the matter of Moses' war victory over the Midianites, God had previously commanded him to build an army and defeat the enemy. After successful completion of this task, his army takes thousands of war prisoners. Moses then orders his army to kill the remaining men, boys, and women who have already slept with a man, "but all the women children, that have not known a man by lying with him, keep alive for yourselves" (Numbers 31:17-18). If taking a human war trophy based solely on the prisoner's gender and sexual status isn't implied permission to commit rape, I honestly don't know what is. Even God receives thirty-two virgins as his share of the spoils, but they're handed over to the priest for obvious reasons (Numbers 31:40-41).

The "women children" mentioned in the passage certainly included young girls. Some female inhabitants of the city had to have been several years away from entering puberty, but don't pretend these barbaric savages capable of killing defenseless women thought twice about waiting a few years for the girls to mature. Well, what eventually becomes of these foreign women kidnapped in battle?

> When thou goest forth to war against thine enemies, and the Lord thy God hath delivered them into thine hands, and thou hast taken them captive, And seest among the captives a beautiful woman, and hast a desire unto her, that thou wouldest have her to thy wife; Then thou shalt bring her home to thine house; and she shall shave her head, and pare her nails; And she shall put the raiment of her captivity from off her, and shall remain in thine house, and bewail her father and her mother a full month: and after that thou shalt go in unto her, and be her husband, and she shall by thy wife. And it shall be, if thou have no delight in her, then thou shalt let her go whither she will; but thou shalt not sell her at all for money, thou shalt not make merchandise of her, because thou hast humbled her. (Deuteronomy 21:10-14).

More Old Testament Atrocities

One other mistreatment by omission should come to mind upon completion of reading the Pentateuch: the failure to mention the explicit impermissibility of sexual relations between fathers and daughters. The only such instance that comes to mind is the record of Lot's daughters getting him drunk to become pregnant by him (Genesis 19:30-38). However, the author tells the story using disturbingly tranquil commentary. Had God considered this a reprehensible act, one would assume that it would be noted in some way for its distastefulness. In fact, Moses provides a long list of people with whom we are not to have sexual contact in

Leviticus 20:10-21, but noticeably absent from this list is the debauchery of a father with his daughter. We also know from previous analyses that daughters are the sole property of their fathers. Finally, we can safely assume that these father-daughter relationships existed thousands of years ago, as they secretly do now. The omission of this regulation can only lead to the conclusion that it was permissible, or at least somewhat condonable, for a father to rape his daughters.

The historical books, Joshua through Esther, begin the popular trend of multiple-wife lifestyles. Among those who have several wives and/or concubines are Gideon, Elkanah, David, Rehoboam, Abijah, and Solomon, who I believe is the winner with 700 wives and 300 concubines. Even so, divinely inspired biblical authors wholeheartedly claim that God looks upon these men favorably. Would we expect God to view these individuals in a positive light if this lifestyle was displeasing to the almighty?

We find several more cruelties perpetrated against women in these historical books. Such atrocities include a woman given away as a prize (Judges 1:12-13); a woman offered as a sacrifice (Judges 11:29-39); married daughters given to other people (Judges 15:2); rape, murder, and mutilation by a mob; (Judges 19:22-30); abduction of virgins (Judges 21:7-23); purchasing of wives (Ruth 4:10 and 1 Samuel 18:25-27); and God punishing David by allowing his son to sleep with his wives and concubines, an act for which the women were later imprisoned (2 Samuel 12:11-12, 16:22, 20:3).

If you read the book of Proverbs, you will find more sayings than I care to list that reiterate how women can be evil, strange, adulterous, foolish, contentious, etc. The book concludes with an observation on the rarity of a virtuous woman. According to the author, if you find one such woman, she's worth far more than rubies (Proverbs 31:10). Enlightened readers, on the other hand, should quickly realize that *all* humans are more valuable than material possessions, regardless of their sex, color, or creed.

The books of prophecy, Isaiah through Malachi, have the most vivid images of God tormenting women. Some examples of God's actions not previously covered include the giving away of people's wives (Jeremiah 8:10), justifying a woman being raped (Jeremiah 13:22), making men "become as women" (Jeremiah 50:37), denouncing menstruation (Ezekiel 18:6), telling Hosea to acquire a wife that he knew would be purchased (Hosea 3:1-2), aborting children in their mothers' wombs (Hosea 9:11-12 and 13:16), ridiculing an army by labeling them women (Nahum 3:13), and taking part in a war concluding with women being raped (Zechariah 11:4). Again, I don't feel there's any reason to worry over such matters because none of this will ever happen due to direct intervention by the fictitious version of God depicted in the Old Testament.

New Testament Atrocities

The outlook doesn't substantially improve for women in the New Testament either. The author of Ephesians insists that wives should submit to their husbands in *everything* (5:22-24). While it's true that the author later instructs men to love their wives and treat them well, what does a devout Christian woman do when her husband decides to break the bounds of his instructions by asking her to embrace something she knows is evil? Remember, the woman has no right to divorce the man. In addition, the author fails to mention the existence of any out clause for her in such a situation. It would appear as though she has no choice but to comply with his orders if she is to obey the words in the scripture.

The authors of Colossians, Titus, and 1 Peter all agree that women should submit to their husbands (3:18, 2:5, and 3:1, respectively). The books of Peter also forbid women to wear any type of decorative jewelry to adorn their bodies (1 Peter 3:2-6), refer to women as the weaker vessel of the couple (1 Peter 3:7), and deem Lot to be a righteous man even though he once offered his daughters as a suitable alternative for homosexual rapists surrounding his house (2 Peter 2:8 referring to Genesis 19:4-8). A man with the immoral qualities of Lot cannot be regarded as righteous unless you discount the inherent rights of all people, more specifically, the inherent rights of women.

The author of Timothy also follows suit with his bigoted opinions of women. Like Peter, he says that females shouldn't wear decoration or try to usurp authority over their husbands. Instead, women should remain silent and fully submissive to them. As he also declares that Adam was not the one who was deceived in the Garden of Eden, Eve is clearly the party implicated as being responsible for the downfall of man (1 Timothy 2:9-15). This author isn't particularly kind to widows either. He says we should leave these women in need because their rewards will arrive as an answer to prayer. A widow experiencing pleasure while she's still alive, on the other hand, is already dead in the afterlife. In the author's eyes, the only respectable widows are at least sixty years old, have had only one husband, and have been well known for their positive accomplishments in life. In contrast, younger widows aren't worth assisting because they eventually remarry, become idle, or venture from house to house with their gossip (1 Timothy 5:5-15).

As we discussed near the beginning of this book, Paul is no doubt the single most important figure in getting Christianity to where it is today. Unfortunately, he is also one of the most sexist people you'll find in the New Testament. Paul is very adamant in his belief that women aren't useful for much more than sexually satisfying their husbands. He even remarks that it's good for a man to refrain from touching a woman, but he realizes the need for a man to have sexual contact and permits each to have a wife (1 Corinthians 7:1-2).

Paul also tells a story in his letter to the Romans about men "leaving the 'natural use' of the woman" to have sexual relations with other men (Romans 1:27). The passage is more or less saying that the natural use of a woman is to function as a derogatory sexual outlet for a man. He continues to spread his bigoted beliefs in a letter to the Corinthians by unambiguously declaring the man to be the head of the woman, similar to the way that Jesus is the authority figure for men. Paul also says women, who are the glory of men, were made for men, who are the glory of God (1 Corinthians 11:3-9). The clearly implied chain of importance goes *Christ* first, *man* second, and *woman* last.

Paul also establishes a few ground rules before the men can bring their women to church. The women are to choose between concealing their heads and having their hair completely shaven. Later, Paul takes away the latter choice by declaring a shaved head to be a disgrace in need of covering (1 Corinthians 11:5-7). He also doesn't permit women to speak in church because that also is a shame. If they have a question concerning the material, they must ask their husbands at home. Paul also reminds us once again, "they are commanded to be under obedience" according to the law (1 Corinthians 14:34-35). If you ever attend a Southern Baptist church, you will notice that its members tend to remain clung to these values in some fashion. Unfortunately, some ultra-conservative members continue to take these biblical guidelines into their homes.

Are Women Equal To Men?

Dozens more examples of cruelty to women exist throughout the Bible, but I feel this will be sufficient in making my case. Women had suffered terribly for thousands of years because of what *men*, not any god, wrote in the Bible. To some extent, women still endure coarse treatment stemming from their own religious beliefs and those observed by their husbands. I hope you realize that the authors of the Pentateuch were not divinely inspired to write declarations of women as the sole property of men. Instead, the books should once again read as though some group is depending upon the gullibility of the people to serve their own desires. In essence, the Old Testament authors misled the New Testament authors into believing that they actually recorded the "wonderful" and "loving" God's authentic orders. Not knowing any other society than the one in which they were raised, the New Testament authors felt compelled to endorse these regulations.

Many Christians continue to adhere to these cruel, senseless, and morally bankrupt codes, but most have illogically reasoned their way out of following God's eternal commands. Many Christians have declared that the Old Testament regulations died when Jesus arrived, but three key verses can once again tell us that this simply isn't a valid deduction. "Think not that I am come to destroy the law, or the prophets: I am not come to destroy, but to fulfil" (Matthew 5:7). "For verily I say unto you, Till heaven and earth pass, one jot or one tittle shall in no wise pass from the law, till all be fulfilled" (Matthew 5:18). "And it is easier for heaven and earth to pass, than one tittle of the law to fail" (Luke 16:17). Furthermore, as the New Testament instructions postdate Jesus' life, the failed suggestion doesn't even attempt to resolve the problems created by New Testament authors. Even if we allow the repeal of these old traditions, does this act justify centuries of biblical oppression? For the reasons presented in this chapter, I urge all men to use their intrinsic common decency, not the Bible, when deciding how to treat a woman.

GOD'S STANCE ON SLAVERY

The common apologetic response to the question of how God feels about slavery is that he *definitely* opposed the historical tradition. The long-time practice of holding innocent individuals against their will could very well be the worst crime humankind has ever committed. The Hebrew god, who is purported to love his people to a degree that we could never comprehend, would certainly have to declare some explicit opposition to slavery, wouldn't he? Truth be told, the Bible contains not one mention of God's desire to end slavery. Out of all the "thou shalt nots" and multitude of rules that he provides for us; out of all the chapters that God spends giving us intricate directions for making candles, tents, and temples; and out of all the chapters that God inspires the authors to spend on telling us who begat whom; not once does he *ever* take the time to abolish, admonish, or reject slavery.

Because God is omniscient, he knew a time would arrive when the results of his silence would include the capture, torture, castration, dehumanization, and/or murder of tens of millions of Africans around the world. Even with his unlimited knowledge, God still neglects to spend two seconds of his infinite time to ensure that we have his documented denouncement of slavery. Using elementary deduction and common sense on this scrap of information, we're already able to conclude that it wasn't displeasing in the eyes of the Hebrew god for a more powerful individual to own a lesser.

Does the presumably apathetic preference of God toward slavery mean that we're left with a distant ruler demonstrably indifferent toward the institution? In such a case, perhaps he wants us to use our judgment on whether or not it's morally acceptable to own other people. Regrettably, an in depth analysis of the Bible tells us that this cannot be the case either. As hard as it may be to accept, even for those doubtful of the Bible's authenticity, God and the multitude of his appointed biblical authors are strongly vocal in their advocation of slavery. In fact, prior to the American Civil War, slaveholders worldwide used many of the passages we'll examine to justify their nightmarish treatment of kidnapped Africans.

The orders supposedly given by God are clear enough that I can honestly see how a mentally conditioned Christian would condone or support slavery. If society taught such individuals from birth that the Bible is infallible, even when it drastically varies from their own understanding, many slaveholders would separate from generated cognitive dissonance by submitting to the presumably superior knowledge held by the higher power. Those who broke free from the Christian mindset, illogically justified their way around it, or never supported such religious hatred would eventually coalesce as the abolitionists.

In this modern age, we'd like to pretend that the upcoming passages couldn't be found in the Bible. Even so, that won't make them go away. Again, the church often neglects the Old Testament due to the uneasy feelings that its controversial topics, such as slavery, create. Consequently, this chapter may be the only opportunity that Christian readers have to investigate what information we can extract from these slavery-related biblical passages. Certain verses will prominently show that the so-called divinely inspired people speaking on behalf of the Hebrew god unequivocally state that he was in support of slave ownership.

Before we start analyzing specific passages, however, I need to clarify a bit of terminology. The 1600s King James Version of the Bible often uses *servant* in the English translation to describe people with what we'll temporarily designate as "freedom deprivation." Since the Old Testament was written in Hebrew, and the Hebrew term *ebed* has an ambiguous meaning of *slave* or *servant*, some passages might be too vague to translate effectively without supplemental information. However, the New Testament was penned in Greek; and the Greek words *doulos* and *douloi*, meaning *slave(s)*, are most often used to describe people with freedom deprivation. The Greeks had an alternative word, *diakonos*, for a hired servant or assistant. The authors only use this term when the circumstances obviously depict a voluntary work service.

Because the writers of the New Testament knew exactly what they meant when using the term *doulos*, we can conclude that *ebed* refers to a slave when spoken of under the same *doulos* circumstances. We also have the luxury of relying on the enormous amount of context clues provided in Old Testament passages. Be careful not to let the KJV Bible fool you with its use of the term *servant* or any derivatives of the word (bondservant, maidservant, manservant, etc.) throughout the Old Testament unless they're used in the proper context. The New International Version and many other modern translations of the Bible wisely correct most of these assuredly intentional mistranslations.

The "Origin" Of Slavery

The first biblical mention of slavery occurs during the lives of Noah and his three sons. After the flood, one of Noah's sons, Ham, discovers the only man worthy enough to save from the flood lying naked and drunk in a tent. As Ham informs his brothers Shem and Japheth about their drunk and naked father, the two of them cover him up without looking. When Noah finds out about the seemingly harmless incident, he curses Ham's son, Canaan, and orders him to be a slave to his two uncles. On this day, slavery is supposedly born (Genesis 9:20-27). Thus, the origin of slavery arises from a single young man whose father made the "mistake" of seeing *his* father in the nude. I find it entirely fitting that the root of slavery would be as ridiculous as the institution itself. As a matter of much lesser importance, God punishes yet another individual for the actions of someone over whom this young man has no conceivable control.

The Bible later tells us that each of Noah's sons went their own ways and repopulated the earth. We know Shem and his descendants stayed in the Middle East because Abraham, David, and Jesus were among his recorded descendants (Genesis 11:10-26, Matthew 1). In pre-Civil War America, slaveholders often speculated that the descendants of Ham and the cursed Canaan eventually ended up deep into Africa. For this reason, they deemed the kidnapping of innocent Africans to be perfectly justifiable since the righteous Noah initiated the practice. Moreover, God has already established his acceptance of punishing the offspring of those who make mistakes, as was the case for Ham and Canaan.

Although slaveowners based their rationalizations solely on faulty premises, such deductions created a logical conclusion once you ignore their uninformed fallacy of accepting the Bible as indispensable truth. In this somewhat more enlightened society, most of us obviously realize that slavery isn't a logical or humane concept. We should say the same about the decision to punish one person for the actions of another. I wish we could also say that God has made similar improvements.

At one point, God even informs Abraham that his descendents would be slaves for four hundred years sometime in the near future (Genesis 15:13). What God is actually expressing to Abraham is that he's not going to do anything to stop this imminent enslavement. Back in the real world, however, archeological evidence indicates that slavery existed throughout the region well before the lives of Noah and Abraham. Thus, these aren't the true historical origins of slavery. However, if you believe that the Bible is free from error, your blind assumption forces you to deny the obvious conclusion based on scientific evidence and accept the orders contained in the rest of this composition as God's true desires.

A Slave Or A Servant?

As I alluded to earlier, there's a clear distinction between a slave and a servant. We can best describe a slave as an involuntary possession of another person. One of God's popularized Ten Commandments orders us to not "covet thy neighbor's house...wife, nor his manservant, nor his maidservant, nor his ox, nor his ass, nor anything that is thy neighbor's" (Exodus 20:17). Upon first glance, it may seem that there's a distinction between the specifically listed items and anything a person can physically possesses. Actually, those were just redundancies of common objects to which a person might claim ownership. It's perfectly reasonable to assume that a person can own an animal or a house, and we know from the previous chapter that women were the possessions of men. It's also reasonable to assume that we can say the same for slaves, the final article from the list, since they are, by definition, possessions of the owner. In short, slaves have no liberties and are at the mercy of their masters.

A servant is someone who chooses to do work for another person, usually in exchange for compensation. Servants are free to depart as they please and aren't subject to the cruel treatment endured by slaves. Many Christians, at least the ones who take the time to read the Old Testament, honestly accept the KJV translation that leads them to believe that all instances of *ebed* refer to a servant or someone who volunteered to become a slave. First and foremost, no one volunteers to be treated like a slave. The other half of this hypothesis clearly doesn't hold water either when Leviticus 25:39-40 is considered. Within this passage, God informs the Israelites that there may come a time when one of their fellow compatriots will become indigent and have no possessions left to impound. If someone sells this hypothetical individual to pay his debts, the owner is not to treat him like an *ebed*, but as a "hired servant."

If all the references of *ebed* in the Old Testament refer to a *servant*, as the apologetic hypothesis maintains, the passage from Leviticus actually reads, "Don't treat him like a servant, but as a hired servant." Why is there a distinction between the treatment of a servant and this hypothetical man, who the owner should treat as a hired servant? Since there's no defining difference between a servant and a hired servant, the KJV translation and Christian interpretation are 100% redundant. On the other hand, there's an enormous contrast between a *slave* and a hired servant. *That* must be the precise distinction attempted by the passage because its words could not possibly serve any other purpose. Slaveowners treated their slaves differently from the way people treated common servants, and that's the reason why these instructions were included. In short, God didn't want his chosen people treated like slaves. The alternative conditions endured by foreigners are what follow in the next few sections.

Your Rules For Owning Slaves

As with everything else in the Bible, there are rules accompanying slave ownership. You may wonder how slaveowners were supposed to treat their slaves during their involuntary stay. Did God explicitly allow slaveowners to beat their living property? Absolutely! If a man hits his slave hard enough to keep him down for a day or two, but the slave gets back up, "he shall not be punished: for he is his money" (Exodus 21:21). It doesn't get any clearer than that. God believes that a slave is nothing more than a financial investment of the owner.

The only way that the law can distribute a punishment for the physical onslaught is if it results in the slave's death, yet the author doesn't list the exact punishment.

However, if a slaveowner knocks out a slave's teeth, the slave is to go free as compensation for his injuries. The same goes for a strike to the slave's eye resulting in a loss of sight (Exodus 21:20-27), but I'd hardly consider inherent freedom to be a fair compensation for permanent blindness. If God doesn't approve of a regular slave beating, why does he provide these guidelines in the Bible?

We've established, at the very least, that God condones the beating of slaves, but is the practice encouraged? The educative Proverb 29:19 informs its reader that a slave "cannot be corrected by mere words." First, that's an obvious error since there's certainly at least once instance in which a slave was corrected through verbal discipline. More importantly, this verse paints one of the darkest pictures in the Bible. If God's book says slaveowners can't correct their property by verbal reprimand, what's the prominent and likely alternative? The Bible has already informed us which punishment is legally substitutable.

Another right of slaveowners is to collect a compensation of thirty shekels of silver in the event that another man's ox gores his property (i.e. slave). That's the equivalent of $60 US in today's currency, the exact value of a woman. Sixty dollars seems like a low price for the well-being of another individual, but after all, he *is* just money. As you should expect, there's no mention of compensation for the slave if he happens to survive the attack (Exodus 21:32).

If you buy a fellow Hebrew, you can only keep him for six years. Once this time has elapsed, he's free to leave. However, there's a catch. If the owner provided him with a wife, she has to stay with the master because she is his property. If the couple gave birth to children over the preceding six years, God also considers them the property of the owner. With these factors in mind, the man has the option of staying or leaving. If his final decision is to remain with his wife and children, the paroled Hebrew must agree to become property of his family's owner for life (Exodus 21:1-6).

In a nutshell, a man can leave his wife and kids behind in order to earn his freedom; otherwise, he can stay with them, give up his freedom, and resign to share their fate. As hardly any honorable man would choose to leave his family behind in such a selfish act, I must admit that this is quite a clever ruse conjured by such a primitive mind. I'd imagine that almost all men of moral character faced with this critical decision would feel compelled to remain onboard as a slave. As a direct result of this "decision," the slaveowner can now claim that the man is staying on his own accord.

Another regulation involves buying a "maidservant." If a man sells his daughter to be the wife and sex slave of another man, she doesn't have the inherent right to freedom after six years that the Hebrew men enjoy. The new owner has total discretion in deciding whether to keep her or set her free. If, however, he bought her as a present for his son, he must grant her the rights of a daughter. Although if you've read the previous chapter in this book, you'll realize that a daughter's rights can't be overwhelmingly abundant. The only way this woman can ever be given her freedom is to be deprived of food or clothing by her master (Exodus 21:7-11).

A counterargument often developed by apologists references Colossians 4:1. In this verse, the author suggests that masters should be fair to their slaves. I suppose that the Christian mind believes this is somehow supposed to override every other instruction handed down to us, making the slavery issue magically disappear. Besides, what is *fair* to them other than respecting God's established laws? This passage doesn't condemn the beating of slaves; if anything, it *encourages* it! As we will later see, this isn't the only mention of slave treatment and behavior in the New Testament. Most of the authors order the slaves to be completely obedient and to refrain from questioning their masters.

How You Might Have Become A Slave

A number of unfortunate factors place an individual at risk for becoming an Israelite's slave in the Old Testament. The quickest way is to be caught stealing. If the perpetrator swipes someone's property and can't generate some type of restitution for it, the thief is to be sold into slavery in order to compensate the owner for his losses (Exodus 22:1-3). Personally, I've always felt that we needed tougher laws to deter shoplifting, but I hope we can all agree that God's solution is excessive. These obviously weren't favorable times for people born with kleptomania, which, by the way, is a genuine medical disorder currently believed to be caused by a serotonin imbalance. God essentially turns a blind eye and doesn't make allowances for the genetically predispositioned lawbreakers that he creates.

While Joshua is traveling across the desert to slaughter his countless enemies, he meets a group of Gibeonites pretending to be someone Joshua doesn't want to kill. When Joshua solves the reason for their curious actions, he interrogates them as to why they were behaving deceitfully. As they respond by acknowledging their awareness of how many people he has killed, Joshua decides to spare their lives and make them slaves instead. When you examine the context of the passage, it appears that the decision to make slaves out of the Gibeonite race will always apply because that's where these people are "even unto this day" (Joshua 9:22-27). As a result, you would have already been a slave if you were born from Gibeonite lineage.

Another unfortunate circumstance pushing half the population into considerable danger of becoming a slave is to have been born female. From the time a girl is born, she is the property of her father. The ownership is transferred once the father sells her to another man to become his wife or concubine. From the previous chapter, we know that the wife is to be totally subordinate and fully submissive to the husband in every way, regardless of extraneous circumstances. She is not to question her husband, and the New Testament authors disallow her to participate during worship. In essence, she has no real freedom. If you don't feel this is an example of slavery, I'm afraid you've missed the point somewhere along the line.

If your parents were evil, you stood a good chance of becoming a slave. Your enslavement, however, wasn't a result of your parents selling you for money or anything like that; it was because God wants to punish *them* for *their* actions. He says anyone who doesn't obey his commandments and statutes stands to face a number of curses. The divine hex of particular interest is "thou shalt beget sons and daughters, but thou shalt not enjoy them; for they shall go into captivity" (Deuteronomy 28:15,41 and Joel 3:8). This is yet *another* example of God threatening to punish children for sins that their parents committed. As I've alluded to several times throughout this book, God has a strange sense of justice when deciding proper punishments. Of course, the people who anger God also stand a significant chance of being sold into slavery, but we'll discuss that notion later on.

How To Go About Acquiring A Slave

As if sending people into slavery wasn't treacherous enough, God also educates the Israelites on how to obtain slaves for their own personal use. The people who God prefers that they purchase have origins from the surrounding "heathen" nations. It's also permissible to buy the children of foreigners visiting the Israelite regions. God wants his chosen people to buy only foreigners as life-long slaves because buying a fellow Israelite to serve for more than six years is explicitly disgraceful to him. The purchaser's newly acquired possession is to remain in the family for as long as the property is still breathing. If the owner dies, the male children should inherit the slaves previously owned by their father (Leviticus 25:44-46).

Slaves are also obtainable from the spoils of various wars taking place at the orders of God. When the almighty delivers the enemy into the hands of his people, he orders the men to be killed, "but the women, and the little ones...shalt thou take unto thyself" (Deuteronomy 20:13-14). From this demand, it's reasonable to assume that the captives wouldn't desire for the aggressors to uproot them from their land. Even so, God ignores their wishes because he apathetically allowed their society to become conditioned to worship other deities. As a result, the Hebrew barbarians no doubt raped the women and young girls while they molded the boys into laborious slaves. I have no doubt about the absolute impossibility for anyone to provide true justification for this occurrence. God, once again, demonstrates that he can be pure evil.

Rules For Slaves To Follow

The rules we've covered thus far were divine guidelines on how to conduct your-self around your slaves. The slaves, too, had rules to follow if they wanted a chance to see the glory of God in the afterlife. Paul addresses slaves in his letter to the Corinthians when he tells them that they shouldn't be distressed about the time they spend as *douloi* (slaves) because free men are also slaves to Jesus (1 Corinthians 7:21-22). I sincerely hope Paul wasn't deluded enough to genuinely think that his statement was an appropriate analogy or a comforting message for the beaten and oppressed. Other than Paul admitting we have no choice but to enslave ourselves to Jesus in order to avoid eternal damnation, you may also find it deeply disturbing that the man most responsible for starting the Christian explosion encouraged slaves not to stand up for their basic human rights.

Any decent person knows that this lifestyle is humiliating and demoralizing, not to mention just plain wrong, because freedom is essential to a healthy and happy existence. I'm sure Paul would have ceased his apathetic attitude toward their predicament if he had switched places with one of them for a while. To be fair, how-ever, Paul sincerely thought Jesus was going to arrive and whisk everyone away to Heaven within a few years. Thus, he believed that the slaves shouldn't do anything to jeopardize their chances for an upcoming ticket to paradise. He also thought slaves should go free if they had that option. However, Paul's beliefs in Jesus' expedited visit were incorrect, and he didn't consider the ramifications of being wrong. In reality, I think that Paul truly wanted people to be good to slaves, but he was obviously under the false impression that the Old Testament had legitimacy. However, the Christian crowd must necessarily believe that Paul's words are divinely inspired. In such a sce-nario, God knew slavery would continue for nearly two more millennia, yet he allows Paul to encourage suppression of rebellious feelings.

The author of Ephesians also says slaves are to be submissive. "[*Douloi*], be obedient to them that are your masters according to the flesh, with fear and trembling, in singleness of your heart, as unto Christ." He orders them to follow this rule, not only to please their masters, but also to please God (6:5). We've already learned from the Old Testament that nothing indulges God more than an obedi-ent foreign slave; this author simply reinforces the notion. In essence, he unwit-tingly used a scare tactic of which he was also a victim. If God is pleased with obedient slaves, what does this say about his feelings toward the practice?

The author of Colossians agrees that *douloi* are to be submissive to their mas-ters "in all things" (3:22). It's true that the slaveowners have guidelines as well (4:1), but are the slaves allowed to break their own guidelines if commanded to commit immoral acts? The author does a very poor job of clarifying this perplex-ity. Since an out clause isn't provided, as was the case for the female slaves (i.e.

wives), we can only assume that the text means exactly what it says. Thus, God wants slaves to be obedient regardless of the treatment received.

Peter, who goes more into depth when dispersing his orders to slaves, also reaffirms this idea. They are to be completely obedient and to fear their masters, even the ones who mistreat them (1 Peter 2:18). In other words, no matter how bad they beat you, abuse you, starve you, or rape you, don't act with disobedience. There's no need to pretend that Peter wasn't aware of how some masters treated their slaves. Even in those circumstances, he wants them to be fully submissive. We can reasonably infer that God wants a slave to just sit and watch in the not-so-hypothetical situation that the master is raping his wife. Why can we make such a drastic inference? The same answer as always: divine inspiration. By this point, we should really begin to wonder how the Bible is repeatedly able to top its own record-setting level of disturbance.

The author of the first letter to Timothy says that slaves should look at their masters with utmost respect (6:1). This might be hard to do if disrespectable masters are beating and raping their family members at will. In the last known set of biblical instructions for slavery, the author of Titus says that slaves should be educated on how they can be completely obedient to their masters (2:9-10). I'm afraid to ponder what he may have had in mind.

Once again, to be fair to Paul and the other New Testament authors, they were normal individuals unaware of the lack of reliability held by the Old Testament. No god is going to punish slaves for standing up to their masters, but we should expect neither the authors nor the slaves to realize this fact because, centuries ago, superstition evidently superseded common sense. When Christians insert the notion of divine inspiration into the Bible, however, this rational explanation becomes inadmissible. Christians must then accept the explicit words authored in the New Testament as perfect representations of God's desires.

Who Is The Ultimate Slave Trader?

If you can't already correctly guess the answer to this question, you apparently haven't been paying close attention. In addition to the commands that God gives for the Israelites to acquire slaves, the instructions that he provides to the Israelites on where to locate slaves, the rules that he gives for possession of slaves, the threats that he makes to convert people into slaves, and the times that he destines certain people to become slaves, God allegedly trades more slaves than any known individual in history. To be fair about it, if you wish to call it that, God often forewarned his people about a series of curses that he would bring upon them if they didn't listen to his voice and follow his commandments. The hex in which we're interested at the moment is the promise of serving the enemy tribes as a slave with a "yoke of iron upon thy neck" (Deuteronomy 28:48). That day certainly came, and it did so more than once.

After Joshua dies in the book of Judges, the Israelites turn their backs on God. Of course, this further ignites the inextinguishable fury within God's heart. As promised before, he sells them to a group of raiders (2:10-14). After God feels that he taught them a sufficient lesson, he makes them a free people once again (2:16). However, as they soon return to their evil ways, circumstances force God to teach them a lesson once again, which makes you wonder why he let them go free in the first place. He then peddles them off on a King of Mesopotamia. When the people of Israel are once again slaves, they cry out for God to save them. After letting them serve eight years, he figures that the King has served his purpose. Now, God sends an army led by Othniel to defeat the King and retrieve his chosen people. As long as Othniel lives, the Israelites remain faithful to God. When Othniel dies, however, they once again return to their evil ways of idolizing other gods. Thus, God allows Eglon, King of Moab, to take them as slaves. Again, the people cry out to God for freedom, and, again, he sends relief in an individual named Ehud to kill the King and free the Israelites. Ehud lives another eight years, but the situation changes when he dies. I hope that you're starting to get the idea by now.

As the Israelites once again become evil, God sells them to Jabin, King of Canaan. For the third time, God sends relief and frees his people (Chapters 3-4), and their subsequent freedom lasts forty years. For the fourth time, the Israelites, who obviously didn't learn their lesson, become evil again. God then delivers them in a battle to Midian and the Midianites. When the Israelites cry out for God as you might have anticipated, he sends Gideon to free them yet again by delivering the Midianite army into his hands (Chapters 6-7). Once Gideon dies, the Israelites return to serving other gods *again* (8:28-35). I know this story is getting old by now, but you should see the absurdity in an omniscient God taking this route to teach people a lesson.

By this point in the tale, God seems to ignore their misbehavior for a while before delivering them into the hands of the Philistines and Ammonites (10:7). When they ask for help, God reminds them that he has already freed them on four separate occasions (five, counting the Exodus). He then suggests that they should call upon the gods that they turned to earlier for help (10:14). Even so, God shows a hint of benevolence by setting them free again. The chore of liberating them on this occasion falls upon Jephthah (Chapter 11). As Jephthah dies and the Israelites become evil for an *unprecedented sixth time*, God delivers them to the Philistines for forty years (Chapters 13-16).

The point of all this mess is that God sold or delivered his own people to be slaves on six different occasions because they didn't want to worship him. Do people dumb enough not to stick with a god who undeniably helps them out on such a regular and reliable basis really have the capacity to follow directions? Doesn't this story read more like a fairy tale or a fable with an intended moral than an actual historical account?

The threat of slavery didn't end with the Philistines though. In Jeremiah 15:14, the author reminds us that God will once again sell people into slavery if he chooses to exercise his unlimited power. Such a divinely inspired passage could serve as a perfect justification for those opposing the abolitionist movement. Even so, I fail to see the point in rewarding the Israelites for doing things that God more or less forces them to do, such as worshiping him, when the alternative is a severe punishment of lifelong enslavement. Yet, God does the same thing to us by allegedly offering us eternal paradise as opposed to eternal damnation in Hell. Do believers in these situations *really* have a choice? Aren't we also slaves to this god's desires?

The Racist God

I hope you realized long before reading this chapter that enslaving the innocent is wrong. There's a huge problem, however, in reconciling this belief with the postulate of a "wonderful" and "loving" biblical god because this deity repeatedly commits heinous acts that we inherently know are immoral. Time after time, God sells slaves and orders people to take others as their slaves. He has rules for slaveholders, and the divinely inspired writers of the New Testament have orders for the slaves.

This is the thought that I'm hoping Christian readers will consider among themselves: "I feel that God is a wonderful and loving creator, yet the men who wrote the Old Testament say that God encouraged people to make slaves of foreigners because they worship different gods. He also allowed women to live as slaves because the men believed that females were the inferior gender. These aren't wonderful and loving decisions. The Old Testament writers even say that God sold slaves and gave rules to Moses permitting his people to beat the male slaves and rape the female slaves. This does not seem right at all. *Did God actually say and do all these horrible things, or were the authors probably trying to advance ulterior motives by tricking a gullible audience into believing that these ghastly commands were truly of divine origin?*"

As the events of Genesis are purported to have started taking place at least 3000 years before we know of anyone who recorded them on hardcopy, no primary eyewitnesses were around to testify for or against the legitimacy of these claims. If you decide that God actually said the things written in the Bible, it certainly throws out the notion that he's "wonderful" and "loving." If, on the other hand, you decide that God would never make the aforementioned suggestions, it certainly brings the validity of the Bible's content into question. Think about it for a while.

Reality And The Bible

MOSES AND OTHER HISTORICAL FABRICATIONS

If you've elected to read the preceding selections in this manuscript, you will have noticed that I often refer to the first five books of the Bible as the *Pentateuch*. In Greek, the term simply means "five volumes." Scholars often refer to Genesis, Exodus, Leviticus, Numbers, and Deuteronomy using this collective term because many of our predecessors erroneously assumed for over 2000 years that Moses personally wrote the books. Knowledge gained through modern scholarship and research, however, allows us to ascertain the logical impossibility of this scenario being true. More than likely, the Pentateuch is the work of several individuals, all of whom lived well after the stories they present and had varying oral traditions of how those events unfolded. Because of this societal concoction, the earliest recorded history of the Jews is afflicted with oft-erratic variance.

In order to consider an extraordinary event for inclusion in the modern canon of actual history, we must either have remaining evidence indicating what took place or obtain a record from a reliable eyewitness who documented the occurrence. We generally accept common daily events as fact because we know that these occasions are consistent and inconsequential in the grand scheme of human history. Extraordinary events on the level of those Moses allegedly recorded in the Pentateuch, on the other hand, should be thoroughly scrutinized before canonizing them as fact.

Two major biblical events that we should expect to be reasonably consistent with coexisting historical records and modern archaeological discoveries are the Exodus and Conquests. As you will see, however, these two hypothetical milestones have little, if any, substantiating support. If we are to ignore this contrary finding and just accept whatever the Bible says as truth, it isn't fair to confine ourselves to the accounts of only one religion. Thus, we would have to accept any and all religious claims, regardless of their absurdity. To avoid such a logical disaster, we must reasonably pursue evidence for claims made by *all* beliefs in order to determine which, if any, has the most reliability as the correct religion. Christianity cannot simply trump other religions because it's the one in which the most faith has been placed. Awarding any belief system with this favorable and prejudicial judgment should be an obvious act of intellectual dishonesty. Besides, if Christianity is the one true religion, it should have no trouble in avoiding claims that are disprovable by scientific and investigative scrutiny.

For our study of who initiated the history of the Jews, there's no better place to start than the beginning. Thus, this chapter will discuss the following: how the Pentateuch came into existence, the standard reasons why Christians still maintain that Moses scribed it, why Christians desperately cling to traditional authorship claims, the contrast in writing styles among the multiple authors, and key pieces of information allowing scholars to debunk the traditional dates placed on the writings.

If Moses Didn't Write The Books Of Moses...

Before we delve into much detail of how we know who wrote what in the early Old Testament, you should have an understanding of the different components combined to form the five books of the Pentateuch. This "document hypothesis" states that there were probably four authors and an editor responsible for the compilation. Since it's currently impossible to determine their hypothetical identities, we commonly refer to them as J, E, P, D, and R for the reasons we'll now discuss.

J received his name because he consistently uses JHWH as the unpronounceable name of God. Issues relating to humanity are the primary focus of his writing. J even extends this humanity-based focus by portraying a uniquely human interpretation of God. This author is compassionate and shows none of the bias against women discussed in *Why Women And The Bible Don't Mix*. Seeing as how J wrote a complete historical record of the Israelites from a Judean perspective, he probably resided within the Southern Kingdom of Judea. Based on clues found within his text, historians typically place a 950-750 BCE date on the work, which is about 500-700 years following the death of Moses.

E, whose primary focus is morality, acquired his name because he consistently uses Elohim as the name of God. E commonly emphasized the second born sons of families because they were of historical and personal interest to the North for symbolic reasons. Since E left us with a complete account of the Israelites from the perspective of the Northern Kingdom of Israel, historians generally believe that this was his domicile. Thus, we already have two independent accounts of early Middle Eastern history. Since the split of Israel took place no earlier than 950 BCE, it's exceedingly unlikely that such a contrasting influence would appear in his work before that time. Consequently, estimated dates for the E document range from 900-700 BCE.

P obtained his name because he was almost certainly a priest. He identifies Aaron, the first High Priest, as his spiritual ancestor. His manuscripts include rituals, laws, sins, chronologies, genealogies, and other subjects of definite interest to a priest. In sharp contrast to J, P doesn't attribute any human qualities to God. The Hebrew terms equivalent to *mercy*, *grace*, and *repentance* don't appear once in P's work, while they're plentiful in the compositions of J and E. Furthermore, P is often cold and harsh with his writing unlike the more pleasant E. These interpretations and attitudes are what we would expect from a traditional church leader. He doesn't include any mythical details, such as the ludicrous claims of talking animals, likely interpolated into history by J and E as a result of popular urban legends. As he was seemingly aware of the books of prophecy, while J and E never gave this indication, P probably wrote his share much later around 700-650 BCE.

D received his name because he was the author of Deuteronomy. It's a good possibility that D wrote many of the historical books as well. It's an even better possibility that he wrote the book of Jeremiah, which contains several carbon copies of statements made in the book of Deuteronomy. If this is the case, the author could be Jeremiah's scribe, Baruch, or Jeremiah himself. D most certainly lived in Israel during a very spiritual era, the same era in which the likely author claimed to have discovered the book. Evidence for the document hypothesis indicates that the person compiling the Pentateuch tacked the author's work onto the end of the compilation. Thus, we would expect it to have been created after, not in concurrent conflict with, the other three circulating versions of Jewish history. It then follows that the author probably finished it shortly before its "discovery" in 622 BCE.

We designate the individual responsible for combining the four accounts into one collection as R because he's the redactor (editor). The process finally came to a conclusion some time around 500-434 BCE, but may have begun as early as the Babylonian Exile of 587-539 BCE. R also adds bits and pieces of commentary to make necessary transitions between the passages. The scholarly community consensually believes this redactor is the biblical priest Ezra.

To illustrate the document hypothesis, we'll take a detailed look at the first eight chapters of Genesis. You may find it helpful to locate and follow along in a Bible before proceeding further.

One creation story scribed by P appears from Genesis 1:1-2:3. Notice that the first half of 2:4 doesn't maintain the flow and seems to segue into the second creation account found in 2:4-2:25. That's likely the redactor making a transition between P's and J's creation stories. J continues to the end of the fourth chapter with some recollections of stories centered on Adam and his children. Chapter 5 then hastily jumps in with some genealogy from P or R, but verse 29, written by J, seems recklessly tossed into the mix.

At the commencement of chapter six, J regains control and supplies a few verses set in the time immediately prior to Noah's flood. This account abruptly stops following 6:8, and P's story of Noah begins with his lineage. Furthermore, this section by P is an obvious repetition of the days before the flood, provided earlier in the chapter by J. Genesis 7:1 seems to pick right back up where J left off

at 6:8. Genesis 7:6, written by P, appears haphazardly thrown in because it inter-
rupts a cohesive story told by J. Verses 7:7, 7:10, 7:12, 7:17-20, and 7:22-23 tell
one full story of the flood (J) while 7:8-9, 7:11, 7:13-16, 7:21, and 7:24 tell
another (P). In chapter eight, J likely recorded verses 2, 3, 6, 8-12, the last part of
13, and 20-22, while the remaining verses stand alone as another complete story
by the author P. If you happen to be carefully reading the texts in their native
Hebrew language, you may even notice the contrasting writing styles of the two
authors beginning to emerge.

How And Why Was The Pentateuch Combined?

This part, we cannot say for certain. It's speculated that a number of Israelites fled
south into Judea with the E document in hand when the Assyrians conquered the
Northern Kingdom in 722 BCE. Consequently, the J document would now
coexist with the E document in this society prior to their combination. Around
this time, P likely became a widespread alternative priestly version of the J and E
records. With these three variant interpretations, no doubt would come arguing
factions. R then saw the need, or perhaps was elected, to combine the contrasting
accounts into a single cohesive document agreeable to all parties. Not wishing to
eliminate any essential parts of the respective documents, R would then combine
the contrasting stories into one quasi-harmonious account and do the best he
could to avoid contradictions, inconsistencies, and repetitions. Because the D
document doesn't step on the toes of the other three histories, the redactor likely
tacked Deuteronomy onto the end for this reason. By 434 BCE, the redactor had
certainly compiled the modern version of the Pentateuch.

There's nothing novel about forming multiple author theories for the Moses
biography. The first known hypothesis was proposed nearly a thousand years ago
when it was discovered that a list of kings in the Pentateuch included some who
apparently reigned following Moses' death. Although the suggestion that Moses
didn't write this passage seems to bathe in common sense, the churches of the
Middle Ages weren't exactly known for embracing such heretical theories.
Centuries later, biblical scholars began to propose that prophets and editors may
have had limited involvement in the compilation. Scholars fortunate enough to
live during the age of Enlightenment in the eighteenth century concluded that
different authors recorded the passages conspicuously appearing twice because
one writer would use the name JHWH and the other would use the name
Elohim when referring to the same god. Triplet passages, the beginning of the P
discovery, were soon uncovered in the years to come. Later still, historians determined Deuteronomy has a style distinct from the ones found in the four preceding books. Presently, we have a four author and one editor hypothesis. This will

no doubt undergo alteration as well if subsequent research provides further evidence relevant to the authorship issue. On the other hand, regardless of what evidence researchers discover, the Christian community may indefinitely hold onto a Moses authorship.

While we're certainly not fully able to explain the origins of the Old Testament with 100% accuracy, we *can* conclude with great certainty that the Pentateuch is a set of conflicting passages scribed 500-3500 years after the events it purports. Ask yourself how much oral tradition can change in a few years; then consider the subsequent alteration of details after 3500 years. Of course, this proposal assumes that an omniscient deity offered no input to this particular set of writers. Since we should be unanimous in deciding that a "wonderful" and "loving" God would have no part in the orders of rape, slavery, and the various other acts of extreme brutality contained within the Old Testament, we should also decide that these hundredth-hand stories were highly unlikely to be scientifically or historically accurate. Similarly, we see the inclusion of ridiculous fallacies in the form of Adam and Noah working unpaid overtime at discrediting their own reliability. Furthermore, we have upcoming archaeological evidence indicating that the Exodus and Conquests didn't unfold the way they were recorded, if at all. Thus, we can certainly challenge the existence, or at least question the true nature, of the people on whom the authors based these stories.

There's ample reason why Christians feel the absolute necessity for Moses to have been the sole author of the Pentateuch. First, we have inclusions of several passages indicating Moses did a lot of the writing. For example, "And it came to pass, when Moses had made an end of writing the words of this law in a book..." (Deuteronomy 31:24). There are also several biblical passages outside the Pentateuch insinuating that Moses was responsible for its compilation. Paul demonstrated his conviction that Moses was an author when he said, "For Moses describeth the righteousness which is of the law" (Romans 10:5). Even Jesus implies that Moses wrote the books: "All things must be fulfilled, which were written in the law of Moses" (Luke 24:44). However, there's no passage in the Pentateuch directly implicating Moses as the one and only author of the present compilation. I also fail to recognize any quotes concretely indicating that the New Testament characters were certain of Moses' solitary authorship. The contemporaneous belief of the New Testament authors may have very well been that Moses only provided a foundation for the Old Testament writings.

For the past 2000 years, the church has merely gone on assumptions when making the attribution of the Pentateuch to Moses. In fact, there wouldn't be any additional errors in the Bible if someone completely debunked the traditional hypothesis. The importance of the authorship question lies with determining the credibility and reliability of the authors, not with demonstrating an additional biblical mistake.

Evidence Clearly Pointing Away From Moses

The best evidence we have supporting the position that Moses didn't write the entire Pentateuch is the description of his death and burial in the last chapter of Deuteronomy. Almost all Christians will make this small concession by admitting that Joshua may have finished the works, but some actually believe that God told Moses what to write beforehand. Nevertheless, the possibility of a second author for the final chapter isn't exactly destructive to the traditional author hypothesis. The more critical discoveries arise from the widespread presence of contradictions and inconsistencies contained within repetitions of stories, such as the creation and flood. A single author would have known better than to write a certain passage, only to contradict it a few sentences later. However, these variations are, indeed, present and lead us to believe that the traditional single author hypothesis is completely discountable. Examples of these contradictions can be found in the next chapter.

The inclusion of city names and tribes yet to exist at the time of Moses' death, approximately 1450 BCE, is equally devastating to the traditional Mosaic authorship claim. Genesis 11:31 says that the Chaldees lived in the city of Ur during the life of Abraham, but historical records tell us that the Chaldees didn't even exist as a tribe until well after Moses was dead. In addition, they didn't become a prominent enough group to occupy a city until the sixth century BCE.

Genesis 14:14 mentions the city of Dan, but the city didn't acquire this name until it was seized one thousand years later via conquest. Genesis 37:25 mentions traders with spicery, balm, and myrrh, but these weren't the primary trade products of the region until the eighth century BCE. Isaac visits King Abimelech of Gerar in Genesis 26:1, but Gerar didn't exist until after Isaac's death and wouldn't have been powerful enough to require a King until the eighth century BCE. Genesis 36:31 says that there were "kings that reigned in the land of Edom," but there's no extrabiblical record of Kings in Edom until the eighth century BCE. Exodus 13:17 details Moses' apprehension toward entering the land of the Philistines in Canaan, but there's zero evidence that indicates the Philistines occupied Canaan until the thirteenth century BCE. In addition, they couldn't have sufficiently organized in threatening numbers until a few hundred years later.

Moses references Palestine in Exodus 15:14, the only known mention of that name for hundreds of years. In Deuteronomy 3:11, Moses also mentions the city of Rabbath and Og's location within the city, but no one outside of Rabbath could have held this information until it was conquered hundreds of years later. Jacob is called a wandering Aramean in Deuteronomy 26:5, but the Arameans didn't have contact with the Israelites until the ninth century BCE. Some particular names mentioned in Genesis 14 and 25 (Chedorlaomer, Kadesh, Sheba,

Tema, Nebaioth, and Adbeel) are consistent with names of people recorded by the Assyrians as living during the sixth through eighth centuries BCE, not a thousand years prior. The writers never provide the names of Egyptian Pharaohs even though Moses would have readily known this bit of information.

The Pentateuch authors claim that many of the leading Genesis characters, such as Abraham, Jacob, and Joseph, rode camels. However, there's no archaeological evidence indicating that anyone domesticated these animals earlier than 1200 BCE. Again, this was hundreds or thousands of years after the deaths of these alleged biblical camel riders. Furthermore, no known person trained camels to carry people and other heavy loads until many years later.

Someone making these aforementioned claims in 1500 BCE would have had no ability to appreciate this futuristic information and no reason to present the information in a fashion identifiable only to a specific group of people living in a specific region during an arbitrary future time period. On the other hand, someone in 500 BCE would have had access to this information but lacked a way to know that the stories presented were historically invalid. Not only do these facts indicate a more recent authorship, they also suggest fabrications or alterations of actual events. Finally, many of the passages state that certain aspects of the Hebrew society are still the same "unto this day" (e.g. Genesis 26:33). This wording greatly implies that the complete record was finished well after the purported events took place.

The Exodus: Timeline Inconsistencies

Now let's turn to the particular account of the Exodus and consider the possibility of such a magnificent event taking place. First, we should recognize the plethora of peculiarities concerning the approximate time that the authors say the enslavement and subsequent Exodus took place. We arrive at the aforementioned 1500 BCE estimate for the Exodus because the three different chronologies used to date it differ by about 150 years but tend to center around the designated 1500 BCE date. We commonly use the most accepted and latest possible date of 1447 BCE because it's the easiest to derive.

1 Kings 6:1 says that Solomon's fourth year as ruler was concurrent with the 480th anniversary of the Exodus. Given that Solomon began his first year of rule in 970 BCE, his fourth year as ruler would have been in 967 BCE. Consequently, the Exodus must have taken place 480 years prior in 1447 BCE. Establishing the exact date isn't as important as obtaining a period to which the events must be bound in order to compare it to established historical events.

According to the Bible, the Israelite slaves were used to build the Egyptian cities of Pithom and Raamses (Exodus 1:11). Since the Exodus took place no later than 1447 BCE, the Israelites would have at least had to *start* construction on Raamses by that time in order for the story to remain reliable. In a great setback to Christian apologists, there wasn't even a Pharaoh named Raamses until 1320 BCE, 127 years after the Exodus. For an additional dagger in the heart of biblical inerrancy, consider Egypt's own records. These archaeological findings state that Egypt's own people built the city and not until it came via order of Raamses II who reigned from 1279-1213 BCE. A Hebrew writing a story of his origins several hundred years after all these events had long played out would have had no way of determining when Raamses was constructed without committing to a thorough investigation of Egypt's historical records. Needless to say, the author didn't have such access and made a poor guess on when the city was actually built.

The Exodus: A Valid Counterargument From Silence

Upon the Israelites' alleged escape from their forced construction duties, Moses parts the Red Sea so that they can cross and escape from the pursuing Egyptians (Exodus 14). This was supposed to be the last that Egypt would see of them, and it *was* as far as the Bible is concerned. Moses seemingly marches his people straight through the other Egyptian regions without contest because the author was no doubt ignorant of the soldiers stationed in the surrounding cities. As you might have subsequently guessed, there are no Egyptian reports of such a massive group crossing these outposts.

The story then purports Moses leading the Israelites into the vast wilderness for forty years of aimless wandering. According to the biblical account, Moses freed 600,000 men in addition to the safely presumed multitude of women and children. If we assume only one wife for each man and only one child for every other couple, which is a very low estimate, there's a total of one and a half million escapees in addition to the "mixed multitude…of flocks, and herds, even very much cattle" (Exodus 12:37-41). After forty years, the count probably swelled to three million, a number in agreement with many religious Jewish sources.

Since we have millions of mouths to contend with, let's look at the problem of finding something to feed them. We'll assume that the Israelites were always proximate to a large water source unless stated otherwise. An average individual requires at least a half pound of food per day to meet typical nourishment requirements. In order to just barely survive, we'll assume that the Israelites had half that amount over the course of forty years. If each person ate a quarter pound of food every twenty-four hours, the entire camp would need 375 *tons* of sustenance every day. While we know that they primarily survived off manna, a dried plant material (Numbers 11:6-9), it's ludicrous to believe that they could obtain this much nourishment day after day without supernatural intervention. From what we've learned about this god's true lack of interaction with the people on earth, such unsubstantiated circumstances were highly unlikely to have ever taken place.

Considering that the Bible provides some precise locations of the events surrounding the desert journey, archaeological evidence of three million people wandering around in a confined area for forty years shouldn't be too difficult to locate. In fact, we know that the Israelites were in Kadesh-barnea for most of their long journey (Deuteronomy 1:19). However, not one piece of evidence of an Israeli encampment or occupancy has ever arisen from the multitude of undertaken excavations. In contrast, civilizations with populations less than three million over their entire time of existence have left behind considerable amounts of remains that inform us of their cultural facets. Furthermore, archaeologists weren't necessarily looking for any evidence from these people; they casually stumbled upon the initial discoveries due to the sufficient number of artifacts large groups tend to leave behind. Asserting that unfound archaeological evidence exists for an Exodus is an absurdly difficult position to defend.

Similarly, we have no evidence for three million people invading the land of Canaan and destroying the inhabitants' possessions forty years after the Exodus (Numbers 33:50-54). Archaeological findings in the form of bodies, waste products, documents, and clothing tell us that the population of Canaan was never greater than 100,000. Thus, we can reasonably dismiss the possibility of a group in excess of one million ever conquering and inhabiting the region.

Fortunately, the Egyptians were much less fond of including hyperbole in their historical records. Of the thousands of fourteenth century BCE Egyptian records uncovered at el-Amarna and Boghazkoy detailing the governments, armies, religions, trade routes, and everyday lives of the people living in the region, none pay any respect to the millions of Israelites allegedly moving about like nomads in Kadesh-barnea. In fact, we don't posses a single mention of Israel made prior to the creation of the 1207 BCE Merneptah Stele. The inscriptions on this essential historical artifact inform us that Pharaoh Merneptah had recently entered Canaan and easily defeated the Israelites. Curiously, just seventy-eight years earlier, Pharaoh Raamses recorded his army as numbering only 37,000. Although Egypt is widely acknowledged to have been the most powerful country in the world at that time, how could an army the size of a small city go on the offensive and defeat three *million* inhabitants in a region with nearly one million men of fighting age? If Merneptah *did* defeat the enormous Israeli army, why didn't he acknowledge such a remarkable, unrivaled victory in his writings, and why does the Bible neglect to mention this humiliating defeat?

The Exodus: Bogus Solutions

Because attempts to justify the number of Israelites have consistently fallen flat, apologists have often sought a way around this perplexity. Sound familiar? The Hebrew word used to describe thousands is *eleph*. In a couple of the five hundred or so instances in which the Old Testament authors utilize the term, it meant an army or clan. If this was one of those highly unusual cases, apologists could claim that Moses freed six hundred *families* instead of six hundred thousand men. This gives us roughly 1500 people escaping from Egypt. Even if we allow the convenience of the word just happening to mean something else at the whim of the apologist, the tale still has unanswered problems. The archaeological evidence and Egyptian historical records for this smaller group of people are still absent. More importantly, there are no longer enough of them to invade and take the land of Canaan. When one difficulty is resolved, another takes its place.

As a way of solving the Egyptian silence, Bible defenders have proposed that the records *did* include the Israelites' stay in their country. A writer named Manetho of the third century BCE wrote that, according to some mythical books, a group of people known as the Hyksos invaded Egyptian land and took over the leadership for five hundred years before Pharaoh Ahmose ejected them in 1570 BCE. Some apologists looking for any loophole claim that the Hyksos are a reference to the Israelites. However, several reasons why this isn't the case should already be painfully obvious. The dates are way off; the Israelites didn't invade Egypt; they didn't stay five hundred years; and Ahmose didn't run them off. While the stories are in no way congruent, the Egyptian tale may help explain the provenience of the biblical legend.

Another difficult aspect of the accord for an apologist to defend would be the Israelites' total lack of faith in their god's abilities. After God frees his people from captivity and performs all the plague miracles to ensure their freedom, they *still* don't trust him. Since they think that they're going to die when the Pharaoh decides to chase after them, they complain about the method used to release them from Egyptian custody. Consequently, God has Moses part the sea in order for them to cross and lure the Egyptians into their watery graves. Just a few days later, they complain about an onset of dehydration. Consequently, God provides them with water. Forty days following *that* incident, the people complain about having no meat. Consequently, God sends them a multitude of quail. A while later, the Israelites once again think that they're going to dehydrate even though God provided them with water on the previous occasion. Consequently, God provides them with water once again. When the people complain again about not having any meat, the divinely delivered quail fly in once more. Later still, people start complaining about having no land to call their own. When God is about to provide them with some land, they doubt that they can defeat the multitude of inhabitants to obtain it. Instead, they all desire to return to Egypt as slaves rather than fighting and dying in the wilderness.

The Israelites obviously have zero faith in God even though he performs unbelievable miracles for them on a consistent basis. Why, then, are they so skeptical of a god who has provided them with so many blessings in the past? Why would they later turn their backs on such a powerful confederate? It doesn't make any sense for the Israelites to be so thoroughly convinced that they were going to die when the supernatural interventions of God save them time after time after time. This is another great reason why the story is probably an exceedingly ridiculous fable with an intended moral, much like the repeated enslavement story discussed in the previous chapter.

The Conquests

As I mentioned in *The Flat Earth Society*, God grants Joshua's request to make the sun cease its motion so that he can defeat his enemies in the daylight. Since no society with astronomers recorded this unique event, the ball really started to roll on determining the legitimacy of events claimed in the conquest accounts of the Pentateuch and historical books. Subsequent thorough scientific analyses turn up some very interesting facts relevant to these biblical endeavors.

The size of the army Joshua used to conquer his enemies is astonishing even by today's standards. As I alluded to earlier, the greatest nations of the era had no more than 50,000 soldiers serving simultaneously. The military that Joshua claims to be under his command, however, even outnumbers the current United States Army. While there was an astounding amount of soldiers numbering in the hundreds of thousands during Joshua's conquests, there were over one and a half *million* enlisted by the time David was King. Such an outlandishly sized army could have easily conquered the entire ancient world unopposed if the enlisted men so desired. However, there's no contemporaneous record of an existing force even a *tenth* of that size. In addition, the population problem arises once again because the Israelites could not have possibly grown to this size over such a short amount of time when you necessarily take the subpar living conditions of the era into consideration.

The consensus of archaeological findings, such as the nearly exhaustive collection of proposals reviewed by William Stiebing in 1989, points away from Moses or Joshua ever conquering the cities claimed by the Bible. We know that the conquests directed by Moses had to have taken place during the time that he and Joshua lived concurrently (approximately 1550-1450 BCE), while the conquests following the Pentateuch must have taken place between Moses' death and the lifetimes of his various successors (approximately 1450-1200 BCE). Of the four cities that the Israelites take via force in Numbers 21 (Arad, Hormah, Heshbon, and Dibon), none exhibit any clear evidence that they were occupied during the required period. Areor's remnants, another city claimed to have been conquered while Moses was still alive, offer no credence to the claim that the city was occupied any earlier than two hundred years following the alleged victory (Deuteronomy 2:36).

Although Joshua's most famous battle takes place in Jericho long after the death of Moses, there's overwhelming archaeological evidence that suggests the city was destroyed before Moses would have even been born (Joshua 6). Likewise, impartial archaeologists aren't ready to conclude that the cities of Ai, Gibeon, and Hebron had occupants at the same time that this so-called historical book claims they were destroyed (Joshua 7, 9, and 10, respectively).

Occupational eras of the remaining cities will vary according to different sources, possibly putting their demise around the time of Joshua's conquests. However, the fallacies presented about the other cities demonstrate the need to seriously question the Bible when attempting to place an accurate date on those remaining towns. Even if future findings confirm the dates provided by the Bible, there's no evidence that any "Joshua" was doing all the conquering.

Unless there's compelling evidence to the contrary, we should always give reliability and precedence to correspondence written at the time of the event rather than propagandistic records compiled hundreds of years afterwards. You should realize by now that the Bible is anything *but* compelling evidence. The blatant signs of a more modern authorship, the lack of documented eyewitnesses, and the obvious embellishments clearly indicate that we should take the aforementioned accounts with a handful of salt.

The Significance Of Moses' Absence

Since Moses didn't write the outlandish stories found within the Pentateuch, we must consider the fact we only know of his existence through oral tradition a millennium in the making. With this in mind, could he have been a legend based on a real person? Is it possible that he's a complete work of fiction?

The Law of Moses, supposedly handed down by God himself in Exodus, is probably patterned after the Code of Hammurabi, which was written well before 2000 BCE. This date places the code's origins several centuries prior to Moses' trek up Mt. Sinai. Both codes of conduct contain similar guidelines along with similar punishments in lieu of following the established rules (murder, theft, perjury, adultery, etc.) Simply put, several moral codes existed in the Middle East prior to these unoriginal directions from Moses.

Aspects of Moses' birth are likely to be a copy of King Sargon of Agade's early years as well. Like Moses, Sargon was also said to have been placed into a basket on a river as a baby. The important difference is that Sargon's story was purported a thousand years prior to the same affair Moses allegedly endured as a child (Exodus 2). Is it possible that the original tellers of the story could have based the legend of Moses on this historical figure? Minor details like these add up to further challenge the legitimacy of Moses' existence, and we should not honestly dismiss such parallels as mere coincidences.

Implications Of A Fabricated History

If no "Moses" or any other individual from the contemporaneous era wrote anything in the Pentateuch, how do we really know that God carried out and ordered all the monstrous deeds preserved in those books? We can't be certain of the records for two simple reasons: the stories are utterly ridiculous, and we can scarcely consider hundredth-hand accounts to be reliable. That's why we must analyze the veracity of even the simplest of claims made in the books of Moses to render a verdict on their proper place in history.

The truth is that Moses couldn't have realistically written the books, and we have no reason to believe that he was an actual historical figure. Because the majority of the Old Testament was critically inaccurate in its detail, we cannot conclude that the events contained within are factual and accurate without further evidence. Since the required evidence is completely absent, we should only conclude that the books from Genesis to Job are mythological or greatly exaggerated legends.

The balance of the Old Testament is nothing but songs and prophecies of a god no longer in contact with anyone but a handful of prophets who, as we will see in *A Different Future*, also display a total lack of credibility. By the time the Israelites had a compiled history of their origins, no one ever claims that God had such liberal verbal and visual contact with anyone. All of a sudden, God seemingly ceases to exist from the observable world, a world in which no supernatural events take place. No known Hebrew authors make extraordinary claims in the multi-century span between the documentation of these events and the beginning of the Common Era. In fact, the Israelites existed pretty much as we do now: living normal lives and never recording any verifiably miraculous acts.

How It Came To Be

One man under the divine inspiration of God didn't write the Pentateuch; it was the product of several different perspectives of a common legacy passed down by fallible oral tradition for hundreds of years. When we analyze the texts, we clearly observe

the Pentateuch as a convolution of several works from different authors with interpolated segues to signal subject transitions. Considering these observations, we cannot possibly anticipate the Pentateuch to be 100% accurate in its detail.

Following the Assyrian invasion and Babylonian Exile, conditions were certainly indicative of a rising necessity for a cohesive religious society. Perhaps these
tales arose from the necessity to instill fear into the hearts of Israel's stronger enemies. Consequently, it would be very likely that these bits of propaganda were
intended to be nothing more than methods of keeping superstitious enemies at
bay so that such forces wouldn't overrun the demonstrably inferior and ill-
equipped Israelites.

Exaggerated oral traditions and urban legends during this highly superstitious
era no doubt played a large role in forming the first draft of the Old Testament.
The seemingly countless number of horrible acts carried out by God, recorded in
the Old Testament, and discussed in the previous three chapters of this book
weren't the result of angry divine interactions. Instead, these tales of unfathomably enormous armies and insanely angry deities were undoubtedly the product of a vivid human imagination. Thus, we cannot reasonably attribute the
earliest writings of the Bible to an omniscient deity, much less the "wonderful"
and "loving" Christian god. In short, the historical account left by the Hebrews is
a problematic report filled with wild, unsubstantiated, ridiculous, and extraordinary claims without a shred of evidence to back it up.

THIS WAY AND THAT: BIBLICAL CONTRADICTIONS

When a series of fallible authors attempt to create a cohesive testimonial manuscript, one would expect to find contradictions among accounts of those claiming to be witnesses and/or reporters. We could say the same for a group of conspirators convening to invent stories for whatever purpose they might have in mind. On the other hand, when billions of people deem a certain collection of accounts to originate from the inspirations of a perfect God, there's a reasonable expectation that the facts presented should be free from contradictions.

In the case of the Holy Bible, there's an overwhelming amount of inconsistencies between its covers. However, you must be careful with the plentiful lists found across the Internet and within certain publications because many of the so-called contradictions are justifiably harmonizable. Estimates of these occurrences are often in excess of one thousand, but conservative skeptics offer a number only in the dozens. Most Christians, of course, refuse to budge from zero under the guise of divine inspiration.

I'm confident that there are at least one hundred contradicting passages that should be classified as "irreconcilable through rational means," but such a list would be too laborious to compile and too boring to read if I were to include them all here. Consequently, I'll limit our overview to around forty of the best examples and explain why there's a contradiction in cases when it's not painfully obvious. While many liberal Christians will accept that there are complications due to obvious human authorship, quite a few still hang onto the ridiculous notion that the Bible is the infallible and inerrant word of God. We'll look at some of the apologetically proposed solutions to these difficulties, and I'll specifically explain why they don't fully solve the problems at hand.

Interwoven Myths Of The Pentateuch

As we concluded in the previous chapter, Moses was not the sole author of the Pentateuch. Furthermore, we should give credit for the books to no less than four distinct writers. Because we have a variety of authors present, there will subsequently be divergent details in their recollections when we come upon doublet and triplet passages. As these discrepancies are most noticeable in the creation and flood stories, this is where we will begin our analysis.

The more popular creation account found in the first chapter of Genesis is the one written by the author P. In his account, he provides a very rigid timeline covering a course of six days on the creation of the earth's contents. Genesis 2:4 begins a more relaxed creation account by J, thus there's a repetition of the story with several different details this trip around.

According to the popular P version, God produced the animals before he created Adam (Genesis 1:25-27). However, J says just the opposite. By his account, God first created Adam and then produced the animals so that Adam wouldn't be alone. Unable to comply with God's request to find an animal that would be sexually pleasing to him, Adam is put to sleep so that God can remove one of Adam's ribs to build Eve (Genesis 2:18-25). To further complicate matters, P completely ignores the story of the rib and implies that Adam and Eve were made simultaneously *after* the animals were assembled (Genesis 1:27).

Needless to say, both creation accounts cannot be true since they directly contradict one another. Apologists will often claim, without substantiation, that segments of each story were not written chronologically. As is the case with all contradictions, they begin with the erroneous premise of the Bible being perfect and mold the facts to fit this belief. When you read the passages from an impartial point of view, however, you'll understand how unlikely it would be for their proposal to match the truth. It's highly illogical to assert that the animals came before Adam when the author mentions that God created them following the realization of the man's loneliness. Be cautious of the NIV in this passage, as it disingenuously slips "had" into verse 19 in order to alter the verb tense into past perfect. No such tense shift is present in the original Hebrew language.

The redactor interwove the two flood stories even tighter than the creation myths, often flip-flopping between authors after each verse. P once again manages to write the more popular version of the story in which the animals board the ark as a couple, male and female (Genesis 6:19, 7:8-9, 7:15). On the other hand, J records the number of clean animals taken as "sevens" and the number of unclean animals as "twos" (Genesis 7:2). While this may seem like a change of plan or further clarification to those who believe Moses wrote these commands, the more respectable document hypothesis allows us to see contrasting versions of the same legend.

After the flood, P purports the sons of Noah traveling in separate directions because of their different languages (Genesis 10), yet we see that the world still has only one language when construction begins on the Tower of Babel. The needlessly agoraphobic God divides the one and only world language only after becoming fearful of being spotted from this tower (Genesis 11:1-8). The Pentateuch authors provide us with two completely different explanations for the world's many languages.

What Is God Like?

The drastic alteration of God's personality is the quintessential biblical contradiction. His attitude goes from that of a vocal, evil, and vengeful god in the Old Testament to a silent, benevolent, and forgiving god in the New Testament. It's ridiculous to imagine a perfect, eternal being undergoing this 180-degree makeover at some arbitrary and unverifiable point long in the past. The real reason behind this change is the Bible's allowance of representation by no less than two dozen authors living centuries apart. Since fallible authors void of divine inspiration should have variant perspectives on the nature of God, we should not be surprised when we encounter the anomalous behavior change between the two testaments. Still, this doesn't explain why people were applying this new personality to the Hebrew god at the start of the Common Era.

The likely answer to this riddle may be related to the life cycle that all ancient religions have undergone. Belief systems must evolve with their followers or face extinction. Perhaps people grew tired of the threats made in the Pentateuch and felt there were no true rewards or consequences for their actions. Out of their desires for change, they may have created the Christian notion of Heaven. By this point, someone obviously grasped the notion that you could catch more flies with honey than with vinegar.

As I've said many times before, we have conflicting opinions on the omniscience, omnipotence, and omnipresence of God. Hosea would have us believe that God's knowledge is limited: "They made princes: and I knew it not" (Hosea 8:4). Pentateuch author J would have us believe that God cannot be everywhere: "And Cain went out from the presence of the Lord" (Genesis 4:16). The author of Hebrews would have us believe that there are some things even God cannot do: "It was impossible for God to lie" (Hebrews 6:18). These passages fly in the face of everything that the Bible and contemporary Christians claim about God's infinite qualities.

Similarly, an omnipotent creator would have unlimited power. However, consider this ages old question: "Can God make a burrito hot enough that he can't eat it?" This might seem silly at first, but it demonstrates a fundamental flaw in the existence of an omnipotent being. If he can eat any burrito he makes, he can't make one hot enough; thus, he's not omnipotent. If he makes one too hot to eat, he can't bear the product of his own creation; thus, he's not omnipotent. As I hope you realize from this illustration, an omnipotent being cannot exist. There can be no power strong enough to make squared circles, duplicated unique items, or any other interesting paradoxes that you can imagine.

What about the human qualities of fury and fatigue? Can God experience these feelings? With the new biblical insight that you should have gained over the past few chapters, it should be immediately obvious that God has the capacity to become quite upset at times. Nahum provides us with a nice example: "God is jealous, and the Lord revengeth; the Lord revengeth, and is furious" (1:2). Even so, Isaiah unambiguously claims that God told him "fury is not in me" (27:4). If fury is not in him, how can he experience fury? Even though it may be superficially obvious that God wouldn't experience fatigue, it wouldn't be wise to jump to such a conclusion. According to Jeremiah, God says, "I am weary with repenting" (15:6). According to Isaiah, however, "The everlasting God, the Lord, the Creator of the ends of the earth, fainteth not, neither is weary" (40:28). Either God can experience fatigue or not. Either God can experience fury or not. Nahum, Isaiah, and Jeremiah simply presented their contrasting, divinely uninspired, human interpretations of their god. In the process, they inevitably end up contradicting one another.

How about those who call out to this mysterious being? Will he always save them? Most Christians believe that God will acknowledge these cries for salvation because most Christians only read the New Testament. After all, Paul proclaims, "whosoever shall call upon the name of the Lord shall be saved" (Romans 10:13). Contrast that statement with the one given by Micah: "Then shall they cry unto the Lord, but he will not hear them" (3:4). In other words, Paul claims that God will save *anyone* who calls out for the Lord. However, Micah provides a specific situation in which Paul's unconditional statement wouldn't apply. Sure, one can try to assert that Paul was referring to the time before judgment while Micah was referring to the time after judgment, but this doesn't validate Paul's statement. He plainly tells us that *whosoever* calls to God will be saved. If we only had Paul's statement to go on, and we were given the scenario of people crying out to the Lord as described in Micah, we could only assume that God would save them. Such an assumption would be contradictory to what Micah claims. If Paul was simply being careless with his diction, consider what other important information he might have neglected to mention.

God's Ambiguous Life Guidelines

Is it permissible to swear when making a promise? Pentateuch author D says we should "fear the Lord thy God; him shalt thou serve, and to him shalt thou cleave, and swear by his name" (Deuteronomy 10:20). However, Jesus instructs his followers to "swear not at all" (Matthew 5:34). An apologist will typically claim that the words of Jesus override all divergent information, but this line of reasoning fails to harmonize the contradiction. Even worse, this proposal would result in Christians ignoring large portions of God's perfect law (Psalms 19:7). In case you're wondering, both verses refer to taking an oath, not a degradation of ethical language.

Should we be happy when our enemies suffer? Common decency might lead us to have some sympathy for our adversaries when matters drastically worsen for them, as does the good Proverb 24:17: "Rejoice not when thine enemy falleth, and let not thine heart be glad when he stumbleth." However, we don't need to look far to find portions of the Bible distant from the concept of decency. Psalms 58:10 speaks of a time when the righteous will rejoice after God lashes his vengeance on the wicked. I'm not sure I understand the Bible's position on the issue. Am I correct to assume that God doesn't want us to rejoice when our enemies fall unless he's the one doing the punishing? If I didn't know better, I'd say the Christian god could be quite hypocritical.

Are we supposed to pray in public or private? Most churches observe public prayer in accordance with the author of Timothy, who says, "I will therefore that men pray every where, lifting up holy hands" (1 Timothy 2:8). Okay, but Jesus specifically told his followers to refrain from this behavior. "And when thou prayest, thou shalt not be as the hypocrites are: for they love to pray standing in the synagogues and in the corners of the streets, that they may be seen of men. Verily I say unto you, They have their reward. But thou, when thou prayest, enter into thy closet, and when thou hast shut thy door, pray to thy Father which is in secret; and thy Father which seeth in secret shall reward thee openly." (Matthew 6:5-6). Granted, the people who pray in church aren't doing so just to let others see them, but they're still violating a direct order given by Jesus to avoid prayer in public. Jesus was clear in his desire of not wanting his true believers to have commonalties with the hypocrites who pray in public for counterfeit reasons. Even so, Christians continue to pray in church. Do the words in Timothy now trump the lessons taught by Jesus Christ, or do Christians not fully read the Bible?

Has God declared it permissible to be wealthy? Psalms 112:1-3 says, "Blessed is the man that feareth the Lord, that delighteth greatly in his commandments. His seed shall be mighty upon the earth: the generation of the upright shall be blessed. Wealth and riches shall be in his house." Considering that one obtains these riches for fearing God and following his commandments, it's safe to say that these verses look favorably upon those who earn their wealth in this manner. On the other hand, Jesus says, "it is easier for a camel to go through the eye of a needle, than for a rich man to enter into the Kingdom of God" (Matthew 19:24, Mark 10:25, Luke 18:25). Why would God bless the righteous with riches when it's impossible for rich people to go to Heaven? Yet again, the perfect Bible fails to be consistent with its moral guidelines.

Does God save his followers according to their faith or by the works they do while on earth? This is a fair question and one deserving of an honest answer if we're to do what's necessary to please God. As there are several contradictions on this matter, let's look at only one example. The letter to the Ephesians says, "For by grace are ye saved through faith; and not of yourselves: it is the gift of God: Not of works, lest any man should boast" (2:8-9). In other words, we are saved by our faith and not through our works. Compare that with this passage found in the book of James: "What doth it profit, my brethren, though a man say he hath faith, and have not works? can faith save him?…Even so faith, if it hath not works, is dead, being alone" (2:14-17). Now, works are essential requirements for entering into Heaven. While Christians feel that they should satisfy both requirements to be assured of a spot in the afterlife, this measure doesn't sufficiently solve the contradiction. Again, two fallible authors yield two contrasting viewpoints.

Should we love the members of our family? Of course we should, right? Jesus says, "If any man come to me, and hate not his father, and mother, and wife, and children, and brethren, and sisters, yea, and his own life also, he cannot be my disciple" (Luke 14:26). In other words, Jesus tells his listeners to hate their families and themselves before they follow him. Contrast that surprising declaration with "honour thy father and thy mother" and John's words: "he that loveth not his brother whom he hath seen, how can he love God whom he hath not seen" (Exodus 20:12 and 1 John 4:20, respectively). What about Jesus' famous command that we "love one another" (John 15:17)? I wouldn't have an answer for these discrepancies without modifying the obvious connotations of the passages. Once again, imperfect authors provide contradicting guidelines. It should be obvious that Jesus' behavior in this passage is totally opposite of what most people have perceived for centuries. His statement simply goes against the way decent people are raised to respect their families.

Since passages like this are extremely disturbing to apologists, they try to find ways to alter the meanings in order for the Christian Jesus blueprint to remain unbroken. Luke 14:26 is certainly no exception. When discussing the matter with semi-informed opposition, you'll often hear the assertion that the original Greek word for hate, *miseo*, can also mean "to love less than." In other words, these Christians believe that Jesus said to love your family less than you love God. While this might be consistent with orthodox belief, you can be positive of one thing: there's no truth to this interpretation, whatsoever. No other contemporaneous records, including the other forty New Testament uses, ever suggested *miseo* could have this proposed definition. In fact, *miseo* is an extreme form of hatred, not your every day disgust. Nonetheless, Christians truly believe this proposal because they, once again, start with the faulty premise of an ideological Jesus and only accept the most likely interpretation consistent with this belief. This line of rationale lies far outside the bounds of reality.

Did the arrival of Jesus serve to repeal the Laws of Moses? For those who like this justification for ignoring the Old Testament, Jesus provides a rebuttal: "Think not that I am come to destroy the law, or the prophets: I am not come to destroy, but to fulfil. For verily I say unto you, Till heaven and earth pass, one jot or one tittle shall in no wise pass from the law, till all be fulfilled. Whosoever therefore shall break one of these least commandments, and shall teach men so, he shall be called the least in the kingdom of heaven: but whosoever shall do and teach them, the same shall be called great in the kingdom of heaven" (Matthew 5:17-19). Jesus clearly instructs his followers to maintain their observance of the old laws. Furthermore, if the Old Testament "law of the Lord is perfect" (Psalms 19:7), for what conceivable reason would it ever need an overhaul?

The apologists' claim that the old law has since collapsed seemingly has no merit with the Bible. Nevertheless, the author of Hebrews says, "But now hath he obtained a more excellent ministry, by how much also he is the mediator of a better covenant, which was established upon better promises. For if that first covenant had been faultless, then should no place have been sought for the second" (8:6-7). Now, this writer claims that the Laws of Moses given by God *did* have faults and require a replacement in the form of a new covenant. If someone argues that the Psalm is no longer valid because its self-proclamation fell under the Laws of Moses, an imperfect set of guidelines, this person has just replaced the contradiction with a blatant error committed by the Psalmist.

The Background Of Jesus Christ

The ability of the Bible to provide a consistent background for its main character astonishingly begins to falter even before Jesus came into the world. The genealogies provided in the books of Matthew and Luke yield an excellent example of an error avoided by one author but overlooked by another. Because of this human mistake, the Bible ends up containing yet another contradiction.

In the first chapter of Matthew, we see the ancestry of Jesus spanning from King David to Joseph, Mary's husband. The complication with this genealogy is the absolute lack of a blood relationship between Joseph and Jesus. As the story goes, Jesus, a man without an earthly father, was born from a virgin impregnated by God. If the Matthew genealogy is true, Jesus was not a descendant of David. Consequently, he could not be the Messiah allegedly prophesied to arise from the line of David (Psalm 132:11). As you should expect, this was obviously not the author's intent. Seeing as how the author of Luke probably realized that tracing Jesus' lineage this way would be a blunder, he created his own genealogy passing through Heli. Even though Luke is specific in stating that Heli is Joseph's father, I have given Christians the benefit of the doubt that he is Joseph's father-in-law instead of a second father. To very little surprise, Heli and Mary just so happen to be descendants of King David as well (Luke 3:23-38). The Bible has now begun to insult the intelligence of its audience.

Accounts also differ from Matthew and Luke on when Jesus was born. The more popular account of Matthew has King Herod alive at the time of Jesus' birth (Chapter 2). From several historical sources, we know Herod's reign ended in 4 BCE with his violent death. Thus, according to Matthew, Jesus must have been born in or before 4 BCE. The date later designated as Jesus' birth is misplaced, but there's nothing biblically wrong about that. However, Luke says that Mary was still with child at the time Quirinius was conducting a census as Governor of Syria (2:1-5). According to meticulously kept Roman history, Quirinius couldn't have carried out this census until at least 6 CE. Thus, according to Luke, Jesus must have been born in or after 6 CE. In order for the two accounts to be harmonious, Jesus had to be born before 4 BCE and after 6 CE: a feat impossible even for a supernatural being. The two accounts provide a ten-year discrepancy in need of a difficult resolution.

To rectify this insurmountable problem, Christians have desperately proposed, without justification, that Quirinius was a governor twice. They say this earlier phantom governorship was held sometime before 4 BCE in order for Luke to be consistent with Matthew. Here's what we know from Roman history: Quintilius was governor from 6 BCE to 3 BCE; Saturninus was governor from 9 BCE to 6 BCE; Titius was governor from 12 BCE to 9 BCE; Quirinius, the governor in question, didn't obtain consulship until 12 BCE, making him ineligible to hold Syria's office of governor before that time; no one ever held the governorship of Syria twice; Josephus and Tacitus, the two most important historians from the early Common Era, never mentioned Quirinius holding the post twice; and there would be no reason for Quirinius to conduct a census prior to 6 CE because Judea wasn't under Roman control until that time. A few contributions of irrelevant evidence and several wild explanations claim to rectify this obvious contradiction, each one through its own unique method, but they're all nothing more than the most outrageous "how-it-could-have-been-scenarios." The two accounts contradict greatly over the time Jesus was allegedly born.

The Death Of Jesus Christ

Shortly before Jesus' crucifixion, Peter's master tells him that he will choose to disavow any knowledge of Jesus on three occasions. After these events manifest, a rooster will crow to remind him of Jesus' words. In Matthew, Luke, and John, Jesus warns Peter that all three of his denials will take place *before* the rooster crows (26:34, 22:34, and 13:38, respectively). In these three accounts, the situation unfolds exactly how Jesus predicted. The rooster crows after, and only after, Peter's third denial is made (26:69-75, 22:56-61, and 18:17-27, respectively). However, the details are different in Mark. Here, we see Jesus warning Peter that the rooster will crow after his first denial and crow again after his third denial (14:30). Of course, this is exactly how the events play out (14:66-72). This is an undeniable contradiction without a rational explanation. If Mark is correct, the rooster crowed after the first denial even though Jesus said, in the other three Gospels, that it wouldn't crow until after the third denial. If these three Gospels are accurate, Mark is wrong because the rooster could not have crowed until after Peter's third denial.

In addition to the problem of the crowing rooster, the identities of the people interrogating Peter over his relationship with Jesus differ among the four Gospels. In Matthew, the subjects were a damsel, another maid, and the crowd. In Mark, the subjects were a maid, the same maid again, and the crowd. In Luke, the subjects were a maid, a man, and another man. In John, the subjects were a damsel, the crowd, and a servant of the high priest. While it may be possible to justify a harmonization among two, possibly three, accounts, there's no possibility in fitting the four reports into one cohesive tale.

Once Jesus was summoned before Pontius Pilate, Matthew claims that Jesus "answered him to never a word" (27:13-14). John, however, records a lengthy dialogue between the two men (18:33-37). Apologists often assert that John was speaking of a different interrogation than the one reported in Matthew, but this meritless claim still doesn't resolve the discrepancy. Matthew unambiguously states that Jesus *never* answered to Pilate. If Jesus never answered to Pilate, the discussion recorded in John could have never taken place.

On the way to his crucifixion, Jesus burdened his own cross according to John (19:17). The other three Gospel writers tell us that a man named Simon of Cyrene carried it (Matthew 27:32, Mark 15:21, Luke 23:36). While it's true that *both* may have carried the cross at some point, as many apologists claim, what are the odds that all four authors would foul up by omitting this important detail?

The four Gospels also differ on what they purport was written on the sign above the cross. Matthew 27:37: This is Jesus the King of the Jews. Mark 15:26: The King of the Jews. Luke 23:38: This is the King of the Jews. John 19:19: Jesus of Nazareth the King of the Jews. Mark also claims that the thieves who were executed with Jesus insulted him (15:32), but Luke says that one thief insulted Jesus while the other begged his forgiveness to secure a place in Heaven (23:39-42). In addition, the Gospel writers also differ on what they imply were Jesus' last words. Matthew 27:46 and Mark 15:34: "My God, my God, why hast thou forsaken me?" Luke 23:46: "Father, into thy hands I commend my spirit." John 19:30: "It is finished." Furthermore, the four contradicting authors made similar errors and/or omissions with regard to the number of women and angels visiting Jesus' tomb following his burial. I would never claim that minor variations in detail invalidate a story, but you must agree that writers inspired by an omnipotent deity should perform a little better than they have up to this point. These discrepancies obviously arise from several decades of playing the telephone game.

It's All In The Details

Has anyone ever seen God? According to the Pentateuch, God made an appearance in human form over a dozen times in front of several people, such as Abraham, Jacob, and Moses (e.g. Genesis 12:7, Genesis 32:30, and Exodus 33:11, respectively). However, Jesus and John claim that no one has ever seen God face to face (John 6:46 and John 1:18, respectively).

Was Ahaziah eighteen years younger or two years older than his father (2 Kings 8:26 and 2 Chronicles 21:20-22:2, respectively)? The Bible says that a man was two years older than his father, yet Christians still parade it as perfect! Perhaps these apologists only read the NIV translation of 2 Chronicles, which deceitfully alters Ahaziah's age from forty-two to twenty-two with only a minor footnote. Even more astounding than this perplexity is the exceedingly unfortunate Saul who died via four different methods: suicide by sword (1 Samuel 31:4-5), death by an Amalekite (2 Samuel 1:8-10), death by a Philistine (2 Samuel 21:12), and struck down by God (1 Chronicles 10:13-14).

How did Judas die after betraying Jesus? The popular account of Matthew is that he hung himself (27:5). However, there's a lesser-known account of how he died in Acts. "Now [Judas] purchased a field with the reward of iniquity; and falling headlong, he burst asunder in the midst, and all his bowels gushed out" (1:18). I'll openly admit that the common explanation proposed for this contradiction is one of the funniest things I've ever heard. Evidently, this is what took place: Judas hung himself from an extremely elevated tree branch in the field, the branch snapped, he did a flip to fall head first, and his body exploded upon impact. If someone were to add "how-it-could-have-been-scenario" in the dictionary, the editor would surely have to consider this example for inclusion.

There's even a contradiction related to how the field was purchased. Matthew says Judas took the money that he received as a reward for surrendering Jesus and threw it into a temple. The priests within the temple then used the money to buy a field for burying strangers (Matthew 27:5-7). Remember, however, Acts claims that Judas, not the priests, was the one responsible for buying the field. The most likely reason for this blaring contradiction is a lack of one author's access to the contrasting records of the other. Had something lifted this assumed restriction, we could be reasonably certain that this contradiction would disappear.

In the Gospel according to Mark, Jesus sends his disciples on a journey and tells them to take nothing but their staves and sandals (6:8-9). In Luke, Jesus says to take nothing, provides a list of items that the disciples are to leave behind, and includes staves on the list (9:3). In Matthew, Jesus reaffirms his desire for the disciples to leave everything at home, including *both* shoes and staves (10:10). Such a seemingly inconsequential detail is important for one reason only: demonstrating yet again that the Bible is a fallible record scribed by humans, not the perfect word of an eternal god.

Here are a few more impossible puzzles for you to solve if you ever get bored: "No man hath ascended up to heaven" (John 3:13) versus "Elijah went up by a whirlwind into heaven" (2 Kings 2:11); "And one kid of the goats for a sin offering: to make an atonement for you" (Numbers 29:5) versus "For it is not possible that the blood of bulls and of goats should take away sins" (Hebrews 10:4); "If a man have long hair, it is a shame unto him" (1 Corinthians 11:14) versus "He shall be holy, and shall let the locks of the hair on his head grow" (Numbers 6:5); "The earth abideth for ever" (Ecclesiastes 1:4) versus "Heaven and earth shall pass away" (Matthew 24:35); "And the anger of the *Lord* was kindled against Israel, and he moved David against them to say, Go and number Israel" (2 Samuel 24:1) versus "And *Satan* stood up against Israel and provoked David to number Israel" (1 Chronicles 21:1); "Walk in the ways of thine heart, and in the sight of thine eyes" (Ecclesiastes 11:9) versus "Seek not after your own heart and your own eyes" (Numbers 15:39); "That Christ should suffer, and he should be the first that should rise from the dead" (Acts 26:23) versus Lazarus rising from the dead months ago (John 11:43) and the previous resurrection miracles of Elijah centuries in the past. Did the fig tree cursed by Jesus wither immediately (Matthew 21:19-20) or overnight (Mark 11:13-21)? Did Jehoiachin reign three months and ten days when he was eight (2 Chronicles 36:9) or three months when he was eighteen (2 Kings 24:8)?

"Even The Stuff That Contradicts The Other Stuff"

This chapter is but a small sample of possible biblical incongruities. God's holy word contains contradictions of every kind from cover to cover within accounts of important events, rules for worship, how to get to Heaven, the nature of God, historical records of birth and rule, and the teachings of Jesus. Realizing the existence of such contradictions would destroy the ideal quality of the book many set out to explain by any means necessary. An impartial ear can often translate common justifications for these problems as "the Bible says something it doesn't mean" or "the Bible means something it doesn't say." These dishonest and inconsistent apologists feel that as long as they put a nonsense scenario out there that's capable of satisfying the contradiction, it's up to everyone else to prove it wrong. This is a very dishonest and implausible attempt at holding the Bible to be perfect. Even worse, it doesn't work because anyone can do that to *any* book. If all else fails, they often brush aside unexplainable predicaments as "the incomprehensible and mysterious ways of God."

The contradictions exist for a reason. First of all, as I've said so many times before, there was no true divine inspiration from God guiding the authors to write their material. Each person wrote through his own limited interpretations and experiences because no one honestly expected the collection of books to grow in popularity to their current state. In addition, no one had any way of knowing which books were going to be enshrined in the Bible and which ones were destined to face omission. It would have been too daunting of a task for the authors to check every historical record for contradictions with their compositions. Instead, it's likely that most authors simply tried to keep a steady theme set by preceding authors. As time progressed, the new generation of authors obviously sensed that the Israelites needed a new God. As the Gospel writers were perhaps aware of a growing disdain for the threats from the cruel god of the Old Testament, they set out to create a new one in their own image.

Absurdity At Its Finest

No reader can truthfully deny that multitudes of curious occurrences are readily observable in the Bible. To a Christian believer, these strange events are nothing more than the mysterious ways of God. To a freethinker, the alleged phenomena are an indicative subset of the widespread superstitious beliefs held by our ancestors. There are hundreds, if not thousands, of ridiculous statements made by the authors of the Bible. Whether you enjoy reading about plumb lines or talking donkeys, the Christian religion carries more than its fair share of absurdities. In fact, some of the biblical reports are illogical enough to disqualify explanations through supernatural means! As was the case for contradictions in the previous chapter, I forced myself to limit this overview to a small fraction of those eligible for this frank discussion. It's my hope that this chapter will provide additional fuel for thought in the fight against religious conditioning.

Highly Suspect

Before we leap into the solid cases for biblical absurdity, we'll begin by discussing some quite comical passages that *could* possibly have some far removed explanation for their content. Let's first consider the sex life of Abraham and Sarah. Because they're upset over failing to give birth to any children, God has pity on them and tells Sarah that they will soon have their wish granted. God maintains his promise, and Sarah eventually has a child. Soon after, Abraham finds another wife and has six more children with her. Going solely on this information, these events don't seem too unlikely if we ignore the divine intervention. However, there's an extremely questionable part of the story that wasn't mentioned. Sarah was close to one hundred years old when she gave birth, and Abraham was well over the century mark (Genesis 18:11-15, 21:1-2, 25:1-2). Even worse, Noah was five hundred years old when he had three sons (Genesis 5:32).

The Devil finds God one day, and they thoroughly analyze Job, a wealthy and righteous man who is essentially perfect in God's eyes. God points out Job's good behavior to Satan, but Satan disagrees with him and says that Job would curse the name of God if all his possessions were taken away. The bet is on, and God permits Satan to do anything to Job as long as he doesn't permanently harm him. Satan, whose location was previously unknown to the all-knowing God, once

155

again leaves the presence of the omnipresent Lord (Job 1:1-12). God evidently stands idle while the Devil torments Job by stealing his possessions, slaughtering his livestock, murdering his family, killing his workers, and afflicting him with diseases. Withstanding even the most tumultuous of misfortunes, Job remains loyal to God and doesn't curse him. I'm honestly not sure what other details could be added to this story to increase its fairy-tale connotations. Why does God feel the need to punish a respectable person in order to prove a point to Satan, and why doesn't Satan just accept the statements of an omniscient being? Since Job was written around the same time as the Pentateuch, you should now be able to understand where the absurdity in this myth might originate.

While Moses was perched atop Mt. Sinai waiting for God to deliver his commandments, he goes without food and water for forty days and forty nights (Exodus 34:28). I can't think of a justification for including such a statement unless the author was unaware of anyone ever suffering from dehydration. The author, in this case, could have thought that Moses went through serious agony during those forty days but eventually surmised there was no permanent risk to his health. While going without food for forty days and surviving is feasible for those who condition themselves to do so, we know today that there's no realistic chance of survival without water for this extended period. Most people cannot survive five days under such grueling circumstances, while fourteen days without water would certainly weed out even the most conditioned participants. We should obviously file a report of a man going forty days without food and water under "highly suspect."

God laid down a strangely curious law when he declared that any man with damaged or missing genitals, as well as any man who doesn't know the names of his ancestors to ten generations, cannot enter into religious congregations (Deuteronomy 23:1-2). First, I don't see how anyone would know another person had a genital abnormality unless someone literally screened the visitors at the door. As for the burden of proving an ancestry, I doubt that any Hebrew was able to keep accurate and truthful records thousands of years ago. How could anyone indisputably prove that he knew his family line that far back? What was to prevent someone from just conjuring up some names so that he could attend worship? If no one knew this person's ancestry, no one could disprove him. Wouldn't the omniscient God realize this futile law wasn't going to work? More importantly, why is God thoroughly preoccupied with the condition of a man's genitals? I know I've mentioned it before, but the whole matter is patently asinine. This is one of the many absurd rules that Big Brother allegedly distributes to keep his society in order. Likewise, instead of including undeniable proof for the book's authenticity, he tells us not to wear a piece of clothing made of more than one fabric (Leviticus 19:19). These examples of God's foolish rules will have to serve for now in order to keep the topic at a reasonable length.

It's a safe wager that the majority of the free world has heard the tale of David slaying the towering Goliath. Most people commonly refer to Goliath as a giant, but a more specific height is given. The Bible lists him at six cubits and a span, which is approximately 9'9" in our modern measurement system. If we were to use known data to compare the rarity of Goliath's height with other individuals, we would find that there may have never been, or ever will be, anyone within two or three inches of his extraordinary eminence. The verifiable record currently stands at 8'11", though the record holder was anything but a robust warrior capable of supporting a 125-pound brass mail (1 Samuel 17:4-5). This monster would have been nothing less than a unique visual spectacle. If the tale of David slaying Goliath is a derivative of some true historical underdog overcoming great odds, wouldn't you find it probable that the giant's height was romanticized by fibbing humans until it reached tall-tale proportions?

Solomon was supposedly "wiser than all men" (1 Kings 4:31). In fact, his wisdom exceeded "the sand that is on the sea shore" (1 Kings 4:29). As wise as this man presumably was, "his wives turned away his heart after other gods" (1 Kings 11:4). I can certainly contemplate a few hypothetical factors that might lead an intelligent person to join a cult promising a better life on a far away planet; I cannot imagine any reason why the wisest man in the region could be led away from what is supposed to be the true god, especially since this being is in direct communication with him. It doesn't make the least bit of sense unless we consider that his infinite wisdom may have told him something about the belief system in question.

As you well know, a rather cartoonish portrayal of God is offered throughout the Old Testament. However, we still haven't fully covered the absurdity of God's presence. Most poets, prophets, and historians certainly believed him to be a human-like personage. God shoots flames from his mouth and smoke from his nostrils like a mean ole dragon (Psalms 18:8). In fact, God has eyes, ears, a nose, a mouth, a finger, a hand, a back, loins, and feet just to name a few of his physical human attributes. God supposedly made man in his own image, but why would an omnipotent, omniscient, and omnipresent spirit have human qualities that provide us with finite abilities? For instance, why does God need feet to walk if he's eternally present? He roars and shouts (Jeremiah 25:30), loves the aroma of burning animals (Genesis 8:21), and wants the fat from animal sacrifices (Leviticus 3:16). God even seems a tad jealous when a woman leaves his word for other men (Hosea 2:7-13). Essentially, the Christian god is "perfect" with imperfect attributes. It's a bit too coincidental for my liking that God made humans in his image when we can more rationally say the exact opposite. This deity isn't benevolent; it's absurd.

The book of Acts tells the reader a story in which a gathered crowd simultaneously understands all the speaking disciples in every language (Acts 2:1-6). While that sounds quite deranged, it's not the point I intend to make because apologists often rely on the divine miracle fallback. When the men in the audience accused the speakers of drunkenness, Peter reminded the crowd of what Joel understood God to say. "And it shall come to pass in the last days, saith God" (Acts 2:17). Peter's speech goes on to explain how unusual events were to be expected when the world was about to end. Thus, he was obviously under the impression that they were living in the final days on earth. Even so, we're still here. It's hardly likely that "the last days" have been the past 2000 years when the earth was supposedly only 4000 years old at the time Peter made this prediction.

James argues that it didn't rain anywhere on the entire planet for three and a half years because Elias (Elijah) prayed for a drought (James 5:17). There's absolutely zero evidence that a prayer answerable only by supernatural means has ever been accommodated. It's highly unlikely that it ceased to rain over the whole earth for that long, and it's even more unlikely that this unusual weather phenomenon would come about because a mortal man prayed for it to take place. The lack of rain would have caused untold devastation by instigating mass dehydration in all living organisms. Of course, no such extreme drought was recorded consistently around the world at any point in history. There's a good reason for this discrepancy: the unverifiable drought didn't happen.

The Greatest Show On Earth

Among all of God's strange and ridiculous regulations, a large portion involves animals. We can find two examples making little to no sense in Deuteronomy. First, God doesn't want anyone to boil a young goat in its mother's milk (14:21). If you're going to boil a young goat in milk, is it that much more deviant to do it in its mother's? Why is an eternal, omnipotent god concerned with such trivial and outdated matters? This god also doesn't want you to plow a field with an ox and a donkey on the same yoke (22:10). God, of course, gives no reason for this useless regulation. Instead of making certain that his holy word included clear abolishments of slavery and rape so that millions of his creations wouldn't needlessly suffer, God decides to set idiotic rules for plowing fields and boiling goats. This should provoke indignation from any moralistically reasonable person, regardless of religious conviction.

In the beginning, when God allegedly created the animals, they were designed to consume plants rather than meat (Genesis 1:30). Even so, there's certainly no reason to believe that the ancestors of present-day predators survived off an herbivore diet. The food chain is in harmony because of the fluctuations occurring due to a rising and falling cycle of predator and prey populations. Withdrawing that relationship would throw the chain into unknown chaos. Furthermore, we have fossil records of these animals purported to be herbivores. Their equipped teeth were intended to initiate and facilitate the digestion of meat, not plants. Six thousand years ago, just like today, many species could not survive solely on plants. In addition, parasites require blood from living hosts. Blood is neither a plant nor a meat. Suggesting that parasites also made their daily meals from plants is increasingly absurd. Science demonstrates that it's impossible for some species to survive on plants, yet the erroneous Bible claims this testable statement isn't true. Do Christians expect everyone to believe that the Bible is correct regardless of what it says?

The prophet Isaiah informs us that a cockatrice, a mythical creature able to kill its victim with a casual glance, will arise from a serpent (Isaiah 14:29). What tangible evidence do we have to believe that a creature with this incredible ability has ever existed? Again, the Bible provides stories that sound like something straight out of a fairy tale. While some animals are certainly capable of killing their prey by biting or strangling them, a look has no anticipated scientific capacity to kill another creature. While there may be some type of alternative mechanism of action for the attack, such as venom sprayed through the eyes, it wouldn't be due to the act of looking. The cockatrice, unicorn, and dragon are examples of mythical creatures in the Bible that fail to leave any reliable evidence for their existence.

In John's Revelation dream, which is conveyed to be an imminent and realistic future event, he sees crown-wearing locusts with faces of men, hair of women, teeth of lions, tails of scorpions, and wings sounding like chariots. These locusts also adorn iron breastplates in preparation for battle (9:7-10). Draw your own conclusions.

Like mutated locusts, talking animals aren't uncommon in the Bible. Everyone should remember the talking serpent tempting Eve in the Garden of Eden (Genesis 3:1), but there's an even more hilarious example of an atypical animal. In this instance, a man named Balaam is riding along on his donkey. When the donkey sits down on him twice, Balaam gives it a beating for its rebellion. When the donkey notices a murderous angel in their path, it sits down for a third time. Of course, Balaam delivers an additional flogging upon the donkey's body. The donkey then *asks* Balaam, "What have I done unto thee, that thou hast smitten me these three times?" Yes, the donkey argues with its master! Then, Balaam, who does not appear to be the least bit surprised that his ride is questioning his motives, decides to engage in a debate with the donkey by claiming that it mocked him by sitting down. Furthermore, he informs his donkey that it would have already been dead if he had a sword nearby. The donkey then outsmarts him by pointing out that he has always let his master ride him but never asked to ride his master. Thoroughly outsmarted and outclassed, Balaam then concedes defeat in his debate with the donkey (Numbers 22:27-30). Seeing as how no concluding comment that I could make here would do this outdated and obtuse blunder justice, we'll move on.

Health And Knowledge

Is the Bible a reliable guide for maintaining good health and expanding our knowledge? Within 2 Chronicles, we learn of Asa contracting an unspecified foot disease. "Yet in his disease he sought not to the Lord, but to the physicians" (16:12). The passage clearly displays a negative attitude toward Asa for trusting doctors more than God. According to the author of this passage, we are to believe that God is a better source than a physician for curing our ailments.

Recall the prayer experiment proposed all the way back in *The Psychology Hidden Behind Christianity*. God *does not* have a higher success rate than physicians for curing diseases. Even so, the Bible wholeheartedly endorses prayer as the more powerful force. Unfortunately, many smaller denominations of Christianity secretly follow this "no physician" guideline. It doesn't work, and that's why it's illegal to enforce it on minors in most of the civilized world. There has never been any scientific study indicating an act of God has facilitated a recovery from sickness. A person will surely die from a fatal ailment if they refuse medical treatment, regardless of whether or not this individual prays to any god. Even so, most Christians believe praying to their god will prompt a divine intervention that has some unknown and immeasurable positive effect on the outcome. While prayer and faith may comfort a patient enough to facilitate recovery, the acts of the divine are worth nothing if no one's paying attention. Such a misguided belief is blindly illogical, patently absurd, and without a place in reality.

The author of the first letter to Timothy advises his reader to drink wine instead of water (5:23). While researchers in the medical profession currently believe that alcohol is beneficial in moderation, consuming enough wine to remain hydrated for the rest of Timothy's life would certainly destroy his liver after a very brief period. Of course, the author was unaware of the biological effects of alcohol on the liver's filtration system because he wasn't divinely inspired with advanced physiological knowledge. Had he been cognizant of such information, this horrible recommendation would have never made it into the Bible.

Briefly returning our attention to John's dream in Revelation, we learn of an angel who holds out a book for John to eat. He consumes it and describes the taste to be as "sweet as honey" even though it made his stomach bitter (Revelation 10:10). Like replacing water with alcohol, eating a book is not a healthy activity. Another book eater, Ezekiel, recorded so many fantastic experiences, I had to give him his own section. We'll discuss his personal endeavors in a moment.

One of the Proverbs offers the universal answer for any nonsensical statements found within the Bible. "Trust in the Lord with all thine heart; and lean not unto thine own understanding" (3:5). The author really went the extra mile to cover all his bases, but the problem with this advice serving as a fallback answer for all discrepancies is that any religion can invoke such an alibi in order to divert attention away from its flaws. This method doesn't automatically dissolve the problems of any text, including the Bible. Simply put, a book isn't correct because the book says so. Accepting this fallacious reasoning, ignoring common knowledge, and refusing to examine what might very well be the truth creates the prototypical mindless sheep.

Paul uses himself as an example for the mindless sheep when he tells his readers that he doesn't want to know anything except Jesus (1 Corinthians 2:2). "That your faith should not stand in the wisdom of men, but in the power of God" (1 Corinthians 2:5). "Beware lest any man spoil you through philosophy and vain deceit, after the tradition of men, after the rudiments of the world, and not after Christ" (Colossians 2:8). In other words, blindly follow whatever the Bible says even when overwhelming evidence arises to the contrary. I'm sorry, but blind faith should never trump the observable world. Even so, billions of people have lived in similar ignorance and subsequently died clinging to all sorts of myths.

God's Necromancers

Moses and Aaron are apparently well known throughout the region for the magic tricks that God teaches them. God demonstrates to Moses how to cast his rod to the ground in order to make it become a serpent. The transformation frightens him, but the serpent becomes a rod again when he grabs it by the tail. God also shows Moses how to make his hand become leprous. He can reverse the spell by touching the leprous hand to his body (Exodus 4:2-7).

When the hour arrives for Moses and Aaron to impress the Egyptian Pharaoh, they perform the rod trick. However, the Pharaoh's magicians are able to follow suit by transforming their rods into serpents. Aaron's serpent rod then eats all the other serpent rods (Exodus 7:10-12). In a second attempt to outperform the Pharaoh's magicians, Moses and Aaron transform an entire river into blood by touching it with their rods. Again, the Pharaoh's magicians are able to replicate the feat. Moses and Aaron, refusing to give up, induce an aggregation of frogs to emerge from the waters and occupy the land. Yet again, the Pharaoh's magicians demonstrate the same gimmick. In a fourth attempt to demonstrate God's overwhelming power over Egypt, Moses and Aaron are able to create lice out of dust. Since the creation of life *ex nihilo* proves too difficult for the magicians, they concede that Moses and Aaron have the true power of God. As an encore, the victorious couple produces plagues of flies, cattle death, boils, hail, locusts, darkness, and the eventual killing of all the firstborn male children previously mentioned in *The Darker Side Of God* (Exodus 7-11).

Even after the unprecedented accomplishments in Egypt, Moses still has a few tricks remaining up his sleeve. He's able to satisfy the water requirements of millions by tapping a rock with his rod (Exodus 17:6). Moses also accomplished the construction of a serpent statue capable of preventing people from dying of snakebite, provided the victims were looking at it while bitten (Numbers 21:6-7). He even supports Joshua's army in its war against Amalek by simply keeping his hand aloft. Whenever Moses raises his arm, Joshua gets the better of Amalek in the battle; whenever his hand falls from fatigue, the fates reverse. Eventually, Moses begins to rest his arm by propping it on a rock. This ingenious tactic enables Joshua to defeat Amalek (Exodus 17:11-13). I'm not sure what possible impact that Moses raising his hand could have on a truly historical battle.

Elijah obtained his meals from ravens that "brought him bread and flesh in the morning, and bread and flesh in the evening" (1 Kings 17:6). Why would ravens do this for him, and how does one go about training these birds to perform such a feat? While there's never been any indication a flock of ravens would bring food to a human on a regular twelve-hour basis, this *is* the man who caused a three-year drought by simply praying to God.

Elijah's successor, Elisha, is yet another biblical wizard ordained with magnificent powers. He's able to separate the Jordan River by hitting it with his cloak and correspondingly able to rejoin it by adding a pinch of salt (2 Kings 2:14-22). In addition, Elisha can make an iron axe head float in the water (2 Kings 6:6). Assuming this axe head wasn't in a shape enabling it to float, he's able to alter the density of iron with no assured scientific knowledge of what enables certain substances to remain above others.

Later, Elisha asks the King to take some arrows and strike the ground with them. The King does so three times, but Elisha becomes irate and says that he would have been victorious over his enemies if the ground had been struck a couple more times (2 Kings 18:19). Again, more biblical daffiness. Even after death, Elisha still isn't finished working his magic. When a corpse is thrown into Elisha's grave, the body jumps back to life after coming into contact with Elisha's bones (2 Kings 18:20-21). Remember, those verse references that you see after each statement mean you can find all this nonsense in the Bible.

Ezekiel

Ezekiel, perhaps the most eccentric man in the entire Bible, claims to see four creatures in a windstorm from what some believe to be a flying saucer. Each of the four creatures had four faces (a man, a lion, an ox, and an eagle) and four conjoined wings. They had human hands under the wings, one on each squared side of their bodies. The feet, which looked like those of calves, shone like brass and were attached to peglegs (Ezekiel 1:4-10). I'm not entirely sure I shouldn't have classified this passage within the animal absurdities, but I decided to keep it here out of obvious confusion. Needless to say, evidence for such avant-garde creatures does not exist. Besides, this make-believe story fits in perfectly among the multitude of other ancient superstitions involving holy animals taking on several forms.

Ezekiel also claims to have caught a side glimpse of God. Evidently, and I use the term loosely, God is an amber metallic color above his waist, on fire down below, and completely encompassed by a rainbow (1:27-28). Ezekiel would later see God again, this time standing next to bodies, backs, hands, wings, and wheels all packed full of eyes (10:12). With all he witnessed, it's far more likely that Ezekiel was on a hallucinogenic trip than a divine inspiration.

As I promised earlier, God gives Ezekiel a scroll to eat. He eats it and, like John, says that it tastes as sweet as honey (3:1-3). Why does God desire to inform us of his atypical obsession with asking people to eat paper? God then turns sadistic and decides to torment Ezekiel by tying him up in his house and sticking his tongue to the roof of his mouth (3:24-26). Prolonging the torture, God forces Ezekiel to lie on his left side for 390 days and his right side for 40 days in order to symbolize the number of years certain regions lived in sin (4:4-6). What enjoyment could this possibly bring to an omnipotent being? Not thoroughly satisfied with his brutal deeds thus far, God commands him to bake his bread using human dung. After Ezekiel pleads with him to reconsider, God, an omniscient being who should have already known that he was going to go with Ezekiel's alternative plan, changes his mind and lets him use cow dung instead (4:9-15). Did God just get a sick satisfaction out of making this poor man think that he was going to have to eat something baked from his own waste?

God forces Ezekiel to shave his head and gather the hair into thirds. He burns one pile, strikes one with a knife, and scatters the last into the wind (5:1-2). What purpose could these uncanny orders serve? Ezekiel also claims that God informed him of his anger at a wall destined to be destroyed (13:15). Why is God angry at a wall? Nearer the end of his time together with God, the almighty takes Ezekiel to a location filled with bones. Here, God tells him to give an order for their assembly. Once Ezekiel follows this strange demand, the skeletons grow flesh and inhale a breath of life. Now, the skeletons are an army (37:1-14). Why do so many Christians claim to know so much about the omnibenevolent creator? God isn't concerned with giving heartfelt rules for ethical conduct; he wants to waste time watching people play with their hair.

Jesus

While I consider exorcism more of a scientific error than an absurdity, there are definitely some aspects of Jesus' demon-removals that fit better in this section. According to Matthew, Jesus once encountered a couple of men possessed by devils. As they ask Jesus for a cure, he approves their request by driving the devil spirits into a drove of pigs. Possessed by demons, the pigs leap off a cliff and plunge to their deaths. The witnesses in the town then turn against Jesus as a result of his decision to drive the swine insane (Matthew 8:28-34). Why would a man this powerful not just cast the spirits deep into space or somewhere else out of harm's way? Why intentionally kill innocent animals to make people turn against you? Nevertheless, Jesus also donned his disciples with the mystic power to perform exorcisms (Mark 3:15). Even so, there has yet to be a reliable documented case containing evidence that spirits had possessed a human being. On the other hand, the science of so-called "possessions" closely resembles the effects of neurochemical imbalances.

Now let's see what Jesus says about faith. First, if you have faith the size of a mustard seed, you can *literally* cause a mountain to jump into the sea by telling it to do so (Matthew 17:20 and 21:21). Christians living today have endless faith that Jesus spoke only the truth, but no one has ever been able to move a mountain even one inch by using this incredible method. It's absurd to think that anyone could accomplish such a remarkable feat, and it's absurd that the son of God would assert such a false and preposterous claim. Has Jesus just demonstrated himself to be a liar? The only other possibility is that Jesus spoke of some physical component to faith that's required to grow to the size of a mustard seed, but this proposal is as equally ridiculous as the previous claim. This interesting character also announces that every person who came before him was a thief and a robber (John 10:8). I find it very difficult to imagine a world without a single person who didn't steal something prior to Jesus' arrival.

Jesus also purports some questionable aspects about gaining admittance into Heaven. Most of us are aware of the more common requirements, but there are quite a few of which many Christians are obviously unaware. Jesus says, "it is easier for a camel to go through the eye of a needle, than for a rich man to enter into the kingdom of God" (Matthew 19:24). Are we really to believe that it's easier for a camel to walk through the eye of a needle than for a rich man to meet the commonly accepted requirements? If not, Jesus offers no clear standard by which a person can enter into Heaven. If Jesus truly means what he says, it's yet another outright contradiction. Rich people are more than capable of satisfying the requirements set by many other New Testament authors.

Staying with this notion of having to earn Heaven for a moment, Jesus also claims that anyone who says "thou fool" is in danger of Hellfire (Matthew 5:22).

Yet, in Luke 11:40, he calls a group of people "fools." While the authors of the two passages record different Greek words, the meaning remains the same. How absurd is it when a perfect person who lays down standards of how to avoid Hell remains flawless even though he breaks the same standards strong enough to put a regular person in Hell? Additionally, what kind of example does he set for his followers? It seems as though the hypocritical Jesus is above his own laws. Once again, different authors predictably yield different interpretations.

Jesus provides his followers with instructions for helping out their fellow man. First, he advises you to turn the other cheek if someone hits you. Such a recommendation would eventually end in death if one continued to follow Jesus' advice when faced with a vicious adversary. Second, if someone steals from you, offer him more. Following this godly advice would eventually cause you to leave yourself with nothing. Third, give whatever someone asks from you. This advice could be deadly as well, depending on what the person asked for. Fourth, never ask for anything you gave away (Luke 6:29-30). All of these are good in principle, but there's no limit to them because people will definitely take advantage of someone following this advice to the letter. Thus, I feel the need to take it upon myself to encourage the few of you who want to obey Jesus to place reasonable limits on his philosophies. The majority of followers already know better than to obey Jesus in this instance. Yes, almost all Christians blatantly and hypocritically disregard many of the teachings provided by their Lord and savior simply because they're lethal, hazardous, or inconvenient.

Matthew 21:22 is Jesus' most damaging statement against the legitimacy of Christian faith. He says, "And all things, whatsoever ye shall ask in prayer, believing, ye shall receive." In other words, you will receive anything you pray for as long as you believe that you'll receive it. That statement is undeniably false, and we can easily demonstrate it as such. Apologists have tried to justify this statement over the years by postulating that Jesus' statement is true only if the request is in God's will. However, there is no biblical text supporting the inclusion of God's will into the words from Jesus' mouth. He says if you believe, you will receive. End of story.

If a request were already in God's will, however, what impact would the prayer truthfully have? If the request isn't in God's will, he won't answer it no matter how much one prays. Thus, God's will, not prayer, is the sole determining factor for future events. Once again, since it's impossible to shift from the future that God envisioned at the beginning of time, prayer can have no effect on the outcome. Even so, Jesus repeats this promise no less than three additional times in John's Gospel (14:12-14, 15:7, 16:23-24). The red text is there for everyone to see these claims. I really can't emphasize enough how damaging these statements are toward the assertion that Christianity is a legitimate faith.

Iron: God's Kryptonite

The Bible contains farces that even an act of God cannot explain. After the creation, God asks Adam to look over the animals and find one "suitable" for him (Genesis 2:18-20). The all-knowing god is absolutely clueless as to what kind of partner Adam might desire. Did he not already realize that he was going to make a woman for him? Isn't it also disgusting for God to propose that Adam should find an animal to be his sexual companion?

Two additional stories in Genesis seem relevant to about every topic we cover: Noah and Babel. During Noah's flood, God kills almost the entire world population of humans and animals because the people are evil. Why would an omniscient god lack the common sense to get his creation right the first time so that he isn't required to redo everything? Afterwards, he promises to never do it again because humans are evil (Genesis 8:21). As stated before, God admits that the flood solved nothing. Several years later, groups of people assemble to build a tower so that they can see God in Heaven. Since God doesn't like this seemingly impossible idea of people spotting him, he confuses their language to cease construction on the tower (Genesis 11:1-8). The people may not have realized that God didn't actually live on top of a dome over the earth, but God should have been aware of this information for obvious reasons. We've looked deep into space with telescopes, but God didn't stop us on those endeavors. Why would he think that these primitive people could see him? Is this when he moved from the earth's dome to the outer boundaries of the universe? What about all the other authors who claim to have caught a glimpse of God? The Tower of Babel myth is definitely one of the most absurd stories ever told. Even so, a good portion of the world still ignorantly accepts it as truth. That's a shame, too.

Later in Genesis, God asks himself if he should hide his plans for destroying Sodom from Abraham (Genesis 18:17). Why would God not know what he's going to do, and how could Abraham's knowledge of the matter have any possible outcome on God's ultimate decision to exercise his infinite power? On the other hand, perhaps God has good reason to worry since we've already established that he isn't all-knowing or all-powerful as the Bible claims.

When God is preparing to go on another murdering spree, he tells the people of Israel to smear blood on their doors so that he'll know which homes are occupied by his chosen people (Exodus 12:13). With this directive completed, he's free to kill all the Egyptian firstborn male children without accidentally harming an Israelite, but why does he need blood on the doors to serve as a reminder if he knows everything? Jonah, like Cain before him, was able to leave the presence of God (Jonah 1:3). According to Zephaniah, God will search through Jerusalem with candles and find people who scoff at him (1:12). Why would God need candles to see in the dark?

Judges 1:19 says that God was with the men of Judah in a battle, yet they couldn't drive out the enemies because the other side was riding upon chariots of iron. If God is with someone, shouldn't this person be able to do the miracles that every other God-accompanied individual performs? Honestly, did authors bother to proofread their work centuries ago?

Whatever's Left

Since I couldn't think of a way to categorize many of the remaining biblical absurdities that I wanted to include, we'll just take a blitzkrieg approach at covering them. Abraham has a picnic with God (Genesis 18:1-8). Lot's wife is turned into salt for looking at the destruction of a city (Genesis 19:26). Jacob wrestles with God and defeats him (Genesis 32:24-30). God becomes a burning bush while talking with Moses (Exodus 3:3-4) and has intentions to murder Moses' son because he wasn't circumcised (Exodus 4:24-26). God will kill Aaron if he goes to minister without wearing a golden bell and blue pomegranates (Exodus 28:31-35). God says that we can cure leprosy by killing a bird, putting the bird's blood on another bird, killing a lamb, wiping the lamb blood on the leper, and killing two doves (Leviticus 14). A storm is stopped because Jonah is tossed into the sea (Jonah 1:15). God says that he will eat some people like a lion (Hosea 13:8). God stands on a wall and hangs a plumb line in front of Amos (Amos 7:7-8). This people-eating god decides to reveal himself to Amos via a plumb line demonstration but not to all the people currently killing each other over who is holding his true book!

God says that Joshua's army can destroy the city walls of Jericho by marching around them and blowing horns (Joshua 6). Wine makes God happy, or at least that's what the vine says (Judges 9:13). Samson claims his strength originates from his long hair (Judges 16:17). David buys Saul's daughter with two hundred foreskins (1 Samuel 18:27). People who don't believe in a god fail to do anything good (Psalms 14:1, 53:1). People are cured from their illnesses by touching Paul's handkerchiefs and aprons (Acts 19:12). A person who eats only vegetables is weak (Romans 14:2). It's wrong to take a dispute into court (1 Corinthians 6:6-7). Nature teaches us that it's shameful for a man to have long hair (1 Corinthians 6:11-14). Anyone who doesn't confess Christ is an antichrist who deceives others (2 John 1:7). If you don't repent your sins, Jesus will attack you with the sword in his mouth (Revelation 2:16). As a way of discerning people, the righteous eat all they want while the wicked don't have anything to eat (Proverbs 13:25). What correlation does eating have with faith? Are Ethiopians wicked? Is that why God allows thousands of them to die every day?

All Of This Is In The Bible?

I hope this chapter has brought some of the absurdities contained within the Bible to your attention. As I stated earlier, this is a mere fraction of those actually told by the Christian text. I encourage you to do an impartial reading of the Bible and consider the others you will no doubt encounter.

Many of the referenced passages in this paper were guided by superstition and deceitfulness on the part of the authors, particularly those of the Pentateuch. Even Jesus made absurd statements because he was ignorant of many aspects of human behavior. When absurdities like these appear in other religions, no Christian would think twice about the validity of the events because no Christian is conditioned to accept those sources as absolute and unquestionable truth. As a result, they immediately dismiss the fictitious accounts. Because, and only because, the aforementioned absurdities are in the Bible, Christians fully accept the comical blunders out of fear and ignorance.

As it stands, people were a lot less knowledgeable hundreds of years ago. They had no reason to disbelieve the accounts of God and were very much afraid to make statements as bold as the ones in this book. Conversely, Christians continue the tradition of blindly accepting whatever the Bible says even though we know the problems are there. Like the careless and negligent ostriches of the biblical universe, everyone has seemingly buried their heads deep in the desert sand.

A Different Future

Prophetical books were presumably included in the Bible to offer the reader insight into the days of supernatural extravaganzas yet to come. Fortunately, the test of time has shown the majority of these bleak prophecies to be total bunk. In fact, there hasn't been a single verifiable prophecy fulfillment outside of those incredibly obvious to predict. As a few notable zealots have often altered clear meanings of specific terms or taken passages out of context in order to create biblical intent in lieu of their agendas, we'll take a realistic approach toward studying the fulfillments in question so that you can better understand why the apologetic methods of interpretation aren't reliable.

Even Jesus was among those guilty of making false prophecies. The most condemning of such prophetic statements were his predictions of a return to earth during the long-passed era that he designated. Even though you've no doubt been repeatedly told that the Bible doesn't indicate when Jesus is going to make his return, such statements are demonstrably false. The truth is that Jesus failed to follow through on the promises unambiguously included in the text as his own words. I imagine such a bold declaration may be difficult to swallow at first for two primary reasons: you've received an overwhelming wealth of information to the contrary, and it seems that Christianity would crumble at Jesus' failure to reappear. Probably for these very same reasons, early Christians found a way to circumvent the problem and convince their associates not to renounce his imminent return.

Prophecies Yet To Be Fulfilled

We'll initiate our discussion of the future according to the Bible by looking at prophecies very unlikely to be fulfilled due to a variety of current circumstances. Isaiah predicts, "Damascus is taken away from being a city, and it shall be a ruinous heap" (17:1). Damascus, the largest city in Syria with a population of sixteen million inhabitants, is now the most ancient capital in the world. It's highly unlikely that Damascus will be in ruins any time in the foreseeable future unless massively cataclysmic natural forces are doing the destruction. In such a scenario, we should deem Isaiah's conjecture as painfully obvious with respect to the eventuality of these types of predictions. Nature will inevitably drive all cities to

169

become ruinous heaps, but not in a manner shocking enough to warrant special mention from an infallible prophet.

Isaiah also warns, "for the nation and kingdom that will not serve [God] shall perish" (60:12). I agree 100% with his assessment, but to reiterate, nations and kingdoms won't perish based on their refusal to worship Isaiah's interpretation of God. Nations and kingdoms will eventually fade from existence because it's the nature of a dynamic global society. Countries are established, conquered, and reconquered in continuous cycles. If we leave the verse alone in its obvious intention of conveying a causal relationship between the downfall of a region and its refusal to worship God, we should note that this prophecy remains unfulfilled.

Isaiah, Ezekiel, and Zechariah offer an additional geographical speculation by guessing that the Nile River will eventually run dry (19:5, 30:12, and 10:11, respectively). The Nile is currently the largest river in the world and has never given any indication to reinforce the claims of these three prophets, but again, nature will take care of the Nile one day. What factor of this natural event is important enough to warrant special consideration? Every river will cease to run at some point; every mountain will crumble to the ground one day; every living being will be erased from existence after a matter of time. Such developments will play out in natural cycles, not because oblivious ancients prophesied that they would take place.

Ezekiel also expresses that a time will arrive when the people of Israel "shall dwell safely therein" (28:26). It seems rather obvious that every country would enjoy an era of peace at some point during its existence. Ironically, Israel is one of the few to fail in ever obtaining this luxury. Based on events from the past few decades, the chances of Israel realizing Ezekiel's promise don't seem to be improving. Instead of peace and freedom, the country has witnessed the occupation of several foreign states, such as Rome and Palestine.

Jeremiah predicts, "...at that time they shall call Jerusalem the throne of the Lord; and all the nations shall be gathered unto it, to the name of the Lord, to Jerusalem" (3:17). To paraphrase, every country will come together and worship the Hebrew god one day. Barring a return of the universe's creator to set the record straight on which religious interpretation is, indeed, correct, there will certainly *never* be only one religion. Every passing year produces a growing and diversifying number of beliefs, sects, denominations, and cults. Even if God *did* appear before us, as I proposed before, many countries and religious groups would absolutely refuse to accept the truth because it's [insert the local evil spirit here] trying to tempt them away from the true god(s).

Prophecies That Cannot Be Fulfilled

The prophets of the Old Testament also offer several predictions that are either provably false or unattainable due to the constraints placed upon them. In addition, there are several still-outstanding prophecies that cannot be fulfilled due to cultural changes that have taken place since the prophets recorded their predictions.

Isaiah and Jeremiah both speculate that Babylon will never be reinhabited after its fall in 689 BCE (13:19-20 and 50:35-39, respectively). Withstanding the wisdom of God's appointed speakers, Nebuchadnezzar II reconstructed the city less than a century later. Babylon would thrive until Alexander the Great conquered the city in 330 BCE. Isaiah and Jeremiah have unquestionably demonstrated their prophetic incompetence once again. Why has God provided his inspiration to those who transmit blatantly false information to their readers? Well, this magnificent holy invention of the people is flawed as well because God says he'll make Babylon "perpetual desolations" in Jeremiah 25:12. I suppose the all-knowing god of perfection prefers to demonstrate his changing desires instead of his omniscience.

Jeremiah declares Hazor to be a region of enduring desolation while it serves as a dwelling place for dragons (49:33). As common sense told you before reading contrary information in the Bible, there's no reliable reason to accept the existence of mythological dragons at any point in the past. Furthermore, Citadels remained in Hazor until the first century BCE. Nevertheless, as I've mentioned before, predicting that a city will undergo desertion is as easy as predicting that the sun will shine tomorrow. Nature will eventually satisfy these vague and unconditional predictions.

Jonah also enjoyed a short six-verse stint as a reliable prophet. In 3:4, he says Nineveh will be overthrown in forty days. However, God scratches the foretold destruction of the city in 3:10. This is an extraordinary example demonstrating the flaws even the "divinely inspired" carry over into their works. If Jonah was stimulated to write an outright mistake, what falsehoods *without* subsequent corrections may have found their way into the text? Being swallowed by a fish, perhaps?

Egypt, the former nemesis of Israel, has predictably found itself at the losing end of several Old Testament forecasts. Jeremiah tells us that God will kill all the Israelites migrating into Egypt "by the sword, by the famine, and by the pestilence and none of them shall remain or escape from the evil that I will bring upon them" (42:15-18). Even so, I believe we can be reasonably certain that people from Israel have journeyed into Egypt without suffering God's wrath. Since Egypt is no longer an archenemy of Israel, would God even display his anger at the Israelites for trying to get along with their neighbors? Correspondingly, Isaiah predicts that there will be five cities in Egypt to undergo a language conversion to the Canaanite tongue (19:18). This prophecy has failed to be the least bit accurate, and the language of the Canaanites is now dead. There's virtually no chance a dead language would make an appreciable return, much less one triumphant enough to satisfy the conditions Isaiah has set forth.

A few verses later, Isaiah alludes to a coalition among Egypt, Assyria, and Israel (19:23-25). This affiliation has also failed to take place, and Assyria is no longer a nation. Even if Assyria reformed and made a pact with modern-day Egypt and Israel, the new Assyria wouldn't necessarily be valid toward fulfilling the prophecy because it's not the same country to which Isaiah was clearly referring. If this man truly had a gift for seeing the future, one would certainly expect him to mention such a significant detail. If Isaiah wasn't divinely inspired with futuristic knowledge, one might expect him to earn the same low success rate as you or me for predicting the future. So you must ask yourself, which of these two scenarios have we witnessed thus far?

Isaiah also informs Jerusalem of a time when the "uncircumcised and the unclean" will no longer visit the city (52:1). This transcendentally imposed impediment has yet to be set in effect, and there's no credible reason to believe it ever will. The notion of "uncircumcised equals unclean" is superstitious, ancient, and nonsensical. We can reasonably assume that uncircumcised men have consistently resided in Jerusalem since its foundation. The chances of a government passing a law in this modern age in order to enforce such senseless views are exceedingly remote. Besides, Jerusalem has much larger problems to contend with than the condition of its male inhabitants' reproductive organs.

Ezekiel purports God making claims that the Ammonites will be "no more remembered" (21:32). The difficulty with accepting this bold declaration is the very act of this statement's inclusion into the Bible. Ironically, the Bible would need to become obsolete if we were truly to forget the Ammonites. If this happens, however, the prophecy is no longer of importance because no one will remember it! God seriously fouled up on the logical consequences of this one.

Amos and Ezekiel claim that the Israelites will enjoy a permanent place of residency while God protects them from encroaching enemies (9:15 and 34:28-29, respectively). First, the Israelites have never enjoyed a home of undisputed territory. Second, we've never witnessed God lifting a finger to save the hapless Israelites from their enemies. Third, this omnipotent being apathetically watched in unnervingly lonesome silence as Hitler exterminated his chosen people by the millions. With these facts in mind, suggesting that God protects the Israelites in some immeasurable fashion is disturbingly wicked.

A common underlying theme of false biblical prophecy is the prediction that all these events are to take place sometime in the immediate future. Joel, Obadiah, and Zephaniah claim that the day of reckoning is "near" (2:1, 1:15, and

1:14, respectively). Keep in mind that the human race was supposedly only 3500 years old during the lives of these prophets. As was the case for Peter defending the actions of the multilingual disciples, it would be erroneous and extremely foolish to assume that there was any implication "near" could have meant 2500+ years from the time that such allegations were made. These predictions failed, and they will certainly continue to fail. Although these instances do a sufficient job of removing credibility from biblical scribes, we'll look at some much more devastating "near" prophecies very shortly.

Isaiah 7:14

The Old Testament contains a seemingly endless list of scriptures that Christians point to as references for the foretelling of Christ. Since there's no reliable evidence that anyone can predict the future to a respectable degree of accuracy, the burden of proof is on those who assert that people capable of this gift once existed. As you should already be able to tentatively conclude that the Old Testament prophets were void of this talent, you might have quickly deduced that apologists have taken these verses out of context or ran some translatory manipulation on them in order to make the upcoming proposals feasible.

From my experiences, I've noted approximately fifty passages consistently used to support the quasi-reality of a fulfilled prophecy. Since debunking all these claims would require a retort lengthy enough to lose the majority of the audience's attention, we'll analyze what I feel are the ten most popular claims that biblical apologists offer in defense of prophecy realizations. Unless you wish to do some independent research on the validity of these reports, you'll have to trust me again when I say that not one of the overlooked passages has any more foundation in reality than the ones discussed at length in this chapter.

We'll begin with the verse that I believe Christians most commonly cite as a prophecy fulfillment. Isaiah 7:14 reads, "A virgin shall conceive, and bear a son, and shall call his name Immanuel." Even so, the claim of a prophecy fulfillment fails miserably due to both context and content of the message.

Let us consider the content of Isaiah 7:14 first. In this passage, the English word *virgin* was translated from the Hebrew word *almah*. However, the most accurate term in the Hebrew language for conveying a sexually untouched woman is *betula*. *Almah* is a general term for a young woman, not necessarily a virgin. If Isaiah wanted his audience to believe that a virgin was going to give birth to a child, he had a much better word at his disposal. One would do well to think that he should utilize this more specific term for such a unique event so that his contemporaries wouldn't first have to know that he was invoking the much less anticipated, potentially vague meaning of *almah*. Furthermore, Proverbs

30:19 is extremely detrimental to the *virgin* translation of *almah*: "The way of an eagle in the air; the way of a serpent upon a rock; the way of a ship in the midst of the sea; and the way of a man with [an *almah*]." Since the term doesn't necessarily mean *virgin*, one must look for the obvious connotation of the original Hebrew word. With this responsibility in mind, virgins don't have children. In all reasonable likelihood, *almah* refers to a young woman in this passage. Even so, Matthew 1:23 may have tried to relate the Immanuel birth to Jesus by altering the obvious content of the Old Testament prophecy. Ironically, even the Greek word *parthenos* used in Matthew doesn't necessarily mean *virgin*, as repeatedly demonstrated in Homer's *Iliad*.

A second and seemingly more overlooked clue in the passage's content is the name of the child, Immanuel. To put it in the simplest of terms, Jesus' name wasn't Immanuel. The fact that Immanuel means "God with us" doesn't make one iota of difference because hundreds of Hebrew names have references to God. For example, Abiah means "God is my father," which, in my opinion, would have been slightly more impressive. The verse plainly declares that she "shall call his name Immanuel," but the so-called Messiah's mother called him Jesus.

As for the contextual misapplication of Isaiah 7:14, one must read the chapter in its entirety since this supposed prophecy is part of a larger story. Within this passage, a battle is about to begin in which Rezin and Pekah are planning to attack Ahaz. God informs Ahaz that he may ask for a sign as proof that this battle will never ensue. Ahaz is reluctant to put God to a test, but Isaiah interjects and declares that there will be a sign. God will reaffirm his reliability on the issue when a young woman gives birth to a son named Immanuel who will eat butter and honey. Before this boy can choose evil over good, the land will fall out of the grip of Rezin and Pekah.

We can continue studying context by reading ahead to Isaiah 8:3-4, where we find a prophetess who has recently given birth to a son. This is immensely more likely to be the child that Isaiah wanted us to believe he predicted, especially when you figure in the fact that Isaiah 7:14 uses the more specific term *ha-almah*, translated as *the* woman, to specify a particular woman most likely known by the author and his audience.

When you consider the most accurate translation of *almah*, the actual name of the child, the context of the message, and the contiguous birth of an ordinary child, this passage is in a different ballpark from reports of Jesus' birth from his virgin mother. Even though the case for Isaiah 7:14 appears solidly shut, we should consider two more questions. If Isaiah wanted to predict a virgin birth story, wouldn't he have drawn more attention to the most important and unique event in human history? If God were truly interested in convincing more people of Jesus' authenticity, wouldn't he have Isaiah make a more direct and less disputable prophecy?

More Alleged Prophecy Fulfillments

A lesser-known prophecy made by Isaiah reads, "for unto us a child is born, unto us a son is given: and the government shall be upon his shoulder: and his name shall be Wonderful, Counseller, The mighty God, The everlasting Father, The Prince of Peace" (9:6). This sounds like the version of Jesus we've all heard, but where is the textual evidence of a link between him and this verse? The Jews have always maintained that this passage, full of usual praises given to a King, refers to King Hezekiah. Furthermore, the following verse says that this individual will run the government with great power while sitting upon the Throne of David. Jesus never sat upon a throne or ran a government "upon his shoulder." Since a plethora of circumstances could make bits and pieces of a prophecy come true, a divinely inspired prediction for the future should be clear and accurate in all of its details if we are to accept the legitimacy of such a bold statement.

We can also find another supposed reference to Jesus as the subject of Isaiah 53. In the last part of Chapter 52, God mentions one of his servants who will be exalted, only to be later despised, rejected, oppressed, afflicted, imprisoned, judged, acquainted with grief, wounded for our sins and transgressions, and loaded with iniquities. The man in question was sans deceit or violence. On the surface, there seems to be a strong correlation with Jesus; once we vigorously inspect all the facts, the analogy once again fails. One of the poorest translations possible fuels the misdirection. The grief acquainted with this servant is actually sickness, from the Hebrew word *choli*. God "putting our iniquities on him" is better translated as "hurting him with our sin," as if to punish him. Furthermore, this superior translation parallels better with the physical injuries he sustained in the previous verse. The *children* this man had (Hebrew word *zera*) are direct descendants, not a spiritual family as it has been suggested in order to add credence to apologetic claims. Finally, Isaiah claims that the oppressed and afflicted man never opened his mouth. How can such a statement apply to Jesus who did a *lot* of preaching and correcting? Can we honestly state with reasonable certainty that this was a divinely inspired passage referring to Jesus Christ?

The delusional author of Matthew would like for the reader to believe that Jeremiah correctly predicted the timeframe of Jesus' birth by asserting that a girl named Rachel crying for her dead children is a reference to King Herod's alleged child massacre in the era of Jesus' birth (Matthew 2:17-18 referring to Jeremiah 31:15). First and foremost, no historian contemporaneous with Herod's reign ever mentioned this incredible act of brutality. In addition, if you continue to read the passage Matthew referenced, as all honest researchers should, you'll discover God telling Rachel that their deaths were not in vain because the people will return to their homeland (31:16-17). With a modest background in Ancient

Middle Eastern history, one can easily surmise that the passage in Jeremiah refers to the Babylonian captivity, not the time of Jesus' birth. Since there are no true prophecies of Jesus' arrival, apologists must resort to grasping straws that appear increasingly remote.

Daniel 9:24-27 proclaims that in seven sets of seventy weeks (490 weeks), a ruler will arrive and reconstruct a city. The Hebrew word for week, *septad*, actually means *sevens*, but the Israelites commonly used the term to refer to a set of seven days. In order for the upcoming prophecy to fit, disingenuous apologists must alter the obvious meaning of *septad* to *seven years* in quintessential *post hoc* fashion. Nevertheless, even if we give the benefit of the miniscule doubt to the apologists and assume that *septad* refers to a set of seven years, the arrival of this ruler would take place in 55 BCE. We know the starting point of the time in question because the passage refers to Cyrus' order of cleansing the city in 545 BCE. Thus, prophecy inventors must once again alter the obvious intent of the passage and claim that Cyrus' heir, Artaxerxes, was the one who gave the order. This puts the new date of arrival around 39 CE, approximately seven years after the presumed death of Jesus. Next, the apologist must shorten the length of a year by averaging the length of a solar year and the length of a lunar year in order to make the prophecy fit nicely with the year of the crucifixion. Even when you allow all of these absurd leniencies, there's no potent evidence to support the notion that this passage refers to Jesus in any way, shape, form, or fashion. Jesus wasn't a ruler, and he didn't rebuild any cities. Even so, a few Christian zealots would like the world to believe that this is a fulfilled prophecy. Would these same apologists bend over backwards to support the text if such statements were found in the Qur'an?

Hosea 6:2 reads, "after two days will he revive us: in the third day he will raise us up, and we shall live in his sight". This might seem to be another loose reference to the death and resurrection of Jesus if you haven't read the passage in its proper context. The preceding verse, an important piece of the whole picture, concerns a group of people who will return to God in order to be restored through him. After two days, God will revive the people; on the third day, they'll arise so that they can live in his sight. When a more thorough analysis replaces the shallow one, the reader will discover that the verse has nothing at all to do with Jesus. This claim of a prophecy fulfillment is just another use of a passage out of context in order to meet an apologetic agenda.

Hosea has another supposed Jesus prophecy in the first verse of Chapter 11: "When Israel was a child, then I love him, and called my son out of Egypt." This is supposedly an allegory for Mary and Joseph fleeing the country. In this case, Jesus would be represented in the verse by "Israel." If the reader takes time to review the next verse, as it would only be responsible to do so, the lack of merit in the apologetic interpretation becomes obvious. In 11:2, we learn that Israel sacrificed to

Baalim (Baal) and "burned incense to graven images." The Jesus of the scriptures certainly wouldn't be guilty of observing this blasphemous ceremony. A realistic investigation would lead us to believe that the verse is a certain reference to the Israeli Exodus from Egypt. As authors often refer to groups and countries in the singular form throughout the books of prophecy, this conclusion is far more sensible than the apologetic stretch.

Micah offers another Jesus foretelling of great popularity in the Christian crowd, but it fails to hold the aforementioned qualities of valid prophecy fulfillment for several reasons. The passage in question says, "but thou, Bethlehem Ephratah though you be little among the thousands of Judah, yet out of thee shall he come forth unto me that is to be ruler of Israel; whose goings forth have been from of old, from everlasting" (5:2). Once again, a quick sweep across the surface might lead the reader to believe that this verse is about Jesus' birth. Such an assertion is especially convincing with the inclusion of his hometown, Bethlehem, but you might wonder what role "Ephratah" serves in this passage. We can find the answer all the way back in 1 Chronicles 4:4. There, we learn that Bethlehem Ephratah was a person: Bethlehem, the son of Ephratah. In essence, the prophecy refers to the line of descendants from that individual. Even if we blindly assume that Ephratah was a more specific location within Bethlehem rather than a people, apologists still have the problem of Jesus never having ruled Israel. The authors of Matthew and John both conveniently leave Ephratah out of their references to this prophecy (2:5-6 and 7:42, respectively). This disingenuous act can only be the result of a desire to add credibility to an otherwise convincingly weak case. Furthermore, if the ones making this claim read to verse six, they would discover Micah predicting that this same individual will lead a battle against Assyria in order to deliver people out of slavery. No record of Jesus ever performing this noble deed exists, nor would we expect one to.

Zechariah informs us that a just King will arrive in Jerusalem riding upon an ass and a colt (9:9). In fact, Jesus *did* ride into Jerusalem on an ass and a colt according to the account given by Matthew (21:1-7). The primary problem of claiming a miraculously fulfilled prophecy in this instance is the awareness of Matthew and John (12:14-15) that Zechariah had made the prediction. The others involved, including Jesus, were almost certainly aware of the Old Testament passage as well. In fact, Matthew 21:4-5 says, "all this was done, that it might be fulfilled which was spoken by saying…thy King cometh unto thee, meek, and sitting upon an ass, and a colt the foal of an ass." To paraphrase Matthew, the disciples had Jesus ride into Jerusalem using this method just so that they could fulfill the prophecy. You must forgive me if I personally deem this quasi-actualization unimpressive. Had the group honestly been unaware of the forecast, there might be the slightest hint of some underlying validity for those presenting this claim.

For the final investigated prophecy, we'll switch gears away from Jesus for a moment. The author of Mark implies that the arrival of John the Baptist satisfies Malachi's prophecy of God sending Elias/Elijah forth "before the coming of the great and dreadful day of the Lord" (Mark 8:28 referring to Malachi 4:5). He makes this erroneous proposal because the observers thought John was the reincarnation of Elijah. Making people *think* something has happened isn't the same thing as the event actually taking place. Since John himself even denies being Elijah (John 1:21), we can safely assume that he's not involved with Malachi's prophecy.

I hope that these passages will be beneficial toward demonstrating the absence of a verifiable prophecy fulfillment concerning Jesus' birth or any other futuristic happenings. The fact that Jesus and the Gospel writers deceitfully invented their own prophecies and fulfillments, a charge we will now investigate, lends a hand to this assessment.

Jesus makes the claim that his persecution, death, and resurrection are realizations of an Old Testament prophecy (Luke 18:31-33). I assure you that there is no such statement in the Old Testament; I challenge anyone to find it. Jesus also claims that Moses foretold his arrival (John 5:46). Not only is it highly unlikely that Moses wrote any part of the Pentateuch, there's no mention of Jesus in that text either; I challenge anyone to find it. The author of Matthew says Jesus "dwelt in a city called Nazareth: that it might be fulfilled which was spoken by the prophets, He shall be called a Nazarene" (2:23). Not only do the prophets fail to offer such conjecture, there's not a passage in the Old Testament that includes a single word related to *Nazareth* or *Nazarene*; I challenge anyone to find it. Finally, the author of John claims that a prophecy was fulfilled when the bones of Jesus remained unbroken throughout the crucifixion (19:36). Again, there is no such prophecy in the Old Testament; I challenge anyone to find it. No one has brought forth and verified any information with the potential to lend credence to these fortune-telling products for obvious reasons.

The Return Prophecies

This is the part you've probably been anticipating. Did Jesus truly put a time-frame on when he would reappear? When he instructs his disciples to preach the good news on all their ventures, Jesus warns, "Ye shall be hated of all men for my name's sake: but he that endureth to the end shall be saved. But when they persecute you in this city, flee ye into another: for verily I say unto you, *Ye shall not have gone over the cities of Israel, till the Son of man be come*" (Matthew 10:22-23). In comprehensible modern English, Jesus is saying that he'll return to earth before the disciples finish their journeys to all of Israel's cities. The word of God has long completed its travel throughout the region, but Jesus continues to fail Promise Keeping 101.

When Jesus' disciples beg him to avoid any actions with fatal consequences, he comforts them by proclaiming, "For the Son of man shall come in the glory of his Father with his angels; and then he shall reward every man according to his works. Verily I say unto you, *There be some standing here, which shall not taste of death, till they see the Son of man coming in his kingdom*" (Matthew 16:27-28, also see Mark 9:1 and Luke 9:27). In this instance, Jesus unambiguously informs his followers that there were people living on the earth *at that time* who would still be alive when he made his ultimate return.

While preaching to his disciples, Jesus says, "Immediately after the tribulation of those days shall the sun be darkened, and the moon shall not give her light, and the stars shall fall from heaven, and the powers of the heavens shall be shaken: And then shall appear the sign of the Son of man in heaven: and then shall all the tribes of the earth mourn, and they shall see the Son of man coming in the clouds of heaven with power and great glory. And he shall send his angels with a great sound of a trumpet and they shall gather together his elect from the four winds, from one end of heaven to the other...Verily I say unto you, *This generation shall not pass, till all these things be fulfilled*" (Matthew 24:29-34, Mark 14:24-30). Aside from projecting scientifically erroneous notions, Jesus yet again gives a proclamation that includes his return during *that* generation.

In a scene involving Jesus with the high priest, "the high priest arose, and said unto him, 'Answerest thou nothing? what is it which these witness against thee?' But Jesus held his peace. And the high priest answered and said unto him, 'I adjure thee by the living God, that thou tell us whether thou be the Christ, the Son of God.' Jesus said unto him, 'Thou hast said: nevertheless I say unto you *Hereafter shall ye see the Son of man sitting on the right hand of power, and coming in the clouds of heaven*'" (Matthew 26:62-64, also see Mark 14:60-62). Jesus informs the priest that he will personally witness the imminent return of the son of God and gives clear indication that these events will transpire while the high priest is still alive. The high priest is long dead, and Jesus has been truant for nearly 2000 years.

Speaking to a crowd of Pharisees, Jesus preaches about a series of events destined to come upon them that inevitably conclude with their damnation to Hell (Matthew 23). When will these scenarios play out? "Verily I say unto you, *All these things shall come upon this generation*" (Matthew 23:36). The connotation is clear: the events mentioned throughout the chapter were to take place during the lifetimes of those living in *that* generation. In order to defend Jesus' statement, some Christians claim that the makers of the KJV Bible should have translated the Hebrew word *genea* as *age* or *race*. While modern lexicons may support this translation for the very same reason that Christians believe it, what evidences contemporaneous with the era do they have to support this assertion? Nowhere in the New Testament did the translators interpret *genea* to be anything other than *generation*. The obvious choice of translation is also consistent with all other failed return prophecies. Again, they begin with the faulty premise of inerrancy and search for the most likely way to maintain this quality. What religion *wouldn't* survive an infallibility test given such luxurious leniencies?

The celebrated Paul was also convinced that the arrival of Jesus was drawing near. In his letter to the Romans, he says, "now it is high time to awake out of sleep: for now is our salvation nearer than when we believed. The night is far spent, the day is at hand" (13:11-12). In his first letter to the Corinthians, he says, "the time is short" (7:29). In his letter to the Philippians, he says, "The Lord is at hand" (4:5). In his first letter to the Thessalonians, Paul reminds them that "the Lord himself shall descend from heaven with a shout, with the voice of the archangel, and with the trump of God: and the dead in Christ shall rise first: Then we which are alive and remain shall be caught up together with them in the clouds, to meet the Lord in the air: and so shall we ever be with the Lord" (4:16-17). Paul clearly held an unwavering belief that some of those living at the time would serve as witnesses to these divine occurrences. As you will see in the upcoming chapter, however, Paul was making predictions for Jesus' *primary* visit to the earth, long after his alleged crucifixion during a prehistorical era. Nowhere did Paul mention a "return" because nowhere did Paul claim any knowledge of Jesus' earthly residency as told in the Gospels.

A variety of other New Testament authors also believed that Jesus was returning soon. "The day of Christ is at hand" (2 Thessalonians 2:2). "God…hath in these last days spoken unto us by his Son" (Hebrews 1:1-2). "For ye have need of patience, that, after ye have done the will of God, ye might receive the promise. For yet a little while, and he that, shall come will come, and will not tarry" (Hebrews 10:36-37). "Be ye also patient; stablish your hearts: for the coming of the Lord draweth nigh" (James 5:8). "Who verily was foreordained before the foundation of the world, but was manifest in these last times for you" (1 Peter 1:20). "The end of all things is at hand" (1 Peter 4:7). "Little children, it is the last time: and as ye have heard that antichrist shall come, even now are there many antichrists; whereby we know that it is the last time" (1 John 2:18). "The Revelation of Jesus Christ, which God gave unto him, to shew unto his servants things which must shortly come to pass; and he sent and signified it by his angel unto his servant John…Blessed is he that readeth, and they that hear the words of this prophecy, and keep those things which are written therein: for the time is at hand" (Revelation 1:1-3). "I come quickly" (Revelation 3:11, 22:7, 22:12, 22:20). Jesus wasn't the only one on a train bound for misdirection.

The second book of Peter, penned around 120 CE and probably the last of the New Testament Epistles to be completed, came at the heel of the generation promise allegedly made by Jesus. His followers were no doubt starting to become impatient, and they demonstrate a hint of restlessness by inquiring, "Where is the promise of his coming?" (3:4). In order to settle doubts and downplay the "generation" claims, Peter says, "be not ignorant of this one thing, that one day is with the Lord as a thousand years, and a thousand years as one day" (3:8). Unfortunately, Peter's explanation satisfies absolutely nothing. Not once did Jesus offer a return date in terms of days and years. However, Jesus *does* give us a rough timeframe in reference to generations and lifetimes. Jesus did not satisfy the conditions that he personally established in order for all his future worshippers to appreciate. Peter's speculative assertion is an incredibly futile attempt at solving Jesus' perpetual absence.

Looking At The Fortune Tellers

This chapter demonstrates several important points: prophets of the Old Testament made predictions that have yet to come true; predictions made by those same prophets are either erroneous or impossible to fulfill; there are no prophecies from the Old Testament truly satisfied by the alleged arrival of Jesus Christ; Jesus and the Gospel writers invented supposed prophecy fulfillments; Jesus failed to return within the timeframe he promised; and it was commonly believed that Jesus was going to return about 1900 years ago. These factors inevitably subtract even *more* credibility from the authors' claims of divine inspiration.

While we shouldn't honestly expect a self-proclaimed prophet to have the ability to predict the future with any appreciable accuracy, there should be an elevated level of expectation for those who Christians claim that God divinely inspired. The Old Testament prophets are nowhere near meeting this reasonable expectation. What we *do* see is a Nostradamus-like *post hoc* set of poor explanations and analyses of old scriptures undoubtedly designed to invent prophecy fulfillments. Thus, we can conclude that not one of the prophets truly mentions anything interpretable as the supposed arrival of Jesus. Bits and pieces extracted from here and there do not add up to a verifiable resolution of this indispensable difficulty.

Jesus Christ did not satisfy any prophecies made in the Old Testament, and some of the prophetical forecasts that he and the Gospel writers claim as fulfilled weren't even included by any known preceding authors. If we are to consider Jesus' biblical proclamations accurate, he undeniably made several statements requiring him to return within the century. As further evidence in support of this conclusion, there was a consensus among the alleged divinely inspired authors that Jesus would be returning extremely soon. When people thought that the earth was only 4000 years old, "soon" did not mean 2000+ years later, nor will it mean 20,000+ or 200,000+ years later when those times inevitably arrive undisturbed. In short, Jesus defiantly broke his promise of returning. This brings us to wonder how many of Jesus' quotes and workings we can actually consider for the realm of historical plausibility. Consequently, we will explore this essential consideration of utmost importance in the next shocking chapter.

THE FIGURE BEHIND THE LEGEND

The paramount aspect of Christian faith is the unwavering belief that a man named Jesus from Nazareth was the supernatural son of God. This character performed a variety of incredible miracles and attributed their possibility to the faith that his followers held in his Heavenly father. Such an extraordinary being would eventually be crucified for his teachings, as the story goes, only to follow through on his promises of resurrecting from death and returning to his disciples shortly thereafter. Before his ultimate reunion with God, he pledges to redescend one day in order to take all those with him who believe in following his examples. Suffice to say, this is the mother of all extraordinary cultish claims requiring extraordinary evidence. Consequently, this chapter will review all pertinent biblical and extrabiblical evidence that casts doubt on these wild assertions.

At the present, it's honestly impossible to verify or dismiss Jesus as a real person because we lack evidence and crucial eyewitness testimony. Thus, the Christian belief of Jesus being a true historical figure is entirely predicated upon blind faith. Even if we assume a successful completion of an endeavor to legitimize a historical Jesus who lectured on various subjects of life, the burden of proof would still be on the shoulder of the apologist to prove the typical claims of outlandish miracles. Thus, it's these allegations of mystic performances that are relevant to our analysis.

If Jesus Christ was merely an ordinary man with extraordinary teaching abilities, or if he was a legend born from the obvious necessities of turbulent times, the entire foundation of the New Testament quickly implodes. While we're still unable to offer the undeniable proof that contradicts these liberal Christian claims, we *can* easily demonstrate the incredibly overwhelming unlikelihood of Jesus ever having lived a life anything like the one depicted in the Gospels. Such an elementary presentation is, in fact, the intent of this chapter. For now, try to forget everything you know about Jesus Christ so that you may have the benefit of learning about this mysterious figure from a refreshingly unbiased perspective.

Paul's Jesus

The Apostle Paul composed the earliest known records mentioning the name Jesus Christ from 49-60 CE. Even if he truly realized an earthly Jesus, Paul's twelve-year span of writing falls outside the life of his subject. Thus, instead of providing an eyewitness account written while the miraculous events were still works in progress,

God apparently leaves us with a curious absence of any contemporaneous testimonies for Jesus' existence. In fact, there are absolutely no records of an earthly Jesus until several decades after his presumed legacy on earth ended with his crucifixion around 30 CE. We'll return to this essential consideration a little later.

Since Paul was the first known individual to write about Jesus, it seems quite peculiar that he chooses to abstain from mentioning any of the astounding miracles accomplished by his subject. By no means, however, is this consideration a conclusively modern discovery. The early church, notoriously recognized for its own redaction of future biblical works, may have noticed this glaring insufficiency and decided to interpolate four or five statements into Paul's work for a variety of potential reasons. Seeing as how greater than 99.9% of Paul's writings are shockingly void of details on Jesus' life, the handful of upcoming passages should already be held suspect.

Although we can attribute large portions of the New Testament to Paul, scholars have generally refuted the idea of one individual being responsible for the completion of the traditional Pauline works. Such is the case for the phrase "who before Pontius Pilate," which appears in the sixth chapter of 1 Timothy, one of the New Testament works certain to be a second century product. Thus, someone other than Paul likely wrote this passage during a time in which the Pilate story was already enjoying widespread circulation.

Let's begin our analysis of the authentic Pauline books with 1 Thessalonians 2:13-16. Verse 16 is, of course, highly controversial for its direct implication of the Jews as Jesus' murderers. Such an anti-Semitic passage is not only the most out of character of Paul's writings, but it also breaks up a cohesive passage in the letter. Try reading the chapter with an omission of these verses to see if you don't notice a much-improved flow of the text. In addition to the obvious tangent interjection thrown into the fray, the verse is typical of the early church's hatred toward the Jews. For these and some additional reasons far too complex to delve into here, the verse is widely regarded in scholarly circles to be an interpolation.

Another passage often referred to as the Lord's Supper appears in 1 Corinthians 11:23: "For I have received of the Lord that which also I delivered unto you, that the Lord Jesus the same night in which he was betrayed took bread." Four major points cast doubt on the likelihood of this passage referring to the earthly supper purported in the Gospels. First, Paul declares that he gained this knowledge through the Lord. In other words, he was divinely inspired to tell this part of the story. Why would God need to be the one to inform him of what must have been a widely distributed report? Nevertheless, I trust that you vividly remember how accurate these divine revelations tend to be. Second, Paul doesn't offer any seemingly essential details of location or company with the taking of bread. Third, we know final and sacrificial meals are common mythological tales in a variety of other world religions. Fourth, translators rendered the word *betrayed*, a supposed reference to the traitor Judas, from the Greek word *paredideto*, a term that should have been more accurately translated as *surrendered*. Otherwise, we see Jesus *betraying* his life for us in Ephesians 5:2. Such an idea obviously isn't consistent with the Gospel story of Jesus clearly *surrendering* his life to the Roman authorities. Likewise, no contemporaneous documents support the abused English translation of this passage. An individual who incompetently considered the postdated Gospel story was obviously responsible for committing this translatory blunder. For these reasons, there's no rationality in assuming that Paul was discussing a worldly event over a fantastical one. If Paul had finished his letters *after* the Gospels were written, we could reasonably conclude that he was referencing the corresponding Gospel texts. In reality, the Gospel writers arrived on the scene well after Paul and had free access to include this intuitively transcendental event at their own discretion.

A vague reference to Jesus dying and resurrecting quickly appears and fades in 1 Thessalonians 4:14, but Paul offers no crucial details to discern these two momentous developments from mythological episodes. 2 Timothy 1:9 says that God's grace "was given us in Christ Jesus before the world began." The combination of these two statements offers additional credence to the mythological Jesus hypothesis. According to this school of thought, Jesus died and returned in a spiritual form at some point in history long before the Common Era began. Similarly, most of the epistles refer to Jesus as an earthly spiritual presence instead of a formerly living individual. Based on the summation of these letters, it seems the popular belief was that Jesus' spirit had been present since the world began around 4004 BCE.

In his letter to the Galatians, Paul writes about his journey to Jerusalem and his subsequent rendezvous with Peter and James. Even so, he completely fails to relay any details about these crucially important meetings to his readers. The Gospels claim that his two new acquaintances were disciples and close friends of Jesus, yet Paul is completely silent on the subject of their paramount conversations. Surely, they would have been capable of telling him something worthy of writing down!

Because we should find it difficult to accept that Paul would be ignorant of the audience's desire to hear of Jesus' divine birth, teachings, miracles, exorcisms, crucifixion, and resurrection, we should consequently question why he exercises this stunning silence. As I see it, there are several possible reasons for this omission: he simply forgot to include details of Jesus' life in his enormous volume of work, God allowed the important documents detailing the life of Jesus to become mysteriously lost, Paul really *was* ignorant of what people wanted to hear, the events of Jesus' life were not remarkable enough to convey to the readers, or there was no earthly presence to report. We must also wonder why Paul wasn't able to locate someone else in the city who could personally testify to the physical existence of

Jesus Christ and the historical events surrounding his residency. Paul would have had the ability to meet with thousands who had witnessed Jesus' miracles, but what could these people possibly tell him about fantastic events that may have yet to become part of history?

We can find the most peculiar passage in Paul's works in his letter to the Romans. He informs them of the necessity in believing that God raised Jesus from the dead if they want to be saved (10:9). Why would they need to have faith in this phenomenon if there were hundreds of witnesses who could verify the legitimacy of the supernatural claim? The Romans would have had the benefit of studying their own records, listening to eyewitness testimony in Jerusalem, and performing their own investigational research to determine if the assertions of an earthly resurrection were true. However, Paul speaks to them as though they must take the belief by heart rather than through tests of research and validity. On the other hand, if Jesus was the spiritual presence of a mythical figure who resurrected ages ago, Paul's insistence on their blind faith is readily understandable. Furthermore, Paul recalls Elijah crying to God for killing his prophets in the next chapter. Could there have been a more perfect time to initiate a discussion on the crucifixion of the supreme prophet? Instead of undeniable inclusions of stories from Jesus' Gospel life, Paul's writings offer abstract concepts and ultra-sporadic references to vague events appearing independently from the most opportune times. Paul's chosen subject matter of a spiritual presence is extremely inconsistent with that of the Gospel writers' earthly savior.

A Wealth Of Missing Information

As I mentioned earlier, there are no existing records of Jesus made prior to 49 CE. This often-overlooked exclusion might be understandable, perhaps even anticipated, if there were no reputable historians or philosophers around to document the unique phenomena purported by the New Testament. However, this supposed explanation cannot be the case. The quintessential reason is Philo of Alexandria (approximately 15 BCE–50 CE), a devotedly religious Jewish philosopher with a volume of work sizable enough to fill a modern publication of nearly one thousand pages with small print. Even though he was adamant about the legitimacy of the Hebrew scripture, not once does he indicate that he knew the first thing about an earthly Jesus. However, Philo *did* choose to refer to the son of God in the form of *Logos*, which is to say a spiritual medium between God and man. As it stands in the biblical world, the supernatural son of the universe's almighty creator was supposedly performing unprecedented miracles and fulfilling prophecies that this philosopher spent his life analyzing, yet Philo, living well before Jesus' birth and well after the crucifixion, *never* mentions such occurrences! This fact alone should assuredly convince you that the Gospel authors based a great deal of their work on rumors, urban legends, and mere fiction.

Justus of Tiberias (approximately 35-100 CE), born in Galilee, is another fine example of a first century Jewish author who never offered Jesus one line of notation in his works. Justus made extensive historical writings on the Jewish war for independence and other contemporaneous events of local interest, but he never mentioned the name of Jesus *once*. This is undeniably remarkable. Was the earthly presence of the divine not important enough to merit a single mention? The purported rumors on the life of Jesus had at least sixty years to spread to Justus, but he totally neglected them. What possible reason could Justus have to ignore such pertinent information other than its nonexistence?

Pliny the Elder (23-79 CE), a scientist who wrote on a diverse number of subjects, never mentions any of the darkness or earthquake phenomena concurrent with Jesus' crucifixion. Since these events were within his interests of natural history, one would do well to suppose that these inexplicable calamities, if they took place, should have been of some interest to future generations.

Jerusalem born Josephus Flavius (approximately 37-100 CE) is a favorite reference among Christians for Jesus' earthly existence. While he wrote an enormous volume of work covering Jewish history and their ongoing wars, only two short passages out of the enormous 93 CE chronicles mention the name Jesus. As was the case for the handful of alleged references in Paul's works, we should impartially scrutinize these passages before accepting them as valid. As expected, this careful scrutiny demonstrates that the authenticity of these acknowledgements is highly questionable.

> About this time there lived Jesus, a wise man, if indeed one ought to call him a man. For he was one who performed surprising deeds and was a teacher of such people as accept the truth gladly. He won over many Jews and many of the Greeks. He was the Messiah. And when, upon the accusation of the principal men among us, Pilate had condemned him to a cross, those who had first come to love him did not cease. He appeared to them spending a third day restored to life, for the prophets of God had foretold these things and a thousand other marvels about him. And the tribe of the Christians, so called after him, has still to this day not disappeared (Antiquities 18).
> Festus was now dead, and Albinus was but upon the road; so he assembled the sanhedrim of judges, and brought before them the brother of Jesus, who was called Christ, whose name was James, and some others (Antiquities 20).

Out of several hundred pages of work, the preceding material constitutes everything Josephus supposedly had to say about the most important man to ever live. If the son of God were a true historical figure, one would anticipate a much broader explanation by the exhaustive historian.

The first passage raises concern for several reasons: only Christians referred to Jesus with the phrase "a wise man," and Josephus was not a Christian; other sections of Josephus' work are already known to have been altered by the church centuries after his death; the passage was discovered by Eusebius, a man widely known to have forged other material about Jesus; and no other Christian writers referenced the notable excerpt until two hundred years after its supposed documentation.

The second passage is also suspect for at least two additional reasons: even though Josephus was extremely meticulous about referencing his earlier work, the mention of Jesus in Antiquities 20 doesn't refer to the previous mention in Antiquities 18; and "Jesus called the Christ" was another phrase of Christian diction.

Since Josephus' writing style would have been easy to mimic after several days of transcribing, we can establish that there was opportunity in addition to the motive for interpolating foreign ideas into his chronicles. When researching the historicity of Jesus, we should obviously only consider the Antiquities with extreme caution. Even if someone were to prove the passages authentic, a possibility very much in doubt, the first mention of an earthly Jesus meekly appears more than sixty years following his alleged death and resurrection. It's wholly inconceivable to suggest that the life of Jesus was too insignificant to warrant earlier mention.

It wasn't until the second century when undeniable references to Jesus' life began to emerge. Pope Clement I alluded to the blood of Christ in a 101 CE letter to the Corinthians, but that's a vague crucifixion reference at best. Around the same time, Pliny the Younger and Trajan from Bithynia became the first to record the Christianity movement, but they strangely offer no details concerning an earthly life of the campaign's source. Instead, they merely reference other Christian works. Finally, in 107 CE, Ignatius mentions Jesus' birth from Mary during the reign of Herod and his execution ordered by Pontius Pilate. Ignatius was an adamant Christian, but he becomes yet another writer to offer only a crude synopsis of the world's most prominent figure. Suetonius mentions the name *Chrestus* around 110 CE, but there's no clear indication he intended to reference Jesus when he mentioned this common name. In 115 CE, Tacitus possibly becomes the first non-religious individual to include a somewhat complete account on the life of Jesus. Barnabas offers his readers some stories of Jesus' life around 120 CE, but he relies quite heavily on sources that we would later know as the Gospels. Likewise, Polycarp records additional history of Jesus around 130 CE with the inclusion of minor life events. The Gospel of Thomas (135 CE?) offers a complete record of Jesus' known sayings, but it ignores his birth, death, and resurrection.

Of all the writers who attempt to convert people with other faiths over to Christianity before 180 CE, only Justin (150 CE?) and Aristides (145 CE?) choose to include solid references to a historical Jesus. The rest focus their teachings entirely on the spiritual Jesus known by Paul. It would be foolish to assume that the balance of these missionaries would think such undeniably miraculous accomplishments wouldn't be essential in the conversion of those with contrasting religious beliefs. Again, we can only conclude that these authors were ignorant of Jesus' earthly residency or had good reason to consider the Gospels fraudulent. It should be clear by now that stories depicting Jesus on earth were either still in the creation process or considered unreliable by the vast majority of early Christians.

Making A Bible

Until the twentieth century came along, the Christian consensus maintained that the Gospel authors finished their works some time between 50-70 CE, a date based on the inclusion of vague references to the destruction of Jerusalem. With the exception of a few individuals refusing to budge from their own agendas, the Christian community has now conceded that this was an optimistic assessment. Their current estimations are now moving into the early end of the 70-120 CE spectrum provided by unbiased secular scholars. Although there's no direct evidence to contradict the early extreme of that assessment, I find it difficult to accept that no one would reference the Gospels through the first five decades of their existence. Thus, we must consider the Christian silence of the late first century and compare it to the movement's explosion in the early second century.

As a matter of personal opinion, I surmise that 100 CE is an approximate but fair designation (for reasons far too lengthy to discuss here) for the first Gospel. Essentially, one person's guess is as good as any, provided some impartial and unbiased research on the subject is involved. There's simply no foreseeable way for the Gospels to have positively affixed dates from the universally held 50-120 CE composite timeframe.

Even worse than not being able to date the scriptures, we can't be sure of who wrote them. The authors don't positively identify themselves by the names designated in the titles or by any other handle. In addition, not one of the authors claims to have personally known Jesus. This is no surprise for Mark and Luke, but Matthew and John were two of his disciples. Moreover, the Gospels are written in a manner hardly befitting of eyewitnesses: third person. Furthermore, there are no known original documents for the accounts, only copies. Since it's probable that several people handed the tales down via oral recitation before they were archived, thus the "Gospel According to *X*" designation preceding each one, we have a justifiable reason for the glaring complications and contradictions among the four books.

You may have noticed that I mentioned the Gospel of Thomas in the previous section, a reference definitely capable of arousing confusion for readers who have never researched early extrabiblical Christian writings. Instead of there only being four divinely appointed Gospel writers to represent the most important person ever to walk the earth, there were at least a dozen authors who claim to have a unique story about Jesus. Incidentally, there were about seventy-five known Gospels, epistles, and letters eligible for New Testament inclusion; a mere third of these made the cut. Since a number of the Gospels, such as James, Nicodemus, Mary, and Peter, weren't chosen to be enshrined in the Bible, you may be curious who made the decision to include only the four now-canonized versions of Jesus' life.

With the explosion of Gospel accounts in the second century, containment was an obvious priority for keeping the religion within reasonable limits. The first man known to have offered such a proposal on behalf of the church was Irenaeus of Lyon around 180 CE. His idea was to accredit only four Gospels because there were four zones of the world, four winds, four forms of living creatures, four divisions of man's estate, and four beasts of the apocalypse. For these poorly thought-out reasons, Irenaeus believed that there should only be four Gospels accepted by the church. As was the case for the horrendous slave-trading institution having its origins in superstitious nonsense, it certainly follows that the most potentially important books in human history would have been decided in a likewise manner. Instead of God providing an unquestionably fitting reason for these Gospel choices, we have a perfectly appropriate act of senselessness leading to the foundation of contemporary Christian faith. Yet, it's no wonder surrogate accounts, such as the Infancy Gospel, didn't make the cut when you consider that Jesus strikes his teachers and playmates dead for attempting to correct him.

Just like the apologists of every world religion, I could make the same bald assertion that the Infancy Gospel, along with Matthew, Mark, Luke, and John, had God's inspiration to make it 100% accurate. If anyone thinks that they can find a way to invalidate my claim, I'll simply generate a "how-it-could-have-been-scenario" that maintains the Gospel's inerrancy while paying no attention to the improbability and absurdity of my proposed solution.

What if Irenaeus accidentally omitted a fifth truthful Gospel that contained an additional prerequisite for entering into Heaven? Christians won't accept the stated extrabiblical requirement because there are four, not five, beasts of the apocalypse. I trust that you understand the fundamental flaw with the blatantly uncertain Christian system.

The Canonical Gospels

Most likely for no other reason than to round out the beasts of the apocalypse, John was chosen to be one of the four Gospels. For the sake of cohesive inerrancy, it would have been more beneficial in its absence. Although the author doesn't venture too far on a tangent from the life of Jesus depicted in the other canon Gospels, there are some distinguished omissions in this account. The most notable absences are the exorcism of devils, the recitation of the Lord's Prayer, Satan tempting Jesus in the wilderness, the transfiguration, the virgin birth from Mary, the Sermon on the Mount, Jesus' proclamations of his return, and every last one of the parables. Scholars agree that the original Gospel of John started at 1:19 and ended at 20:31. Furthermore, they've determined that the remainder of the book seems heavily edited and reworked. For these reasons, John fails to be an unquestionably reliable and synoptic source of divine inspiration for the story of Jesus.

Scholars unanimously agree that Mark is the most primitive of the four canon Gospels. Its details are relatively less developed, consequently making this biography of Jesus very brief. Interestingly, Jesus' primary biographer was obviously a distant Roman who never knew him. In fact, the original version of Mark doesn't even contain Jesus' appearance following his crucifixion (16:9-19)! This concession is made in the NIV but left out of the KJV. Even though the author was from Rome, he provided enough minor details to have a fair understanding of his subject. Why, then, would he leave out the indispensable element of the world's most important story unless he lived during a period without a resurrection rumor?

Since about 80% of the verses in Mark appear verbatim in Matthew, we can seemingly tell that the author of Matthew used Mark as a template when writing his own account. However, he alters many of Mark's details and adds several stories presumably unknown to its author. The Gospel of Matthew most certainly had a Jewish writer since he strives to correct many of the mistakes arising from Mark's ignorance of local knowledge. Since we have no clear evidence that the author of Matthew was one of Jesus' disciples, we can't rule out the likely possibility of its author simply plagiarizing the Mark account in order to make it more acceptable to residents of the Middle East. It's far too coincidental for the writings to match so well in some passages and contradict in others for there not to have been some minor transcribing taking place. Thus, we'll analyze the contrasting details of the two accounts in order to exemplify the unreliability of the latest God-inspired product.

Mark (1:2) makes an incorrect reference to Hebrew scripture by quoting Malachi 3:1 as being the work of Isaiah. The KJV does not contain this error, although biblical translations concerned more with honesty and accuracy than advancing inerrancy leave the misattribution in the text. Needless to say, the more knowledgeable Matthew author doesn't repeat Mark's mistake. Mark also claims that only God can forgive the sin of another (2:7), but that's a direct contrast to actual Jewish beliefs, which hold that other men can forgive sins as well. Again, Matthew drops this statement from the record (9:3). Mark mentions the region of Gadarenes being near a large body of water, but it's about thirty miles from even a sizable lake (5:1). The Matthew author, realizing that Mark knows next to nothing about local geography, changes Gadarenes to Gergesenes, which is only a few miles from a lake (8:28).

Mark mentions multiple "rulers of the synagogue" even though almost all synagogues only had a single leader (5:22). The Matthew author corrected this phrase so that the reader could ambiguously interpret it as having only one ruler (9:18). Mark records Jesus ridiculing the ancient food laws set by God and Moses (7:18-19), but the author of Matthew, being a Jew, no doubt considered this to be sacrilegious and dropped the passage from his account (15:18-20). Mark also has Jesus misquoting one of the commandments as refraining from defrauding others (10:19). Meanwhile, Matthew strictly adheres to the exact commandments of Moses by omitting this curious deception rule but including the "love one another" summary commandment (19:18-19). The author of Mark strangely refers to David as "our father" (11:10). This is something no Jew would ever do because all Jews weren't descendents of David. Seeing as how Abraham and Jacob would be the only individuals referred to in this manner, the desire for accuracy forces the Matthew author to correct another one of Mark's blunders (21:9).

Mark also gets the traditional date for killing the Passover incorrect (14:12), but the Matthew author settles the mistake by omitting the phrase from his own work (26:17). The very next verse in Mark has Jesus ordering two of his disciples to locate a man bearing a pitcher of water (14:13). In Jewish culture, carrying pitchers of water was the work of a woman. Naturally, Matthew must drop this phrase as well (26:18). On the night of the crucifixion, Mark says that it's the time before the Sabbath (15:42). Being a Roman, the author was obviously unaware that the Jewish day *begins* with the evening. Thus, the evening following the crucifixion wasn't the night before the Sabbath; it was the start of it. Matthew must yet again omit one of Mark's divinely inspired statements in the transcription (27:57). Unaware that the Sabbath had already arrived, Mark's account has Joseph of Arimathaea buying linen to wrap around Jesus' body (15:46). Because it was a sin to make purchases on the Sabbath, Matthew must consequentially drop that detail as well (27:59). Finally, Mark mentions "the fourth watch of the night" (6:48). The Jews actually divided the night into only *three* watches, while the Romans made the division into fourths.

The author of Matthew makes a few additional minor corrections from Mark's account, but I trust that you get the point I'm attempting to convey. However uncomfortable it may feel, the divinely inspired author of the earliest Jesus biography, who seemingly invented details out of thin air, knew very little about what he was writing.

The Gospel of Luke begins with a surmised admission that the author didn't personally experience any of the details contained within his account because he alleges the presence of eyewitnesses but fails to notify himself as one. Like Mark's Gospel, Luke was probably narrated by an individual residing far from Jerusalem because he commits several translational errors when converting Old Testament

Hebrew scripture into Greek. Additionally, in a manner similar to the way in which Mark was penned, Luke's author goes into extensive detail on his explanations of local phenomena but not those pertaining to Rome. Following the lead of Matthew's author, Luke's consistent duplication of Mark's verses seemingly indicates that he also relied heavily on that text when making his report. However, researchers soon discovered that they could not find 230 verses common to Matthew and Luke in the more ancient Mark.

The two more recent authors couldn't have derived identical verses from a sole source void of necessary information. Consequently, we can only surmise the hypothetical existence of an even earlier document used by all three authors as a template. This deduction would eventually become known as the Q hypothesis (from the German *Quelle*, meaning *source*). The canonical appearance of quotes from Thomas' Gospel reinforces the theoretical existence of Q. While Thomas was completed around the same time as John, it offered an entirely different perspective on the mystery of Jesus. Even though the Thomas account is nothing but a series of Jesus' sayings, it may help to explain the origin of other Gospel material. Thus, it's quite possible that a primitive set of quotes served as the foundation from which the Gospel legends arose. In such a scenario, the early Jews may have actually known a man who traveled about and shared his philosophies with a number of audiences. This individual may have even been executed for his heretical teachings. His followers would then collect these teachings on paper, only to later subject them to decades of human hyperbole.

The Conventional Idea

The whole concept of a male god and his son wasn't novel to the world when stories of Jesus began to emerge. Almost all preceding religions and philosophies contain a gender-ridden god of anger who speaks to his chosen people through an earthly medium, most often his son. It's somewhat amusing that the "one and only true God" would choose the exact same tired avenue of communication.

Historians refer to the original concept likely serving as a basis for the exaggerated Jesus as *Logos*, the communicating spiritual medium between a deity and its chosen people. The idea had been floating around for centuries prior to Jesus' arrival and probably started with the prophet Zarathustra who founded Zoroastrianism around 600 BCE.

Even more lethal to the Christian cause is the unoriginal nature of Jesus Christ himself. Around 3000 BCE, the ancient Egyptians had the Sun God Trinity of Atum (father), Horus (son), and Ra (holy spirit). When we take the Egyptian *Book of Vivifying the Soul Forever* into consideration, Jesus appears to be a mere carbon copy of Horus. Supporters of both beings claim that their respective subjects are the light of the world, the way, the truth, and the life; refer to them as good shepherds, lambs, and morning stars; claim that they are children of virgins; associate them with a cross and refer to them as Christ/Krst; claim that they have a revelation and bear witness to the world; claim that they initiate their educations at the age of twelve and have twelve followers; claim that they venture out on a boat with seven other passengers; and claim that they become baptized with water upon which they're miraculously able to levitate. There are few more parallels than what I've listed here, but they're rather loose. This analysis isn't one of those laughable lists in which an author is determined to parallel a given celebrity with the antichrist; these are two sons of gods from Middle Eastern religions, alike in an unforgettable abundance of ways. What evidence do we truly hold that we should reject one while we embrace the other?

The comparison of Jesus to other religious characters doesn't end with Horus. Hercules is another famous legendary figure consistently drawing parallels with Jesus. Both were products of the local primary god and a human mother; both had members of royalty seeking to kill them in infancy; both were travelers who helped people as they made their journeys; and both became widely worshipped as heroes following their deaths. Like Jesus, Hercules is a notable reference in many subsequent historical books. In fact, Josephus and Tacitus both mention Hercules in their exhaustive works. Like Jesus, Hercules failed to leave artifacts or eyewitness accounts for his existence. As you can see, Jesus and Hercules are drifting in the same boat with only one exception: Christianity survived the collapse of the Roman Empire while ancient Greek religions did not. As was the case for Horus, why should Hercules face rejection while Jesus is readily accepted?

Aside from Horus and Hercules, there are hosts of supernatural figures remarkably similar to the Christian one. The stories of Attis, Isis, Dionysos, Mithras, Osiris, Hermes, Prometheus, and Perseus include aspects of sacred meals, fasting, wise men, temporary deaths, violent confrontations, celestial birth announcements, virgin mothers, divine fathers, and insurmountable odds for surviving through infancy. If Jesus is the son of the one true God, why is his origin so pathetically unoriginal that we could have easily predicted it using a random religion generator that contained aspects of preceding superstitious myths? Out of the hundreds of divine creatures allegedly capable of miraculous performances, what actual evidence, not blind faith or gut feelings, tells Christians that Jesus is the force behind their comfortable sensations? Remember, correlation doesn't necessarily equal causation.

Problems Galore

As I mentioned in *This Way and That: Biblical Contradictions*, there's a discrepancy between two Gospel accounts of at least ten years on when the world's savior was born. That's the equivalent of two people disagreeing today on whether Theodore Roosevelt or Woodrow Wilson was President of the United States when Bob Hope was born. However, the potential importance of Bob Hope is nothing compared to that of the alleged son of God. While it's true that we have increasingly accurate records in our modern society, it shouldn't be insurmountably difficult to remember a specific year when an individual was born because biblical authors tend to base their dates relative to concurrent events. Such a comparative detail can hardly be easily exaggerated by the passage of time. If, on the other hand, people whimsically created the birth story decades after its setting, we could anticipate this large discrepancy. Also, remember that the Gospel writers had the advantage of divine inspiration for maintaining consistency. What modern technology could be more helpful in preventing complications than an omnipotent god's assistance? Nevertheless, Christians would like the world to believe that Jesus was born during the distinctive incumbencies of King Herod and Quirinius.

The crucifixion legend has many problems in addition to the previously covered contradictions. Although the Romans rarely crucified thieves, we see them executing one on each side of Jesus. Even though Romans never performed executions so close to the Passover, they ignore tradition and carry out the crucifixions on the day before this sacred observance. While the Romans were meticulous in their documentation, they have no record of Jesus or his crucifixion. The whole idea of this Roman procession should be disconcerting if you consider that Rome, the undeniable democratic leader of the planet, didn't offer Jesus due process.

Yet another reason why it's highly improbable that the son of God appeared in human form was the tendency of religious Jews to be very adamant about keeping a separation between God and the human appearance. The Israelites even rioted on one occasion because a picture of Caesar appeared in the vicinity of their temple. It wouldn't make much sense for them to readily accept a human savior when you take their willful convictions into consideration. Even so, thousands of Jews quickly accepted the notion of Christ. Instead of the immensely popular human Jesus, they most likely acknowledged and worshipped the aforementioned spiritual presence of God's son. As time progressed and the Gospels emerged, however, those in the region who believed that their recent ancestors worshipped a human savior joined the Christian movement. Others who adhered to the traditional spiritual presence remained loyal to Judaism. To this day, the Jews do not acknowledge a human presence as the son of God.

The Truth Hurts, Unfortunately

According to Christian preaching, we are to accept Jesus Christ based on the divinely inspired accounts contained within the Gospels. Fortunately, one can easily demonstrate the fundamental flaw in blindly accepting such outrageous claims. Even though this supernatural being was supposedly performing unbelievable miracles before rising from the dead, historians and philosophers neglected these theoretical milestones in favor of mundane historical accounts. Consequently, we don't have an attempted portrayal of an earthly Jesus until several decades following his supposed execution.

Paul was the most important initiator of the religious movement, yet he never conclusively mentions any earthly activity of his subject. In a nutshell, the Gospels are wholly unreliable because they present obvious ignorance of Jewish traditions, contradiction-inducing variations of oral tradition, a lack of eyewitnesses, extraordinary claims without a shred of evidence, known historical anomalies, inexplicably delayed reporting, probable acts of plagiarism, embarrassing scientific blunders, and unoriginal religious themes invoked many centuries before Christianity ever came into being.

I can think of no more than two reasonable hypotheses for the origin of Jesus Christ. Whichever is correct, either upcoming scenario is incalculably more likely to represent what took place 2000 years ago than the wishful thinking that Christians rapidly but blindly develop. The first possibility, and the more probable in my opinion, is that a respectable teacher from Jerusalem who preached his beliefs to a variety of audiences served as an earthly template for a spiritual entity. While his lessons may have been positively motivating for some, he may have pushed the envelope far enough to warrant his death in the opinions of others. As the gossip of his life spread in subsequent years, his followers probably went into a desperate frenzy to positively determine that sacred Old Testament prophecies foretold the arrival of this well-liked man. Spotting possible links here and there, certain individuals may have combined *post hoc* details, real life events, and the notion of a mythical Christ until the stories were arbitrarily deemed worthy of recording. The only sensible alternative to this "true historical figure" proposal requires us to write-off the stories as total myths arising from known social desperation and ancient superstition.

There's simply no reasonable method of deduction allowing us to accept the legitimacy of Jesus Christ as the son of the universe's omnipotent and omniscient creator. The Christian community doesn't acknowledge stories similar to the ones in the New Testament because they appear in religious texts outside of the Bible. In reality, the Jesus story engages as much sensibility as any other unsubstantiated claims made by a number of ancient religions. For these reasons, we must consider the incredibly dubious set of Jesus biographies to be the final nail in the Bible's coffin.

A FINAL WORD ON BIBLICAL NONSENSE

Using the methods provided in this book, our study allowed us to form hundreds of supporting reasons for the absence of divine inspiration in the Bible's content. Seven essential recurring themes of biblical nonsense are readily noticeable when an unprejudiced, emotionless, and objective analysis of Christianity is undertaken.

The Hebrew god is a loathsome, despiteful, and abominable deity. The Old Testament portrays him as a being that experiences pleasure from distributing strange and ridiculous punishments for breaking his equally strange and ridiculous laws. This being is also guilty of torturing innocent people for the sins committed by others, murdering millions of our fellow human beings, and forcing his own creations into slavery. Furthermore, he unambiguously supports the very institution of slavery and the practice of severely oppressing women into a state of subordination. Had the invented God held the moral fortitude to believe otherwise, he would have surely exercised his unlimited power to ban these customs. Instead, he makes promises to deliver a multitude of cruel punishments, including an eternal torture of unimaginable proportions, for those who refuse to bow down and worship him.

The Bible fails a plethora of independent and unbiased scientific tests. Regardless of what scientific field we review, it's likely to contain evidence contrary to the Bible's claims. Several methods used to date the earth's contents have long refuted the temporal setting of the creation, and attempts to harmonize or independently justify the Genesis account have served as embarrassing examples of biblical apologetics. Noah's flood, a plagiarized story with numerous logical impossibilities, has mysteriously left no signs of its occurrence. The Bible's ignorance of our planet's spherical and kinetic attributes is also readily apparent.

The Bible demonstrates overwhelming evidence of authorship by fallible, divinely uninspired humans. In addition to the previously mentioned scientific flaws arising from an obvious limitation of knowledge and perspective, a seemingly countless number of preposterous suggestions can be found within the Bible. These absurdities include talking animals, miraculous war victories, contradictions in every conceivable category, hordes of failed and impossible prophecies, and an array of additional superstitious beliefs readily accepted by unsuspecting biblical readers. The newly acquired ability to assign a much more recent date to the Pentateuch through analyses of fictitious historical accounts debunks the notion of a Moses/God authorship and assists in the demonstration of the book's human origins. Furthermore, these works contain references to people and places contemporaneous with the Babylonian Exile that took place a thousand years after Moses' death. With this consideration, the reasons for the Bible's flaws become readily apparent. Humans inventing stories set centuries in the past had no reason to anticipate that the fraudulent accounts would ever be unmasked. God did not tell us to kill people with other religions. God did not give us orders to take slaves. God did not intend for women to be socially inferior to men. God did not say that he created the universe only a few thousand years ago. God did not kill the entire world in a flood. There's no evidence God did anything. *Men* were the sole driving force behind the creation of the Bible's shameless hatred and propagandistic intentions.

There are fundamental flaws with the existence of God as described in the Bible. His appointed writers parade him as omnipotent, omniscient, and omnipresent, yet they mistakenly drop several clues that this isn't the case. Using a bit of common sense, we can easily demonstrate that omniscience cannot coexist with freewill. Likewise, prayers are not truly answerable by an omniscient god because he would have already envisioned the concrete results of the future. Furthermore, this strangely gender-assigned deity spends his time giving instructions for trivial superstitious rituals rather than pertinent information for proving his existence, ceasing religious wars, or assisting his creations in their daily lives.

The life account of Jesus Christ is highly questionable. Contradictory to what the Gospel writers claim, there were no prophecies of this terribly unoriginal man. Besides, these writers conveniently stall for decades before writing about the unbelievable miracles allegedly performed by their subject. In addition, contemporaneous historians and philosophers frequently ignored the immensely important stories as if they never took place. Even Jesus Christ himself failed to make a return in accordance to his own prophecies. Prior to the purports of all these magnificent tricks and speeches, Paul tells the story of a completely different concept of Christ based in the spiritual realm that may have served as the basis for the Gospel legends. Although the Old Testament was certainly doomed for dismal failure, the New Testament fares no better.

Christians believe strange things for strange reasons. The expansion of Christian beliefs in the West was predominately dependant upon three factors: Rome's desire for a new moral code and its ability to spread such views, the luxury of the religion having the only dominant and hostile belief system of the East, and its maintenance of isolation from other world religions. Once society met these requirements, the continuance of the religion was entirely reliant upon its individual followers. Parents who unknowingly condition their children to shun logic and reason when confronted with testable and observable Bible-debunking evidence now perpetuate the domination of Christian beliefs. Contributors to our environment deceitfully teach us that certain things are unquestionably true. Such nonsensical ideas begin at an age at which we have yet to behave or think in a rational manner. The same ideas are also continuously reinforced in an isolated Christian environment until they accumulate to a degree at which cognitive dissonance takes over and renders common sense impotent.

Counterarguments used by Christian apologists are often dishonest or irrelevant. Although there's an enormous amount of Christian material claiming to debunk skeptical arguments, you have a duty to ask yourself some uncomfortable questions regarding these works. Can you better describe the apologetic arguments as "how-it-could-have-been-scenarios" rather than probable solutions? Do the arguments originate from a biased researcher with a deep emotional investment or an obvious agenda to prove something one way or another? Do the arguments resort to the use of logical fallacies to reach a desired conclusion? Do the arguments take biblical passages out of context or use a premise that is contradicted by what the Bible plainly says? If you've answered *yes* to any of these questions after considering an apologetic explanation to anything that you've read in my work, keep looking. I encourage you to read books on Christianity by both secular *and* religious authors. You will no doubt discover which group acts as its own worst enemy by grasping at slippery straws to support its erroneous viewpoints. If you've heard an argument that you think solidly disproves something I've written, I hope you'll choose to bring it to my attention [admin@biblicalnonsense.com]. I'd certainly like to be able to respond to any claims made against the ones in this book. I may be able to more clearly explain the problem or, perhaps, correct the mistakes I made. You see, no author is infallible.

As a last request, I would ask any readers who still stubbornly insist that Christianity is the one true religion to allow others, including their children, to observe their own religious beliefs without fear of punishment or disappointment from you. If the truth is strong enough, it will find them. The majority of the world's hostilities would vanish overnight if everyone would adhere to this simple guideline.

With the credibility of the Bible repeatedly demolished, perhaps you have opened your eyes to see the real world. There's no certainty that we experience anything more than the challenges we face in this life. While this thought is probably haunting enough to make a few people want to crawl back into the comforts of religion, you will inevitably learn that such an idea is nothing to fear. Consequently, I hope you'll decide to help others who have fallen victim to conditioned thinking provoked by ancient religions.

One day, perhaps, we'll all be free of conditioned thinking and learn to rely on observable and testable evidence when examining religious claims. One day, perhaps, we can all peacefully coexist. Whatever force might be watching us now probably realizes that the majority of us are currently incapable of achieving these goals. If this being is observing our planet during a search for an enlightened race that's ready for the deepest secrets of the universe, it should probably try us again later.

REFERENCES

Recommended Readings

1. *Evidence that Demands a Verdict* by Josh McDowell
   Apologetic material currently without free access, published by Nelson Reference
2. *The Jury Is In: The Ruling on McDowell's Evidence* by Jeffrey Jay Louder, et al.
   Skeptic material currently located online at www.infidels.org
3. *The True. Origin Archive*
   Apologetic material currently located online at www.trueorigin.org
4. *The Talk. Origins Archive*
   Skeptic material currently located online at www.talkorigins.org
5. *Christian Science Evangelism*
   Apologetic material currently located online at www.drdino.com
6. *The Jesus Puzzle* by Earl Doherty
   Skeptic material currently located online at www.jesuspuzzle.org
7. *Ontario Consultants on Religious Tolerance*
   Neutral material currently located online at www.religioustolerance.org
8. *An Introduction to Logic* by Irving M. Copi and Carl Cohen
   Neutral material currently without free access, published by Dark Alley

Traditional And General References

1. *The Holy Bible: King James Version*
2. *The Holy Bible: New International Version*
3. *The New American Standard Bible*
4. *The Blue Letter Bible*
5. *The Lost Books of the Bible*
6. *Strong's Exhaustive Concordance of the Bible*
7. *The Epic of Gilgamesh*
8. *The Code of Hammurabi*
9. *The Works of Josephus Flavius*
10. *Homer's Iliad*
11. *Vivifying the Soul Forever*
12. *The Works of Philo*

Referenced Books And Articles

1. Kosmin, Barry A. and Mayer, Egon. *American Religious Identification Survey* released by <u>The Graduate Center at the City University of New York</u> in 2001.
2. Beckwith, Burnham. *The Effect of Intelligence on Religious Faith*. <u>Free Inquiry</u>. Spring 1986.
3. Taylor, Humphrey. *Harris Poll #59* released by <u>Harris Interactive</u> on October 15, 2003.
4. Darwin, Charles. <u>On the Origin of Species</u>. London: John Murray, 1859.
5. Eddy, J.A. and Boornazian, A.A. *Secular decrease in solar diameter*. <u>Bulletin of the American Astronomical Society</u>. Vol. 11 (1979): 437.
6. Pettersson, H. *Cosmic Sphereules and Meteoritic Dust*. <u>Scientific American</u>. Vol. 202 (1960): 123-132.
7. Dohnanyi, J.S. *Interplanetary objects in review: Statistics of their masses and dynamics*. <u>Icarus</u>. Vol. 17 (1972): 1-48.
8. Barnes, Thomas G. *Origin and Destiny of the Earth's Magnetic Field*. <u>Institution for Creation Research</u>. Technical Monograph No. 4 (1973).
9. Cowling, T.G. *The present status of dynamo theory*. <u>Annual Review of Astronomy and Astrophysics</u>. Vol. 19 (1981): 115-135.
10. Stiebing, William H., Jr. <u>Out of the Desert?: Archeology and the Exodus/ Conquest Narratives</u>. Buffalo, NY: Prometheus Books, 1989.

0-595-34182-9

ted in the United States
)LV00001B/39/A